Follies in Fragile States

How international stabilisation failed
in the Congo

Ian D. Quick

First published in 2015 by:

Double Loop

the Library Building, SW4 7EB
London, United Kingdom
www.rethinkfragility.com

A catalogue record for this publication is available from the British Library.

ISBN 978-0-9933020-0-8 (ebook-Mobi)
ISBN 978-0-9933020-1-5 (paperback)

Table of contents

Prologue

I first resolved to write a book like this on a balcony in northern Sri Lanka. It was June 2007, and my last night in the port town of Trincomalee before starting a convoluted route out of the country.

As if on cue, anti-aircraft fire had started in the early morning and not let up. Earlier in the year the separatist Tamil Tigers had used tiny Czech training aircraft to drop a few handmade bombs on the capital. The attack was ineffectual and mostly for propaganda purposes. But it had made Navy forces paranoid and now they fired wildly into the air at the slightest hint of an unidentified flying object. Coloured tracers were arcing into the sky over the harbour, accompanied by occasional dull thuds of artillery targeting who-knows-what on the ground.

This made it risky to do one's thinking outside. Local security forces were not exactly surgical in their use of force and on several occasions I had seen them literally firing with their eyes closed after a Tiger ambush, spraying from a rifle propped loosely on one hip.

Still, I was transfixed. I couldn't shake the feeling: *What the hell happened? What have I been doing for the last two years?*

I'd arrived in 2005 with bold ambitions and impossible optimism. The job was coordinating post-conflict programmes with the United Nations. They were premised on a ceasefire signed a few years prior between the Government and the Liberation Tigers of Tamil Eelam—bringing a halt to decades of fighting.

A panoply of development agencies had promptly set up satellite offices along the peculiar 'forward defence lines' that separated the two sides, accompanied by a Scandinavian monitoring mission intended to build confidence during negotiations. For my part in the drama I occupied a UNICEF office in the town of Vavuniya, two-thirds of the way up the island.

I rented the second floor of a house from an intrigued local family, bought a bicycle and an array of bright plastic furniture, and got to work trying to turn around a struggling programme.

The objective was 'peacebuilding', 'stabilization' or 'early recovery', depending on who you were talking to. In practice we helped people who had been displaced by fighting return to their homes and build some sort of future. That meant latrines in remote villages, a grueling four-hour drive from the UNICEF field office, boxes of school supplies, and rehabilitation of tiny feeder roads a few miles long. I spent many hours in new community centers, painstakingly facilitating meetings to decide where the next few micro-projects should go. Through dogged persistence with my UN colleagues I pushed up on-time completion, tightened up contract management, and instituted some rudimentary evaluation processes.

Before long, however, the tit-for-tat incidents started. Concealed claymore mines scattered policemen's bodies across the dusty roads that I biked to work. Government thugs abducted suspected Tiger supporters in unmarked vans and 'disappeared' the bodies, the screaming of families two or three doors down waking me in the night. Over the course of five or six months, this escalated into open battle. There was increasingly frequent infiltration and artillery fire across the forward defence lines. A colossal truck bomb slaughtered nearly 100 sailors at one stroke, the town of Habarana going temporarily insane around me while I pleaded for radio guidance from our security advisers. Afterwards I was transferred between offices repeatedly, sometimes running away from the violence and sometimes towards it.

Then came an end-phase variously described as 'gruesome', blood-soaked' or 'unnecessarily brutal'. (Or, per *TIME* magazine, marking 'the end of human rights'.[1]) Government forces ripped through territory once held by the Tigers and pinned the remnants on a strip of beach on the north-eastern coast. They sealed up this space, over a hundred thousand civilians included, then shelled it relentlessly. In the end they got what nobody expected—a decisive victory after thirty years.

Agitation for a credible accounting of war crimes continues to this day. Meanwhile the political climate became increasingly authoritarian. Power concentrated in the hands of the Rajapaksa clan, upcountry nationalists who could communicate authentically with a frustrated and marginalised peasantry. Their senior advisers went on international tours hawking the 'Sri Lankan approach' to counter-insurgency, although the jury is still out on whether violent opposition will recur.

From the UN perspective, we saw our work disappear under the rising tide of violence. Newly built infrastructure was destroyed—the people that we had 'reintegrated' in their villages were displaced anew by fighting and then again by government fiat. Many of them ended up in giant internment camps set up right nearby my failed 'post-conflict' projects, a poster of a gloating President Rajapaksa towering above the sad little shacks.[2] To add insult to injury, the government successfully pressured international relief agencies into providing health and education services to those detained inside.

The failure was so glaring that it led to the rarest of events in this line of work—a formal inquest. The report of the 'Secretary-General's Internal Review Panel' was released in November 2012. (After the document was leaked, the Secretary-General decided that he might as well just publish it.) The Panel noted a steadfast refusal on the part of the UN leadership team in-country to engage with 'political' issues, which 'seemed to encompass everything related to the root causes of the crisis and aspects of the conduct of the war'.[3] This was linked with 'a grave failure of the UN to adequately respond to early warnings' and failure to establish 'an adequate system to collect information on killings and injuries until the beginning of February 2009'.

For my part, I never told that story that I had been pondering on the balcony. Instead I parlayed the experience into a graduate scholarship and then bigger jobs in bigger crises. I held off the shame and frustration by working on experimental initiatives that challenged the status quo in minor ways: closer integration of the various bits and pieces of the UN; development of new peacebuilding institutions to plug the gaps; and the turn to proactive 'stabilisation' of eastern Congo.

The problem is that Sri Lanka turned out to be just the first time. Over the course of a decade in the aid business, I have acted in the same drama time and again. The same mix of frenetic yet quixotic effort, then the same mix of relief and shame on leaving the stage. Friends outside the aid-worker bubble are often bemused by the track record. In response, I've taken to telling them it's a numbers game:

Well... we're talking huge stakes here, ten or twenty million people. If you get that to work once or twice, over the course of a career, that's still pretty good.

Pull the lens back, and the numbers game is even more apparent. For my personal experience mirrors the much larger narrative of the last ten years, during which enormous ambitions to reshape 'fragile states' have been left frustrated and ultimately scaled back.

The highest-profile cases were certainly Iraq and Afghanistan. In Iraq, the US-led invasion in 2003 was followed by confusion, a slide into near civil war in 2006–07 and then shifts in strategy (the 'surge') that seemed to stem the bleeding. The trauma and expense were astronomical. Credible estimates put war-related deaths from 2003–11 at 461,000, and financial costs to the United States at something like USD 3.1 *trillion*.[4] So it was a sad discovery for all involved that progress was always reversible. Political institutions do not so much evolve onwards and upwards as jump between different states of equilibrium, some of them worse than others.

The point was vividly illustrated while I was writing this Prologue, in early 2014. A resurgent Islamic State of Iraq and Syria had formed opportunistic alliances with tribes in Anbar province. One result was the occupation of parts of the city of Fallujah. Black flags flew over government buildings and the optics, as politicians say, could not have been worse. The US Marine Corps had stormed Fallujah in 2005 in perhaps the bloodiest engagement of the entire war—not long after the failure of an abortive and embarrassing experiment with 'Iraqification' of its security. So interviews with veterans cropped up everywhere. Here is one representative passage:[5]

'No one cares anymore,' he says. 'It's heartbreaking to say it, but it's true.'

Gonzalez is still proud of his service, of his fellow Marines, and what they accomplished in Fallujah. But he now wonders, for the first time, whether that sacrifice was worth it...

Did they die in vain? He pauses for a long time, his eyes brimming with tears.

'It's looking that way,' he says softly. 'For a time I thought it was worth it, and now, you know, I question it. And it's eating me up more and more.'

To my ears this sounded all too familiar. I have lost count of colleagues streaming out of 'stabilisation' and 'post-conflict' interventions over the last few years in the wake of major crises, despondent that they were back behind square zero.

First came the spectacular collapse of Mali in late 2012. A military coup made a mockery of twenty years of international support to democratic governance, support that had been frequently touted as an example for the region. Then a coalition of Touareg discontents and Islamists swept across the country, with only last-minute French military intervention averting a total collapse. A few months later it was the turn of the Central African Republic. A fringe rebel group took the capital by force in March 2013. This was rapidly followed by counter-mobilisation of the cruel and disorganised *anti-balaka* militias, widespread communal violence and targeted ethnic cleansing. Concurrently, South Sudan also slid into serious civil conflict. This was a case that enjoyed many advantages. There was strong interest from the countries that mattered, almost unlimited money and a capable figure at the head of a large UN stabilisation mission. Yet at the time of writing it too remains balanced on the edge of a grave humanitarian crisis.

My own nadir—the failure that has really stuck with me—was in the Democratic Republic of the Congo. Here I worked for two-and-a-half years with the United Nations system to stabilise the country's tragically violent eastern provinces. The net results can be summed up in one incident: the capture of the most important city in the conflict theatre by insurgents in November 2012. This was humiliating for both the Congolese government and its international partners, coming as it did after fourteen consecutive years of UN peacekeeping forces on the ground. It was not a sudden collapse on the scale of those in the Central African Republic or South Sudan, but was all the more depressing for the slow-motion yet seemingly inexorable path that had led up to it. It put an exclamation point on a dismal failure of ambitions to improve the lot of some fifteen million people.

This book is about what went wrong in the Congo. It is an attempt to return to the balcony and this time salvage something from failure. After many false starts that 'something' turned out to be the Five Follies: a short list of propositions on why our hard work never added up to meaningful results. I put them forward not as a grand theoretical scheme but as cautious generalisations about work in this most complex and fascinating of regions.

In early reviews, the most common question was of course: 'Do they apply elsewhere?' The short answer is that I suspect that they do. In fact, an early plan for this book used a different country example for each of the Follies, pulling together the full range of crises in which I've worked. But this proved too hard to follow, and certainly much too reliant on simply asserting the way things were rather than taking the time to demonstrate. Less proved to be more. Here, I feel that I am on safe ground citing a legitimate classic of policy studies, Graham Allison and Phillip Zellikow's study of the Cuban missile crisis of 1962:[6]

> On the one hand, substantive instance; on the other, conceptual argument. Today we must confess that we are no longer certain where one begins and the other ends, or, indeed, which is the head and which the tail of this coin. But we are certain about the impulse that led us to pursue these two aims jointly.

With this in mind, I am writing for two target audiences. The first is the engaged member of the public. There are plenty of people who care about the Congo, and about other nations placed in the 'fragile states' basket. In fact there is enormous latent energy here. Aid professionals respond snidely when this manifests in celebrity activism, or blink-and-you'll-miss-it phenomena like #Kony2012 and #BringBackOurGirls. But ultimately there must be a 'pull' factor for what matters. As a fine study of British governance put it, 'consideration of alternatives is not an agenda item for some grand strategy session of civilian generals; it is part of the evolving societal process by which dissatisfied people try to respond to felt needs at any time.'[7]

This process unfolds in classrooms, editors' offices, places of worship, and a thousand other settings. In this respect, a colleague once noted that 'the distance from the bush to Goma is enormous; that from Goma to Kinshasa greater still. The distance from the bush to Addis Ababa or New York is completely unbridgeable'. I would dearly like to prove her wrong.

My second target audience is the critical practitioner. The few ethnographic accounts that have been written of the aid business tend to report a 'culture of secrecy', and a sense that critical accounts had 'ruptured relationships and broken the rules of fair play'.[8] I think that this is too strong. Day-to-day, aid workers encounter tremendous political and social forces that can bulldoze their best and most painstaking work in an instant. They are also isolated from both those responsible for political oversight and those they are attempting to assist. It is hardly surprising that such conditions result in strong group solidarity against outside criticism, much as one finds in police or military institutions.[9]

Yet I know also that colleagues are not beyond self-reflection. To quote a recent head of the UN Development Programme, 'each of us has had our own moment of truth when the head finally controlled the heart and we came to realise... that things are never simple'.[10] I invite practitioners to relate my account to their own such moment, whether nodding in agreement or shouting in denial.

A note on roles and sources

This book is written in the first person because I was a protagonist, albeit minor, in events. From 2009 to 2011 I worked as an evaluation specialist in the UN peacekeeping mission, called first MONUC and then MONUSCO, in a team charged with coordinating the activities of the wider UN system. The main resource for *Follies in Fragile States* was thus close observation during this period, including thousands of hours of interviews and thousands more of informal conversation. The supplementary resource is part-time involvement before 2009 and after 2011, as an informal adviser, paid consultant, and sometime lobbyist.

My focus is on how international agencies interpreted and reacted to events on the ground, and this means frequent recourse to their internal records. I have noted where to find sources, for those with access to archival material, but do not reproduce anything that could plausibly still be regarded as sensitive or confidential now that we are five years down the road. I also quote extensively from international and Congolese officials, but do not attribute these remarks except where they were made 'on the record' in public forums.

It is an unfortunate fact that ordinary Congolese voices are not so well represented. In fact Chapter 5 concerns precisely this problem: the *de facto* monopoly over serious policy conversations that was held by a small group of officials based in the capital. These individuals' views are amply captured in meeting minutes, strategic frameworks, email correspondence, and thousands of other documents. But there were few serious efforts to capture perspectives from below, and from the periphery. When reconstructing events, this frequently left only the unpalatable alternatives of (i) silence, or (ii) substituting my own recollections for the specific words used. I can only hope that I have handled this dilemma with sensitivity.

Introduction

This book is about efforts to reshape countries in crisis. It reflects on a decade's work around the world, spurred by the realisation that the results have been slim or perhaps even negative.

In one sense, it is the perspective of someone who knows, or suspects, where the bodies are buried. That most interventions in fragile states have not lived up to expectations is plain to see. The question is rather what to do with this fact, because there is both opportunity and motive to ignore it. The opportunity arises because such interventions layer a complex system onto a complex system. A mad jumble of foreign actors find allies and enemies among an equally confusing array of domestic factions, and the resulting mess seems to actively defy attempts to establish causation, contribution or responsibility. The temptation to take this 'out' is ever-present because identities are thoroughly bound up in the job—*we are the good guys*. Self-interest leads us to leave unspoken our failures against declared ambitions, or to redefine them as success against narrow technical criteria.

Here, I try to take failure—both personal and institutional—more seriously. I take a single case, efforts to 'stabilise' eastern Democratic Republic of the Congo from 2007 to 2012, and aim to deconstruct a complex history into a few 'big ideas' on what went wrong.

An inquest is well justified by the case's own merits. Congo exemplifies in many ways the steady expansion of ambitions to reshape fragile states that has occurred in the background of international relations over the last twenty years. And yet, as the *New York Times* put it, 'many critics contend that nowhere else in the world has the United Nations invested so much and accomplished so little'.[1] Core goals to build local capacity and draw down the UN's largest peacekeeping mission were not achieved, and the numbing tide of everyday atrocities ebbed and flowed without much regard to announcements of new peace accords and strategic frameworks. For lack of better ideas this led the Security Council to put ever-increasing stress on 'protection of civilians' under imminent threat, directing twenty thousand foreign soldiers to try and police a vast and restive territory. This approach hit its limits when political re-alignments led rebels to rout the national army and capture the biggest city in the conflict theatre in late 2012.

At the same time, looking at the Congo might tell us something useful about interventions elsewhere. Ambitions to reshape 'fragile states' have grown up incredibly quickly, and the approaches to pursue those ambitions are likewise new and unproven. In the DRC's case I argue that our work was handicapped by a group of dangerous half-truths and peculiar assumptions— the Five Follies. These were system maladaptations attributable more to the politics and economics of intervention than any careful reading of problems on the ground.

As an interpretive framework, this is no doubt too cute by half. But my hunch is that the Follies pose common-sense questions that should be asked for any stabilisation or 'post-conflict' intervention.

The effort is timely, I think, because the 'fragile states' agenda is far from dead. In the Anglophone world, a generation of security and foreign policy professionals has been traumatised its experiences in Iraq and Afghanistan— but circumstances conspire against retirement from the stage. In the course of writing this book two entirely new complex UN operations were launched in Mali and the Central African Republic, while a third was reconfigured in South Sudan. All three were driven by great power interests that are unlikely to disappear. These include: fears of regional destabilisation and transnational terrorism (Mali); Chinese import dependence and aspirations to global influence (South Sudan); and increasingly sophisticated advocacy to mobilise voters in the rich democracies (all three cases).

The suddenness with which all these crises struck was a pointed reminder of an unfortunate fact—that complex problems are frequently also urgent problems. We have no right to sit back and take an experimental attitude, but must rather work it out on the fly.[2] That means learning as much as we can, as quickly as we can, from real, living cases.

Pre-modern medicine

The French crisis consultant Pat Lagadec works on major wildfires, nuclear incidents, liquidity crises and the like. He often writes about *brutal audits*— situations where 'at a moment's notice, everything that was left unprepared becomes a complex problem, and every weakness comes rushing to the forefront'.[3] These are situations that surpass the capacity of existing systems to cope: where normal frames of reference seem to crumble and the outcome that was to be avoided at all costs has somehow managed to occur.

The concept is apt for work to stabilise fragile states. Here international intervention must reckon with enormous political and social forces. We make our best guesses on how to influence them, and where to find the best points of leverage. The problem is that the sheer complexity of the situation means that we can be wrong for a long time without realising. The effects of our actions are delayed, or mutated by contact with the plans and reactions of a hundred other actors. But on occasion a brutal audit comes along and unambiguously disproves our theories. Sri Lanka, the Prologue to this story, was one such case. It has been described as the UN Secretary-General's 'Rwanda moment'; he himself conceded that there had been a 'systemic failure' with 'profound implications for our work across the world'.[4]

There are many other examples. A conservative list, sticking just to the last decade, would include Haiti (2004), East Timor (2006), Somalia (2006), Iraq (2006-07), Côte d'Ivoire (2010), Mali (2012), the Democratic Republic of the Congo (2012), the Central African Republic (2013) and South Sudan (2013-14). Each of these countries received substantial international assistance for stabilisation and governance, and each followed the same trajectory. First, there was a period in which lofty policy goals and realities on the ground were a long way apart—accompanied by optimistic official narratives repeatedly denying the gap. Then, a dramatic failure stripped away all pretence, rapidly growing and metastasising along the fault lines and vulnerabilities that were always already present. Finally a reset and reconfiguration of the work, trying to coax the genie back into the bottle. In some cases the situation recovered; in others it remains mired in a deeply dysfunctional equilibrium.

What should we conclude from this? Is it just a numbers game, as suggested in the Prologue? Is our success rate just *inevitably* low?

The honest answer is: we don't know. In fact, we can't know. Much of the work that is currently attempted to stabilise and reshape fragile states was unknown ten years ago, and virtually all of it twenty years ago. Against this, we are dealing with social and political systems whose evolution is most comprehensibly described in centuries. The consequence is that the data just isn't available. As a perceptive observer of Afghanistan has put it, our 'techniques resemble the early days of medicine, when the human body was poorly understood and doctors prescribed bloodletting, or drilled into skulls to treat madness.'[5]

To grasp how rudimentary our pre-modern medicine really is, consider two trends over the last twenty years. The first is rapid *quantitative* growth. For UN peace operations, the average lifetime cost for missions started between 1985 and 1994 was USD 585 million. For missions starting between 1995 and 2004 it was USD 2.35 billion, a fourfold increase even adjusting for inflation. For those starting between 2005 and 2014 the average cost is already USD 4.29 billion, notwithstanding that the meter is still running for most of them.[6] Likewise for bilateral aid. The OECD's Development Assistance Committee, the club of rich-country donors, didn't even keep a 'working list' of fragile states until 2005. But it recently noted approvingly that total resource flows to these countries have doubled in real terms over a decade, and now account for 38% of total assistance.[7] In the United Kingdom, for instance, this has meant that aid going to fragile states surged from £1.8bn in 2010-11 to £3.4bn in 2014-15.[8]

Concurrent with this has been massive *qualitative* expansion, i.e. growth in the kinds of tasks attempted. Consider the New Deal for Engagement in Fragile States. This is the 2011 product of an elaborate consultative process involving some forty-five governments and most of the key multilateral institutions in the development business. It is intended to map out future orientations for foreign aid to fragile states, with the point of departure five 'peacebuilding and statebuilding goals'.[9] These are: legitimate politics; security; justice; revenue and services; and economic foundations.

This is a remarkably broad remit. The technical and political complexities that confront serious reform in any one of these areas are enormous. But it has become par for the course to intervene in all of them simultaneously. In the UN peacekeeping sector, 'statebuilding' work of this kind was pretty much unknown before 1991. Then came a few initial forays in El Salvador,

Cambodia and Bosnia as Western powers tested the limits of the possible in the post-Cold War environment. From there, it was as if a switch had been flipped. From 1995 onwards, the Security Council mandated UN operations that cut across those big, intimidating themes in no fewer than fifteen countries.[10]

For development agencies there are similarly expansive ambitions. The Millennium Development Goals were formulated in September 2000 to 'create an environment conducive to development and to the elimination of poverty'. The preamble included some aspirational language on peace and governance—but the eight goals themselves related to extreme poverty, primary education, gender equality, child mortality, maternal health, burden of disease, environmental sustainability, and the size of aid flows.[11] Each was subsequently associated with quantitative indicators, compiled and managed centrally to track achievement towards the target year of 2015. As the deadline approaches, expectations have grown for successor arrangements and it is now commonplace to argue for targets on conflict and fragility.

To take the highest-profile example, the UN Secretary-General convened a high-level panel in 2013, including several former heads of state. It recommended targets, among many others, to 'Enhance the capacity, professionalism and accountability of the security forces, police and judiciary'; 'Reduce violent deaths per 100,000 by x [sic] and eliminate all forms of violence against children'; and 'Stem the external stressors that lead to conflict, including those related to organized crime'.[12] Just as for the original Goals, these would be linked with 'precise metrics' for centralised analysis and reporting.

At this point, some caution is surely appropriate. It is clear that these are pressing concerns, and that we do not have the luxury of doing nothing. (Neither did those early medical practitioners!) But it has been a remarkably short span of time in which to invent a wholly new art and science.

The need for prudence is perhaps best illustrated by a quick glance backwards, at the brief history of the aid business. Here it is now conventional to acknowledge multiple 'lost decades' of effort. Successive orthodoxies had to play out at massive scale and for long periods before it was accepted that things were just not working as anticipated—first capital formation in the 1950s and 1960s, then 'basic needs' in the 1970s, then neoliberalism in the 1980s. The profession cycled through each of these in turn before settling into a sort of eclecticism that tends to eschew grand theories.

There is no reason to think the same fate unlikely for the 'fragile states' agenda, which boasts both bolder objectives and country 'clients' who are considerably less able to defend themselves against technocrats looking to test out their bright new ideas. To borrow a metaphor from Karl Popper:[13]

> Science does not rest upon rock-bottom. It is like a building erected on piles. The piles are driven down from above into the swamp, but not down to any natural or 'given' base; and when we cease our attempts to drive our piles into a deeper layer, it is not because we have reached firm ground. We simply stop when we are satisfied that they are firm enough to carry the structure, at least for the time being.

Well—we are a long way out into the swamp, and the building has been built very quickly. And for my part, I think that there is convincing evidence that some of the pillars are rotten.

The Democratic Republic of the Congo is a good place in which to explore this intuition, as among the patients of the new interventionism it is perhaps the longest-standing and most intensively treated. Every year from 2007 to 2012 it hosted the largest or second-largest UN peace operation in the world; was in the top five largest appeals for emergency relief assistance; and in the top ten for dependency on development aid.[14] At the political level, it hosted no fewer than five super-ambassador 'special envoys'. But all this effort did not translate into progress against stated policy goals. This largely escaped comment until the brutal audit came—the split of the *Mouvement de 23 Mars* from the national army and the capture of Goma, the most important city in the conflict theatre, in December 2012. Rwanda intervened directly, threatening a return to the international free-for-all of a decade earlier. The Congolese army was grossly mismanaged and quickly broke and ran, making a mockery of a decade of 'state-building' efforts. The (lack of) response of the UN's peacekeeping force was also widely derided, turning a crisis for the Congolese into a crisis of credibility for the world body.[15]

In the aftermath of a serious crisis event like this, the Harvard leadership guru Ron Heifetz has suggested that effective leadership has two elements. The first is *stabilisation*: stemming the bleeding and buying time. This certainly occurred. The UN deployed its first-ever 'Intervention Brigade' to shift the balance of forces on the ground; huge diplomatic pressure was brought to bear on Rwanda to curtail its meddling; and yet another political framework (the 'Framework for Hope') was agreed between countries in the region. The second element of effective leadership, however, is *adaptation*. This means investigation of the habits and practices that led to crisis and the 'innovation, experimentation and creativity required to learn new ways of doing things'.[16] This certainly did not occur. The story that led up to the fall of Goma wasn't investigated with much seriousness, and the UN and bilateral aid providers managed to avoid serious scrutiny once the initial media interest petered out. For its part the Congolese government failed to do much about the M23's core grievances, up to and including the latter's former combatants starving to death in their demobilisation camps.[17]

Follies in Fragile States attempts to fill this gap. My aim is to decompose 'failure', a complicated historical narrative, into specific hypotheses on 'what went wrong'. Which of our pre-modern medical techniques muddled through to a positive result, and which inadvertently caused harm?

Action and stagnation

The focus of this book is on the Congo's Third Republic, introduced to the world in 2006 with a new Constitution, President and National Assembly. And it is impossible to understand the tragedy of what followed without also understanding the optimism that was present in the early days.

In 1996-7 the First Congo War had seen a modest Rwandan incursion topple the Mobutu dictatorship. It turned out that the latter had been thoroughly rotted from the inside-out by thirty years of kleptocracy: actual fighting was limited, although the human toll was not. But the Second Congo War (1998-2003) was a very different animal. No fewer than seven countries became embroiled on Congolese soil, enlisting or creating local allies and earning the nickname 'Africa's World War'. When the exhausted belligerents finally signed the 2003 Sun City Agreements, the power-sharing government that followed was unsteady and impractical. For many, it was a minor miracle that it was wound up with more-or-less successful elections over the course of 2006. Neighbouring countries refrained from overt intervention, for the most part, as local political factions jockeyed for position. The Government that eventuated was far from perfect but good enough to play ball with the international community—a fact to be signalled in 2010-12 by cancelations of old international debts to the tune of five billion dollars.[18]

The exception to the success story was the East of the country. This is a loosely defined chunk of territory that runs roughly from the southern tip of Burundi up to the top of Lake Albert in Uganda, and a few hundred miles into Congolese territory. It had been the cockpit of the Second Congo War, as the neighbours pushed across the borders and met resistance from both local communities and the national government. And the arrangements hammered out in the Sun City Agreements had not calmed the situation here to the extent that people had hoped. The political and security situation remained precarious, with many factions that had not bought into the new status quo and a steady drip of everyday atrocities.

The biggest single vulnerability was the Congolese army. This was an unstable patchwork of the belligerents left standing at the end of the war, 'divided against itself, with Kinyarwanda speakers poised to fight members of other ethnic groups and to fight among themselves according to the Tutsi–Hutu line of cleavage'.[19] It was clearly ready to fall apart if the right thread was tugged, a scenario that had already knocked on the door several times.

Meanwhile many smaller players felt marginalised by political machinations happening a thousand miles away in the capital. Thorough-going militarisation after many years of bush war meant this translated into dozens of armed groups that never quite demobilised. They retained both capability and willingness to skirmish with each other over resources and more intangible grievances. The most ferocious was the National Congress for the Defence of the People (CNDP, after the French title). This was a descendent of one of the belligerents in the Second Congo War, put together by senior officers who felt they had lost out in the political transition and backed by parts of the Rwandan government. They kept flirting with the new national army but never consummating the relationship, with agreements in 2007 and 2008 breaking down quickly and then yet another tentative rapprochement in early 2009. On each occasion there was a chain reaction among smaller militias who feared being left in the CNDP's sphere of influence as they had been during the war. They were bankrolled by local business and political elites who shared those fears and also by the national army, which kept getting routed on the battlefield.

Sharing this already complex ecosystem were a few more exotic species. Most notable were the Democratic Forces for the Liberation of Rwanda (FDLR), a mutant offspring of the *génocidaires* who had fled from Rwanda into the DRC in 1994. Over time the group had evolved to incorporate parts of the Congolese Hutu community, and lived an opportunistic life with no real political agenda beyond survival. However, its soldiers were relatively well organised and trained and thus often enlisted by local communities in score-settling among themselves. Other factions that didn't fit the usual mould included the FNL, a small Burundian insurgency that found Congo a convenient home, and the ADF, a peculiar Islamist group originating from Uganda. After long obscurity the latter would burst into international prominence in late 2014 after (murky) involvement in a string of gruesome massacres.[20]

All this was in a region where the relevance of the central government had always been in question. Mobutu Sese Seko had been a dictator for thirty-two years, finally dying in 1997. But he had ruled by the judicious distribution of spoils and skilful manipulation of factions against each other, not by an overwhelming concentration of force. The East had not lived under a heavy hand, and indeed had resisted many of Mobutu's centralising efforts.

Two subsequent wars had not improved the situation, with combatants either pulling apart state institutions or else bending them to their will. By any conventional measure—policing, taxation, even physical access—DRC was an archipelago state, barely present outside the major urban centres. Communities functioned and in a few cases even thrived. But in Thomas Hobbes' formulation, they 'lived without a common power to keep them all in awe'.[21] Security, transport infrastructure and most social services were subject to the unofficial motto of the Mobutu period: *débrouillez-vous* ('manage it yourself').[22]

This was most dramatically illustrated by an epidemiological survey that estimated a total 5.4 million 'excess deaths' between 1998 and April 2007— due not to battle but rather disruption of basic sanitation, health services, subsistence farming and trade.[23] (The figure led to the standard media tag 'the deadliest conflict since World War II'.) Day to day, shifting patterns of insecurity continued to keep between one-and-a-half and two million people displaced from their home communities at any one time. For the rest, a survey in 2007 found that about 20% of respondents felt safe meeting a soldier, and less than 40% when meeting a stranger of any kind.[24] The big reason for this was near-total militarisation of competition for economic resources. This ranged from the omnipresent 'checkpoints' on roads—taxing a bundle of cassava here, a few hundred Congolese francs there—through grazing disputes resolved at gunpoint, right up to the big prizes of artisanal mining sites and the cross-border trade of fuel and timber.

Faced with this situation, international actors had enthusiastically taken on public functions. The United Nations Mission in the DRC (MONUC) had been first launched in 1999 and a decade later it had grown to an authorised strength of 20,575 military personnel, 1,440 police and nearly 5,000 civilian staff. Of these 90% were deployed in the East, with their first priority to protect Congolese civilians under the imminent threat of physical violence.[25] In practice this meant a far-flung network of ninety or so field deployments that acted as a sort of UN 911 service in parallel with the national army and police.[26] Concurrent with this, a dizzying array of humanitarian agencies had also set up permanent shop. One representative appeal document asked for funds to underwrite health services for 5.3 million people, and to support the food security of 4.3 million people. It explained that these needs were driven by 'crises' on the one hand and 'general poverty and precariousness' on the other.[27]

Of course all this posed an obvious question: What was the exit strategy? Nobody was comfortable with what amounted to a sharing of sovereign functions.[28] The Congolese government first suggested a drawdown plan for MONUC in 2007, shortly after President Kabila was sworn into office, and then stepped up its efforts aggressively in 2009. The UN's financial contributors were not averse to the idea, with peacekeepers costing USD 1.3 billion annually and emergency relief agencies asking for another seven hundred million on top of that.

The plan, when it came, was not short on ambition. In late 2008 the Security Council directed MONUC to help the central government in 'disarming the recalcitrant local armed groups'.[29] The following year it expanded on this: the UN system was to aim for 'consolidation of State authority throughout the territory'. This included the 'completion of activities of [demobilisation] of Congolese armed groups or their effective integration in the army'; and 'deployment of Congolese civil administration, in particular the police, territorial administration and rule of law institutions'.[30] All this for an area comprising—on the most restrictive interpretation—about 190,000 square kilometres and some fifteen million people.

In formulating these goals, the Council was constantly egged on by Western advocacy groups. In 2009, Human Rights Watch offered a typically optimistic recommendation to the Government and its international partners:[31]

> Develop a new and comprehensive approach for disarming armed groups, including the FDLR, that emphasizes protection of civilians, apprehending those wanted for crimes in violation of international law, a reformed disarmament and demobilization program, and options for temporary resettlement of combatants and their dependents within or outside of Congo.

The Enough Project chimed in with an 'Action Plan to End the World's Deadliest War'. It proposed an American/French/British sally against the FDLR, precise tracing and documentation of mineral supply chains, and 'reform of the Congolese justice system so that it prosecutes the warlords who use rape, village burning, and other attacks on civilians as tools of war'.[32]

Now let's jump forward to early 2013. To put it mildly, all those bold ambitions were not realised. A credible overview from an independent think-tank indicated twenty-four significant armed groups active at this time, the accompanying map a crazy quilt of colour blotches with notations like 'diverse factions of same franchise'.[33] This was fully consistent with intelligence estimates within the UN. I spent a lot of time writing sentences like the following in my cramped office in Goma:[34]

> Security remains the major challenge in many areas. The proximate causes of violence are not yet addressed; and work with civil institutions remains premature. At the same time: There is no political framework for action in the security sector and the role of the [stabilisation strategy] remains limited.

This comes from a public report and is already much too upbeat. We had supported small police deployments to locations where they were shot at, kidnapped and ultimately driven off (occasionally with the collaboration of the local community). In other places, they huddled in rapidly disintegrating tents, derided as the 'UNOPS police' in reference to the UN agency that had procured—and of course branded—their equipment.

In late 2010 a small armed group took over the ultra-remote town of Luvungi, perpetrated some unusually savage violence, and then disappeared back into the bush. Some months afterwards the UN mission prodded Congolese police to deploy in the area, dropping them off in UN helicopters with yet more tents. The press release that followed almost defies belief:[35]

> About a hundred women, the majority of whom were rape victims, met with the delegation on arrival. The mood was festive. Changes were visible everywhere in the town.

> Today, the population feels entirely confident, and can express itself freely. Economic activity around the village is picking up, and the villagers are now contemplating the future, leaving behind a painful past.

The same armed group 're-captured' the town—or rather walked back in with minimal fighting—two months after this press release was written. They killed a few people, assaulted many more, and then left again. Of course this fact was buried in an anodyne UN narrative report rather than a press release, while international organisations squabbled in the pages of *Foreign Policy* over the precise number of victims of sexual violence for the original attack.[36]

In short, something was off. We were speaking a polite language— prosecuting warlords, demobilisation and retraining of combatants, efficient civil administration—in an environment that was considerably more anarchic. Local leaders were playing real politics. They relied on linkages with hugely unreliable armed factions and a thoroughly criminalised economy for any real influence. Our efforts to train them in record-keeping and budget execution were accordingly a little beside the point, or rather didn't take their day-to-day political reality seriously. They were much more concerned about sudden, violent shifts in political equilibrium.

They were frequently proven right, but most definitively in November 2012. This is when the *Mouvement de 23 Mars* captured the city of Goma, shortly after splitting from the national army. This was as unambiguous a failure as one can imagine versus overall policy goals. Government forces had been routed despite maximally favourable operational conditions, the direct support of the UN peacekeeping mission, and the city being indisputably the highest-value target in eastern Congo. It was, moreover, the hub for most international relief agencies, and the small international press corps.

Against this background, 'apprehending and prosecuting' anyone began to look a bit fantastical. Far from drawing down, the peacekeeping budget for Congo actually *grew* by 7% in real terms from 2007 to 2012. After the fall of Goma the UN's presence was further strengthened, with its new Intervention Brigade specifically tasked with combat operations. For the bilateral partners funding aid projects, the picture was no prettier. Twelve of the biggest commissioned an evaluation of their work in 2011 and received a rather blunt response:[37]

> Fundamentally, it is difficult to define the progresses achieved by the interventions towards conflict resolution and peacebuilding, as the contextual analysis is defective. In fact the operational instruments such as humanitarian aid fill the gap left by donor strategies.

Meanwhile the various institutions estimating Congo's overall 'fragility' saw no improvements. They reckoned the DRC to be in company with Iraq at the peak of its crisis in 2006–07, or Sudan just before the secession of South Sudan.[38] In fact the best-known ranking, the Failed States Index, actually pushed the Congo up the table from seventh-most fragile in the world in 2007 to second place in 2012. Experts haggled about the precise trends but could not deny the overall pattern, which is best described as *action and stagnation*.[39]

Each year the UN's Department of Peacekeeping Operations returned to the Security Council for renewal of MONUC's mandate for 22,000 peacekeepers. Each year a funding appeal for humanitarian agencies would circulate for the 'Congo crisis', the world's second- or third-biggest, with an explanation of 'challenges' copied from the previous year's appeal and a few per cent added onto the price tag. That this pattern could repeat itself with little controversy, right up until the brutal audit finally came in late 2012, is a very troubling fact. As the British parliamentarian Rory Stewart has asked about Afghanistan: 'Why was no-one ever exposed? Why did neither colleagues nor bosses nor the public ever challenge such sublime "cautious optimism"?'[40]

The Five Follies

The short explanation is that we were asking the wrong questions. Specifically, we misled ourselves in five key regards:

The makeover fantasy—an untested assumption that formal state institutions were an unalloyed social good. This ignored serious unresolved questions about how these institutions should be governed and to what ends, and prevented identification of widely shared *goals*.

Policy without politics—the failure to understand the fears, uncertainties and interests that lay behind inertia on sensitive issues like security sector reform. This prevented the identification of viable *pathways for change*.

Geography denial—the construction of a fictional entity of 'eastern Congo' that left planning and analysis at unworkable levels of abstraction. This prevented effective *adaptation* to huge variations in conditions across the theatre of operations, and left us with serious mismatches between ends and means.

The coordination fixation—the insistence that more analysis and more planning were the answers to all of the above failings. This put off indefinitely a serious discussion of *wllingness and capabilities*, as major gaps in what international agencies were actually prepared to contribute were never confronted.

The iron triangle—domination of the policy process by a small group of Kinshasa-based officials, rich-country governments, and the expert policy community. This limited *feedback*, the inclusion of crucial ground-truth in the policy conversation.

These are best summarised as respects in which international engagement was unfit for purpose in the DRC. I do not go further and suggest that all can be explained by a lurking ideology (neo-liberal 'empire in denial') or specific professional norms ('the tyranny of experts').[41] Rather each Folly has its own history and reinforcing incentives. It must also be emphasised at the outset that they were shared by many Congolese counterparts, who so often spoke in the peculiar dialects of 'statebuilding' and 'peacebuilding' that they forgot those ideas that were better expressed in everyday language.

Following this overall scheme, the plan of this book is straightforward. The period is 2007-12. The focus is on 'stabilisation', loosely defined as the DRC escaping its dependence on massive foreign security assistance and emergency relief in its eastern provinces. With one eye on this overall goal we pick our way through the Follies sequentially. In each case I reconstruct decision-making in a key priority area, as far as possible letting the original documents and stakeholders speak for themselves. I then compare the assumptions and mental models with how the situation actually evolved on the ground, tracing the actions and reactions of specific individuals, institutions and communities.

The overall effect is to jump in and out, revisiting the same situation from different ground-level perspectives. Figure 1 summarises how we will travel in this regard, superimposing the plan for *Follies in Fragile States* upon a provincial map of the DRC.

We start in Chapter 1 in the company of the Congolese National Police (PNC), following close behind deployments into the province of North Kivu. In Chapter 2 we switch subject to the Congolese Armed Forces (FARDC), tracking perilous schemes to internally restructure and 'integrate' the remaining illegal armed groups in South Kivu. Chapter 3 then jumps to a regional perspective. We turn to frontline civil administrators and add a third area—Ituri district—to compare and contrast the varying situations across the East. Chapter 4 shifts emphasis from Congolese to international institutions, looking at the profusion of international agencies working in-country and their efforts to formulate coherent policy. Finally, Chapter 5 looks at the *grosses légumes*, the Kinshasa-based political elites who dominated the conversation on what ordinary people wanted or needed.

Figure 1: Conceptual map for Follies in Fragile States

Location and primary subject of each chapter

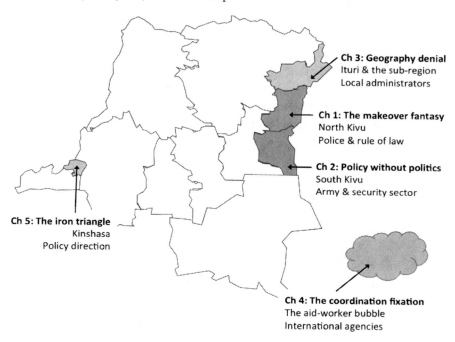

The focus on local and intra-institutional perspectives is partly to avoid the sanitising effects of distance. The tale is quite often bloody, and it is useful sometimes to emphasise that 'stakeholders' deal with real stakes. But it is also because eastern Congo's predicament is irreducibly about trust, risk and historical memory. Discussing any individual 'variable' stripped from its context is thus bloodless in a different way, in that it substitutes an observer's perspective for that of the participants who actually shape events. I aim instead for an approach outlined by Aaron Wildavsky, perhaps the greatest modern observer of how policy is made:[42]

> By quoting extensively from participants, by paying careful attention to the features of their environment as they describe it, and by examining the explanations they give for their own behaviour, we hope to create a recognisable context within which recommended change must take place. Hopefully participants... will recognise in our book the world in which they work and want

to use it both to explain to others what they do and to examine their own behaviour.

The method reacts against the usual practice of international agencies, which is to compartmentalise and focus only on 'their' part of the story. This has been driven home for me many times, but perhaps most vividly in a conversation with a senior UN official in Kinshasa in 2009. He was tall and Scandinavian, fond of loud ties and business jargon that was never used quite correctly. He was also considered a hot talent and knew how to make the right noises to get ahead. I quote:[43]

> At the end of the day... you're not accountable for these overall results. We can't talk about results for return and recovery in general. Accountability is really about contracts, the specific commitments we make in project documents to our donors. That's what we sign on to.

On this view, the proper level of analysis is the project agreement—a few million dollars passed from a single donor (say the United Kingdom) to a single agency (say the UN Development Programme). Most of these projects have success indicators and some are even formally evaluated. The problem is that it ends there, with this very parochial viewpoint. Overall success is not discussed because everybody reserves the right to define it for themselves.

Even where there have been formal post-mortems of strategic failure in fragile states, they have been kept within tight parameters. The Review Panel that followed the debacle in Sri Lanka (Ban Ki-Moon's 'Rwanda moment') was directed unambiguously to the 'final stages of the war', and the 'contribution and effectiveness of the United Nations system in responding to the escalating fighting'.[44] This occluded the uncomfortable fact that the UN system had been present in the country all the way through three decades of violence. (In fact Sri Lanka had often been cited as a success story for development work.) Earlier post-mortems for action in the face of genocide in Rwanda and Srebrenica skirted around the history of policy engagement in precisely the same fashion.[45]

Such tendencies are amplified, or enabled, by a lack of serious outside scrutiny. What is striking about the Iraq and Afghanistan wars, for someone working on lesser-known conflicts, is that they have been *picked to death*. There was heavy parliamentary/Congressional oversight; ceaseless third-party muckraking accounts; credible surveys of public opinion; strong investigative reporting (after a slow start) from an array of news outlets; and a torrent of insider accounts from mid-level and senior-level officials. But we find none of this for those crises which are left to the UN and regional organisations. Accounts from knowledgeable insiders are remarkably rare. [46] The rich countries that foot the bill never regard any individual dossier as a significant political issue because their contributions are individually small. The institutions that are tasked to supervise—the UN Security Council and its African Union counterpart—seem constitutionally incapable of doing so. Meanwhile the media instinctively distrust the official narrative, knowing spin when they see it, but are unwilling to bear the costs of investigative reporting in these very difficult contexts.

Follies in Fragile States is a modest attempt to break those habits. It is muckraking, with a lot of narrative detail and an array of colourful characters. I wrote it in the firm belief that there is 'no arcane form of social science that has to be mastered before one can begin to think about development policy'. [47] Intervention in the Congo—and in other 'fragile states'—is indisputably an area where policy-makers and the public can be informed consumers, and ask the right questions.

1

The makeover fantasy

The wind-up of Congo's transitional government in 2006 kicked off an informal competition for lurid hyperbole. The historian Filip Renytjens declared that 'empirically speaking the Congolese state had virtually disappeared'; the political scientist Jeffrey Herbst concluded that it possessed 'none of the things that make a nation-state'. Still more colourfully, a survey by the World Bank asked ordinary Congolese, 'If the state were a person, what would you do to him?', with 'Kill him' the most common reaction.[1]

Foreign donors and development agencies soon joined in. Normally these institutions are polite to a fault but here the usual euphemisms were discarded due to a happy coincidence of interests—President Kabila's incoming government was keen to distance itself from everything that had come before. Its early policy documents emphasised 'deep-seated dysfunctions that have nearly paralyzed the State structure' and 'bad governance that led to the collapse of the State and plunged the country into war'.[2] International partners soon chimed in, with the Country Assistance Framework defining its challenge as 'building an effective state, in a country where there has never been one'.

In Congo's eastern provinces all this took on a special urgency. The security environment remained fractious, with an array of minor armed groups that hadn't got what they wanted from the political transition. The UN peacekeeping mission (MONUC) had shifted the vast majority of its resources eastwards in early 2007, while humanitarian agencies were still asking for $800m a year for relief work in response to the 'complex emergency'. A working theory was desperately needed on how to proceed, and the (undeniable) weakness of the central government soon came to dominate the debate.

The UN's Department of Peacekeeping Operations had an influential voice given that drawdown of the world's most expensive peacekeeping mission was at issue. Its key early assessments spoke of a 'vacuum' that had been 'exploited' by armed groups. This implied the remedy of 'extension of state authority throughout the territory', comprising most notably police responsibility for public security, an independent judiciary, and functioning civil institutions at national, provincial and local level.[3] A multi-donor evaluation representing most of the major bilateral donors agreed with this diagnosis, asserting bluntly that the 'The key driver of conflict in the DRC is the weakness of the State, even its complete absence, in several large parts of the East.'[4] The Congolese government also got on board. Prime Minister Muzito declared a Stabilisation and Reconstruction Plan for Conflict-Affected areas in 2009, explaining that:[5]

> A durable peace, in this area, is only possible if supported by a complete extension of state authority, the improvement of social services, economic reconstruction and better management of natural resources.

The member states of the UN Security Council initially equivocated, no doubt due to the daunting scope and expense of the task. But by early 2010 they were forced to clarify their position as President Kabila made a surprise demand for MONUC to start withdrawing. The Council's rejoinder was swift, with the categorical statement that any reconfiguration of UN peacekeeping would depend on 'completion of military operations', along with:[6]

> the consolidation of State authority throughout the territory, through the deployment of Congolese civil administration, in particular the police, territorial administration and rule of law institutions in areas freed from armed groups.

This is straightforward enough, and Figure 1.1 faithfully summarises the logic. It comes from a presentation on proposed strategy for the UN system for the period 2010–12.

Figure 1.1: Statebuilding as exit strategy

Source: MONUSCO (2010) 'Presentation on Integrated Strategic Framework'

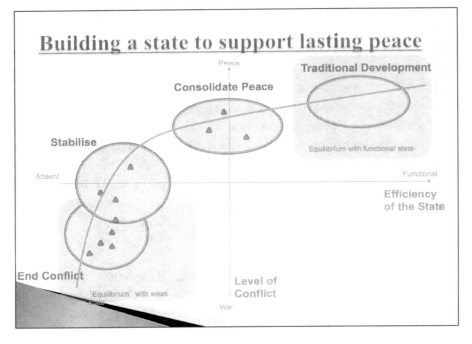

Here 'efficiency of the state' is placed where one usually finds the causal variable, on the X-axis. This is measured from 'absent'—the vacuum once again—to 'functional'. 'Level of conflict' is then the dependent variable. The end-goal is 'traditional development', a code phrase for withdrawing military peacekeepers and leaving civilian specialists in place. Substantial movement towards this goal is expected in the 2010–12 timeframe, with the little red triangles representing programme interventions to nudge things along. To cap it off, another slide is then entitled 'Defining progress: A Congolese state capable of sustaining vital sovereign responsibilities'.

UN documents are rarely so direct, but the chart fairly expresses the main thrust of stabilisation thinking in the DRC. This chapter thus digs into its two major assumptions. We focus on the 'rule of law': the deployment of police, judicial and corrections institutions. Within this frame we look at what happened along the X-axis. Were the central government and its international partners really able to make-over, within a few years, institutions that were starting from a point of 'collapse' and 'deep-seated dysfunction'? To find some answers we track progress on Stability Island, an area in the province of North Kivu where international efforts were heavily concentrated, and logistically a best-case scenario for their success. Next we turn to that rather-too-simple causal relationship: *if* more state 'efficiency', *then* less violent conflict. To test it, we ask: how did local people actually react to the reinforcement of government institutions in the conflict-stricken East? Did deployments like those on Stability Island diminish either motivations or opportunities for violence?

A tour of Stability Island

We received a steady stream of visitors in eastern Congo—or 'missions', as aid workers style such things. These trips usually lasted a week or two. The participants came from the headquarters offices of a confusing of array of agencies in the US, UK, Switzerland, Sweden and a dozen other countries. They were herded onto progressively more dilapidated aircraft to get in-theatre, and then into a carefully orchestrated series of meetings and field trips. (The standard advice from my boss was to 'programme the shit out of them' so they didn't hang around our offices and get in the way.)

The format cried out for simple takeaways—'ground truth'—on a horribly complex situation. Two or three times a week I would guide a gaggle of diplomats, military attachés or aid workers out to the little cafeteria that sat at the back of MONUC's eastern headquarters in Goma. Here I would sketch what we thought this strange animal of 'state authority' might look like when seen in the wild.

Generally what worked best was to concretise things, and the most vivid threat at that time was the National Congress for the Defence of the People (CNDP). We briefly made acquaintance with this group in the Introduction; it consisted of malcontents from one of the belligerents in the Second Congo War who had never quite bought into Congo's new political system. They were encouraged and supported across the border by Rwanda, which sought to protect its local interests. In November 2008 they had routed the national army and occupied Rutshuru, a regional centre an hour's drive north of

Goma. There they massacred well over a hundred civilians within a kilometre of MONUC's local base. Then they marched south, stopping only in a tense standoff with my military colleagues a few kilometres up the road from where we were sitting. Hundreds of thousands of people fled their homes during this course of events. It was, to say the least, a serious black eye for both the Congolese armed forces and UN peacekeeping.[7]

With all that hovering in the background we would try to sketch out a compelling alternative vision. This was often literally lines on a napkin; Figure 1.2 is a photo of a whiteboard version that I produced for a particularly sizeable 'mission'. This depicted our planned 'end-state' for the Rutshuru area. We will call it Stability Island, anticipating a phrase that the chief of MONUC started to use a few years later.[8]

Figure 1.2: Artist's impression of Stability Island
Source: Author files, August 2010

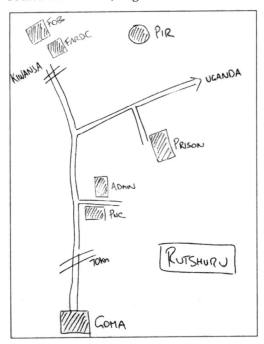

On Stability Island the latest peace deal with the CNDP had stuck, unlike its predecessors. On your right as you disembarked was a new *commissariat* for the Congolese National Police (PNC). This hosted sixty officers, trained and equipped with the lethal and non-lethal tools of the trade. Just across the road stood the new office of the Territorial Administrator with a staff of about forty. Five minutes away was a large new prison meeting international standards. This was to lock up ordinary criminals. To deal with the heavily armed variety, a temporary camp had been set up for a detachment of the *Police d'Intervention Rapide* (PIR), a sort of paramilitary branch of the national police. This was built to last for only about six months and was physically set back from the town as if to emphasise its temporary and urgent character. Meanwhile the security forces—the national army (FARDC) and MONUC's local Forward Operating Base (FOB) were backed off a few more kilometres still.

The overall concept was sometimes summarised as 'state-in-a-box'. Its core feature—the distinction between Stability Island and the 'sea' surrounding it—was to be *law and order*. As a 2009 marketing brochure explained:[9]

Congolese forces have regained control over areas previously occupied by rebels. But getting rid of remaining armed groups cannot in itself ensure stability. Only when responsibility for public order is under police control, roads are reopened and populations returned to their homes can an area be considered relatively stable and on the path to recovery.

Changing this dynamic requires the state to quickly become visible, effective and accountable to people in areas where rebels previously held sway... This includes the deployment of a fully functioning justice system and mechanisms to settle quarrels related to land and property before they turn violent.

These ambitions were translated into a long list of performance indicators, among them: decreased human rights violations by the national army and armed groups; increased utilisation of judicial institutions; and the percentage of the population who felt safe in their community.[10] But to reinforce the idea at a more visceral level we would take officials on driving tours in areas with plenty of new infrastructure. The visual effect is well summarised by Figure 1.3, a slide from a presentation to officials of the central government and several foreign ambassadors.

Figure 1.3: Infrastructure in Masisi centre
Source: MONUSCO (2011) ISSSS Partners Meeting

The overall impression is dramatic. The new blue-roofed buildings seem to dominate the area, towering over the few visible signs of 'old' Masisi. In true PowerPoint fashion labels popped up onto the buildings as you clicked through, making careful note of who had paid for them.

As communication, or as theatre, this worked well enough. This was because we were deploying powerful symbols. The overwhelming majority of our visitors came from rich, strong democracies. Uniformed police, prison guards and court rooms were familiar visual markers for institutions that worked, broadly speaking, to ensure order and stability.

What should have caused greater concern, in retrospect, is who *didn't* buy it. One of the most awkward presentations in my career was in front of an audience of about thirty Congolese journalists. We had assembled them around a horseshoe of folding tables and put up a cloth banner with 'media sensitisation workshop' in hand-painted letters. I gave them the whiteboard version of Stability Island, and lightened the mood with my abominable

Swahili. But they didn't—in fact couldn't possibly—understand the visual grammar in the same way.

What's the point of more officials? You'll dump them there and then they'll have to get by any way they can.

They were referencing an old Congolese joke. Under Joseph-Desiré Mobutu's long reign, people had been said to live by 'article 15', a fictitious constitutional provision to the effect *chacun devait se débrouiller* (each must manage on their own).[11] Its logical corollary was *Système D:* the art and science of getting by. Government officials worked without regular pay or operating budgets, with discretionary bonuses from political patrons, trumped-up fines and kickbacks from service users filling the gaps. This reached its limiting point with the dictator's (possibly apocryphal) comment to the army, 'You have guns—you don't need a salary'.[12]

Two major wars had not improved the situation. In a 2008 survey in North Kivu, when asked 'Who protects you?' a total of 8% of respondents volunteered 'The police'.[13] (Another survey found that just 15% of respondents thought that illegal small arms should be handed over to police.[14]) Meanwhile the justice system was essentially unknown outside major cities, with a total of forty-five decentralised courts for a rural population of perhaps forty-two million people. Even where courts were available there they were considered suspect, with a Gallup poll indicating that 27% of urban residents had confidence in these institutions.[15]

The opinions of international experts tended to be equally unflattering. As we see in Figure 1.4, global rankings for security & justice institutions tended to put modern-day Congo alongside Somalia, or Iraq at the peak of its crisis in 2007–09.

Figure 1.4: Selected indicators for security and justice[16]

Index	Indicator	Ranking
Ibrahim Index of African Governance (2008)	Safety and Rule of Law	50/52 (Africa)
World Governance Indicators (2009)	Rule of Law	206/209 (World)

All in all, there was a colossal gap between what one observed around Congo and what was envisaged for Stability Island. This had two important implications. The first was that targeted institutions would have to ramp up their capabilities very, very quickly to achieve the goals that were set out in our planning documents. (Recall the slide in Figure 1.1, anticipating substantial drawdown of the UN peacekeeping mission within three years.) The second consequence was that institutional reforms were expected to go much further and faster in targeted areas than they were at national level. Planning documents recognised this explicitly, citing 'valid concerns about the quality of the units being deployed' and the need to 'do better than business-as-usual'. [17] UN programmes thus incorporated exceptional measures for Stability Island, including pre-vetting to 'cream' police with clean human rights records from other geographic areas, additional training once these officers were in place, and international teams to provide day-to-day mentoring.

To see how these ambitions played out, let's jump forward a few years. Figure 1.5 is a photo from the formal inauguration of the new police *commissariat* in Rutshuru—the little blue box in the whiteboard map we saw above. The UN used this image many times over in reports to financial contributors, and touted the event as a significant milestone.

Figure 1.5: Inauguration of Rutshuru commissariat
Source: P. Bardoux (2011)

The officers are part of the 'Tiger Battalion' that was deployed to staff the new facilities we were building in the East. They are waiting for a panoply of Congolese dignitaries and the Ambassador of the Netherlands (whose country had paid for the project). And there is certainly the appearance of order. The line is neat; the road is swept and the gutter whitewashed; there is even a brass band. But take a closer look and this picture begins to fall apart. Fewer than half of the officers have a firearm and one of these is missing a stock, rendering it effectively useless. The sword is a cheap fake disguised in garish tissue paper. The uniforms are mismatched with some looking suspiciously home-made—and on the right breast pocket the space to hold the officers' identifying information is conspicuously vacant. More subtly the *commissariat* itself is not in shot, which seems odd for a publication promoting its official opening.

These are hints at quite spectacular logistical problems. The first contingent of the Tiger Battalion landed in Goma in April 2009. The idea was to capitalise on the latest peace accord between the national government and the CNDP by making rapid deployments to Stability Island and its relatives elsewhere. But the plan was so poorly coordinated that the police were left sitting on the patchy grass of Goma's football stadium without shelter or transport. A colleague of mine, a roguish British head-cracker, bent every procurement rule that existed to find tents, water tanks and sleeping mats. All of this equipment was prominently branded by the UN agency that bought it, and the Tiger Battalion acquired the permanent nickname of the 'UNOPS Police'. A further issue was weapons—they had arrived without any. We brokered a loan of Kalashnikovs from the local army brigade. Local contractors rode out to the selected deployment sites and dug out drainage channels and pit latrines, along with rudimentary perimeter lighting. The little encampments ended up looking strikingly similar to the camps for displaced civilians that straggled around Goma and Rutshuru, save only that it was blue police uniforms that hung on the makeshift clothes lines.

Meanwhile the 'state in a box' turned out to be rather difficult to unpack. If we count from that night on the grass in Goma stadium, it was about twenty-one months until the inauguration shown in Figure 1.5, with the other facilities on Stability Island not completed until about thirty months. The reasons always seemed frustratingly banal.[18] Local authorities struggled to identify viable land parcels in negotiation with local communities, having no money to buy it and no coercive authority to simply expropriate it. Provincial-level authorities argued endlessly over blueprints for facilities that had been proposed by their colleagues in the national government in the first place. And local capacity to execute the works was nearly non-existent. Construction of a single police *commissariat* often required four local firms, each paid in multiple small tranches to manage risks of fraud and non-performance.[19]

Meeting day-to-day operating requirements proved equally as difficult. The Prime Minister's Stabilisation and Reconstruction Plan had not led to budgetary apportionments or organisational changes in the ministries that were supposed to deploy staff and supply services. On the ground, this meant that our police counterparts' operations plans listed rations, uniforms/equipment, fuel and transport as simply 'to be provided'.[20] But there were no systems in place to make this happen through supply lines or a cash budget for local purchase. An external evaluation of UN stabilisation programmes described the typical results:[21]

> The team spent a significant amount of time visiting a unit of Congolese police deployed on a hill above the town... The shelter is no longer used, and individuals in this poorly equipped unit now have moved in with local residents since they do not have adequate housing. The team was unable to establish the arrangements under which officers have obtained such local housing. A jeep given to the PNC by donors sits largely unused in a shed due to lack of fuel.

In fact this is already euphemistic—the housing arrangements were attributable to the men acquiring local wives and in many cases small families. This was hardly surprising. They were deployed to the East for years on end with no provision for home leave, and certainly no way of travelling a thousand miles to western DRC to take advantage of it. Like everybody else they also relied on small-scale cultivation to make ends meet, and that meant a family unit to provide the necessary labour.

All this is classic *Système D*. Senior government officials spoke in the peculiar dialects of 'statebuilding' and 'good governance', but an inch beneath the surface it was sheer improvisation, catch-as-catch-can. More formally, this was a problem of policy coherence. What we heard from one partner in government rarely held once we stepped outside their office, with little indication that they were able to motivate, let alone discipline, the various other actors who had to be on board for the plan to work.[22]

Meanwhile—moving on from implementation headaches—what were the impacts on the ground? Figure 1.6 is a photo taken in May 2009 in Kinyandoni, a town fifteen kilometres to the north of Rutshuru. Here we see the immediate aftermath of an attack on one of our new police posts. The Government had deployed thirty officers just one month earlier with UN support, coming from the same Tiger Battalion.

Figure 1.6: Aftermath of an attack in Kinyandoni
Credit: S. Demetriou / MONUC (2009)

On 9 May this unit had arrested an individual nicknamed *Quatre-vingt*. He was affiliated with the Democratic Forces for the Liberation of Rwanda (FDLR), although there were conflicting stories on his precise role. The next morning, the locality chief for Kinyandoni came to demand release of *Quatre-vingt*. Local shops didn't open; the market was unusually quiet. The police refused. Within half an hour the post was attacked by a half-dozen men with small arms. Two police officers were killed and two more wounded, while much of their equipment was torched. A rapid reaction unit of UN peacekeepers

arrived perhaps an hour later but the attackers had left the scene and proved impossible to trace. After-action reports pointed out the obvious: that at least some of the local population was complicit.[23]

In retaliation, the local detachment of the Congolese army (FARDC) 'arrested' Kinyandoni's locality chief and removed him to Rutshuru town. Another customary official came to MONUC to lobby for the latter's release and the full withdrawal of the police detachment from Kinyandoni. He complained that the police officers were idle, that their role was unclear and that they were hostile to the local population. Shortly afterwards the police simply fled the town, joining their colleagues in Rutshuru. There were several near-mutiny incidents, and we had to call in the FARDC to prevent unrestrained shooting by police officers in a near-perfect reversal of the way things were supposed to work on Stability Island.[24]

Faced with these kinds of threat, a UN lessons-learned review concluded that police detachments had 'struggled to define a workable concept of operations'. The population was widely dispersed but the police had no capacity to find, let alone interdict, armed cadres outside urban areas. In fact they avoided leaving main roads for fear of themselves falling prey to opportunistic looting. A follow-up report tortured the English language to square the circle, noting that '[police] units are not deployed in conflict zones, but suffer from repeated raids and harassment from FDLR who are targeting government installations'.[25]

The net consequence was that Stability Island remained heavily militarised. There was no drawdown of the FARDC. The local operating base for MONUC remained on high alert—in fact it put together an elaborate 'Community Alert Network' as a sort of UN-operated 911 service.[26] For the Congolese police units, MONUC arranged for a transfer of more rifles from the FARDC and provided supplementary training in marksmanship and defensive tactics. Joint patrols with local or international soldiers became the norm.[27]

Stuck in this defensive posture, 'law and order' remained a pipe dream. Looting by militias and political killings did not decrease and, in one memorable conversation, a senior civil official complained that militias were 'working in complete tranquillity' just a few kilometres outside town.[28] There was also no indication that the police could deter looting and violence by the Congolese army, vast and under-supplied as it was. In this respect the

Rutshuru area remained in line with the rest of the Kivus, with government security forces responsible for well over 50% of the human rights violations catalogued by humanitarian agencies.[29] (That is, a few hundred reported incidents each month.)

For the local population the net result was continuity rather than change. Oxfam community research in 2012 found that people overwhelmingly preferred to resolve conflicts through unofficial channels, due to a 'continuing failure to properly provide for state security forces' and unchanged 'propensity of many of them to extort money and goods for civilians'.[30] Our own survey work found much the same results—that people remained far more likely to refer problems to shot-callers from the CNDP or other armed groups than they were to go to the 'UNOPS police'.[31] Mob justice remained prevalent, and the civil affairs and human rights detachments of the UN mission assessed that illegal taxation remained exactly as common as before.[32] Meanwhile the only major external evaluation of Stability Island blasted the results:[33]

> A starting point should be that it is unacceptable to pretend that state authority is appropriately restored by facilitating the deployment of underequipped, underpaid, poorly supported Congolese officials…

> Given the extreme difficulties that the Congolese Government continues to have in providing adequate resources, the international community will need to carefully think through its role in this area.

The point can be driven home by taking a few further steps on our tour. In the justice sector, magistrates were a much scarcer commodity than police and could not simply be press-ganged onto a plane. They also belonged to a ministry that was heavily centralised in Kinshasa and notoriously short on resources. A note from the UN coordination team to the Minister of Justice in August 2010, two full years after infrastructure work started, pleaded lamely that efforts 'were approaching the critical phase'.[34] It asked for the establishment of a working group; a process to select magistrates for deployment; and thinking-through of practical requirements for the new facilities to operate. But the problem was never resolved; and no new magistrates started work up to the end of 2012.[35] This made the new, modern prison redundant. In yet another ironic twist, it was used to relieve overcrowding from existing facilities in Goma and Beni, the two main cities in North Kivu.[36] (When the M23 rebellion came at the end of 2012, even those modest gains were erased as the prison was wrecked and the prisoners wandered off.)

In sum, it was pretty clear that the central government had not 'quickly become visible, effective and accountable' quite as we'd planned. What explains this inertia? What was driving passive resistance to finding land for buildings and fuel for police cars? More troubling still—what lay behind the violent resistance to personnel on the ground? The FDLR was frequently caricatured as *génocidaire* bandits, most loudly by the Rwandan government, but clearly there was more than this going on. What was driving segments of local communities to use them as allies against government security forces?

Showdown in Masisi

There was a rather alarming scene in Masisi town in August 2011. Colonel Zabuloni Munyantwari had been appointed commander of police for the surrounding territory a few days before. He had come to take up the post but was now blocked at the outskirts of town. His eighty men stared across a barricade at angry local civilians. On the other side police loyal to the incumbent commander, Colonel Gilbert, riled up the crowd. Much like Zabuloni's men they were mostly ex-militiamen with little experience or interest in peaceful crowd control, and there was a real risk of an ugly confrontation. The senior civilian official was Madame Marie Claire, a tough and experienced administrator. Zabuloni had threatened her on more than one occasion and she had already fled the area to appeal for help to the provincial governor, MONUSCO's head of office, and anybody else who would listen.

A few shots were fired and some scuffles ensued—but in the end Zabuloni backed down. He retreated to his former command post some twenty kilometres away and encouraged the locals there to set up their own roadblocks. A few days later a compromise arrangement was worked out, whereby Zabuloni would instead become police chief in Rutshuru territory and the incumbent there would go to Masisi.[37] The local population didn't seem particularly happy with this arrangement either, but with enough public relations work it went ahead successfully.

What had precipitated the crisis? The UN's official interpretation was that the local population was 'protesting Zabuloni's human rights record'.[38] But this was rather disingenuous. Both Gilbert and Zabuloni had been brought into the National Police from armed groups and as an internal memo noted drily, 'neither can in any regard be thought model police—far from it'.[39]

The problem was rather one of faction. Zabuloni was aligned with the CNDP; Gilbert with an armed group based in the Hunde community that had fought the CNDP from 2007–09.[40] Each exercised fairly effective control over their men and enjoyed (modest) popularity in their heartland areas. But this turned from asset to major liability as they moved around. A long history of local conflict had left communities in a state of mutual suspicion and deeply paranoid about who controlled the security forces. A whiff of this paranoia comes through in the report of a Congolese analyst employed by MONUSCO (the ostensibly neutral party in the dispute):[41]

> Our fear is that the National Police factions will entrench tribalism and implant a parallel police and administration. Why? These police from Masisi were bold enough to chase tax officials from Lushebere to other areas, and the local chief of post deployed his own men to take their taxes for his own treasury. In consequence: The birth of a parallel administration supported by a parallel police.

Colonel Gilbert himself elaborated that 'the Tutsis and Hutus had taken the biggest piece of the cake' in the aftermath of the 2008 and 2009 peace accords, and proceeded to reel off the ethnic/political affiliations of all the commanders and deputies of nearby military regions and police districts.[42] In resisting the appointment of Zabuloni it was clear that he was being egged on by local political heavyweights—who had also procured alcohol and petty cash for the demonstrators on the barricades to help stir up a fight. Their common fear was that losing control of the police force meant vulnerability to intimidation and violence. This would in turn affect access to land, the major productive resource in Masisi territory, and control over illicit tax revenues.

The episode posed some rather serious questions for a strategy premised on the 'extension of state authority'. As an unusually lucid presentation of the national government's Steering Committee for Police Reform once put it, the police force remained a 'mosaic' of elements drawn together from different sources. The most pressing challenge was thus to build a 'republican' and 'apolitical' force, shorn of factional loyalties and subordinate to legal civilian authority.[43] And that challenge was nowhere more obvious than in North Kivu. Peace agreements in 2008 and 2009 had stipulated the 'rapid integration' of thousands of individuals from armed groups into the North Kivu police command. The parameters had been left ill-defined, however, with even the total numbers of personnel very vague and competing demands for ranks and command appointments.[44] In practice, most of those putting on uniforms remained exactly where they were, in the same units and with the same commanders.

The result was a rather blatant struggle for local control. Until the showdown in Masisi, Colonel Zabuloni had worked at the 'parallel' police command in Mushake, a few dozen kilometres to the south-east. There he supervised multiple subordinate detachments, including some cadres already drawing an official police salary, and many more claiming they had a right to do the same. All ignored their notional superiors in the chain of command when it suited them. Unsurprisingly it suited them most where money was involved, and CNDP-affiliated civil officials ran their own taxation system quite openly up until the end of 2011. One UN report reproduced some of their administrative records, detailing imposts for 'dangerous, unhealthy or inconvenient businesses' including hairdressers, micro-cinemas and hardware vendors.[45]

If one travelled north of Masisi town instead of south-east, one found a confusing micro-geography of power with competing police forces associated with Erasto Ntibaturana (also a CNDP affiliate) and the APCLS (a rival group comprised mostly of ethnic Hundes). Both were heavily engaged in taxation and land disputes, with the former implicated in the politically explosive issue of illegal immigration from Rwanda.[46] Most used police uniforms, and some drew salaries. A few miles further west was yet another 'police' affiliated with yet another armed group, the FDN. A UN assessment team observed that the few officers who didn't fall to order were cut off from the outside world because when 'when travelling the road the policemen risk getting caught or arrested by FDN police'.[47]

All this was a long way from the 'vacuum' that all those planning documents had insisted upon. This was demonstrated most plainly in areas where the new Tiger Battalion units ended up co-located with 'rapidly integrated' police. The new deployments created instant contests for jurisdiction, with results that depended upon the local balance of forces. The town of Sake was simply divided, on either side of the market, between the 'UNOPS police' and the 'integrated police'. On a few occasions the boundaries were tested—'our' police attempted to dismantle illegal toll barriers on the road and were summarily run off.[48]

In fact the peculiar situation in Sake was a relatively favourable outcome, because there was a large MONUSCO military base a mile away. As one drew closer to Zabuloni's headquarters in Mushake it became clear who had the upper hand. In one town, a UN police officer reported with a fine sense of irony that the 'the relations between the two units are good, because the deployed unit is marginalised by the [CNDP-affiliated] commander, who does not leave them in a position to work'.[49] In another, parallel police and CNDP-dominated 'customary' authorities forbade the Tiger Battalion unit from doing anything at all and commandeered its holding cells. One visit by UN police officers inventoried the detainees: two thieves arrested by the parallel police and three cases of preventative detention.[50] (The latter included a 'citizen having had altercations with his mistress' and 'a citizen of 45 years, for the reason of contempt towards his uncle'.) The UN officers went on to do what they could, given the circumstances:

> The team strongly requested the authorities, even if they were in zones outside of State control, to scrupulously respect human rights. Some publications on penal procedure were distributed.

The scene is wonderfully evocative of the practical realities. Larger-than-life personalities like Zabuloni and Gilbert protected their own interests, but also represented important local constituencies (however imperfectly). These groups cooperated with the central government sporadically and on limited terms, and with each other even less frequently. It was simply impossible to force them overnight into a unified, centralised command structure.

For Congolese interlocutors this was self-evident—or as one local notable told me, '*plus ça change, plus c'est la même chose...* people have been fighting over who makes the rules here since the colonial time.'

Indeed it is difficult to read the history of North Kivu any other way. The Belgians had arbitrarily reconfigured 'customary' authority in connection with the immigration of Rwandan-speaking peasants in the 1930s–40s. This left many unresolved questions for rights over land and taxation. Just a few years after independence in 1959 the Kanyarwanda War broke out over precisely these tensions, with the trigger an initiative to change colonial-era governance structures.[51] This shaded confusingly into the Mulelist rebellion, a much larger rural insurgency that started elsewhere but cross-pollinated with pre-existing tensions in North Kivu and split communities there into pro- and anti-Mulele camps. Meanwhile central government institutions were rather preoccupied. The 1959–65 period is often referred to simply as *la pagaille*—the chaos, or shambles—as the 'house of cards of the colonial state collapsed' and most trained administrators departed the country.[52] The central government faced two attempted secessions and a second peasant insurgency, much bigger than the Mulelists, along with financial chaos as the colonial-era economy collapsed. The reach and effectiveness of Congolese institutions was rolled back everywhere.

Mobutu's Second Republic (1965–1997) tried hard to reverse the trend and vested executive powers in a network of centrally appointed commissioners and sub-commissioners. The provincial police forces were merged into new national forces, with significant international assistance in the bargain.[53] But both of these systems met their greatest difficulties in the Kivu region. In a detailed study of Zairian statebuilding efforts, Thomas Callaghy highlights the 'local particularism and the power of traditional authorities' of the area in general, and the Masisi territory in particular. He quotes a sub-regional commissioner in 1973:[54]

> [F]or a long time the zone of Masisi has caused us trouble. Spoliation of the land, power disputes and troubles of all kinds live there... my role here is not to remove traditional authorities as some ill-disposed persons contend but rather to search for ways and means of reaching a normalization of the general situation in Masisi Zone.

Another account, of the Shi population in South Kivu, characterises the senior local official as 'more like Kinshasa's ambassador to Ngweshe than the executor of national policy at the local level'.[55]

Attempts to diminish the power of local leaders repeatedly failed. A 1973 law attempted to set criteria for their selection; another in 1974 to transfer them between collectivities just as in the commissioner system. Both were quickly watered down, before being effectively abandoned by 1976. [56] Attempts to reduce the control of traditional authorities over land distribution were equally unsuccessful. The 1973 General Property Law formally established a market system, but by the end of the 1980s just 3% of land was registered under the new system. This left the situation characterised by 'ambiguity, overlapping claims over land, and a de facto dual legal land system'.[57]

Local prerogatives over dispute resolution were protected with equal jealousy. Attempts to introduce new 'peace tribunals' staffed by centrally appointed magistrates foundered almost immediately. [58] Meanwhile, traditional leaders continued to maintain their own police forces. Callaghy reproduces another meeting of regional commissioners in 1971 who fretted that these units were poorly equipped, trained and disciplined and 'supported by the chiefs of the local collectivities because of kinship ties'. Against this, there were 'too few national police and they were poorly equipped, trained and disciplined'.[59] All this led a contemporary newspaper report, no doubt encouraged by the central government, to ask pointedly if Rutshuru territory (the home of Stability Island) was a 'province within a province', and bemoaned that centrally appointed officials became 'mere courtiers and not officials of the state'.[60]

Some commentators go so far as to find the main driver of violence in eastern Congo in this struggle for authority. In 1998, Mahmood Mamdani pointed to a 'crisis of civic citizenship', with local authorities controlling access to land and local governance in favour of some groups and to the exclusion of others. He noted:[61]

In retrospect, one can discern how this produced the environment that incubated the post-1994 crisis of Kivu. The more they were blocked at the local level, the more the Kinyarwanda-speaking minority looked for alternate strategies, both economic and political... When their citizenship was questioned and their right to run for office denied, the Kinyarwanda-speaking minority—

and particularly the Tutsi among them—developed a strategy of entry into organs of the [central] state, particularly the security apparatus.

In recent years Severine Autessere has updated this argument, arguing compellingly that the Second Congo War aggravated the situation.[62] In our case, Muntwari Zabuloni's parallel police could trace its lineage back to the proto-administration established by one of the main belligerents during the war, the so-called Rally for Congolese Democracy-Goma (RCD-G). This group had engaged in clumsy counter-insurgency along ethnic lines, deepening the existing inter-communal rifts. After the war ended, it had then stacked local administrative and police posts once it became obvious that RCD-G candidates would be trounced in provincial and national elections. Other armed groups had done the same when and where they could, to the detriment of communities that had ended the war with little military clout.

A researcher on land conflicts has described the situation that emerged as the *trafic d'influence*, by which armed actors ceaselessly pressured government institutions to align with their interests.

Figure 1.7: Land disputes and the *trafic d'influence*
Source: Beck (2012) 'Contested land in the Eastern DRC'

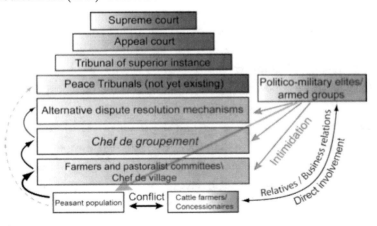

Here is the logic behind the fears of MONUSCO's interpreter on the scene. Colonel Gilbert thought of his militia as a tool to 'defend the population against invasions and land grabs of the former CNDP'.[63] He was hardly about to hand over the tools of coercion in Masisi town—and the authority to judge what was legal and illegal—to Zabuloni as a declared fellow-traveller of that very same group.

The problem was that stabilisation interventions ignored all this. Congolese institutions were instead conceived along the one-dimensional X-axis of 'more' or 'less' state authority that we saw at the top of the chapter. To provide further illustration, Figure 1.8 comes from a 2009 presentation on the concept of operations for the 'restoration of state authority' in eastern DRC.

Figure 1.8: Concept of operations for police deployment
Source: MONUC / UN Police (2008)[64]

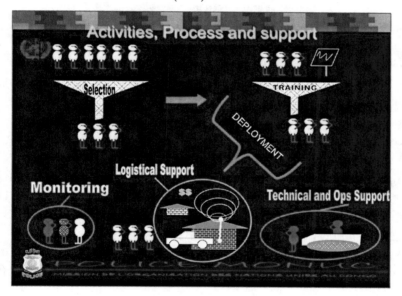

This comes from a Kinshasa-level mixed commission on stabilisation, comprising senior UN police officers seconded from a variety of countries and officers of the Congolese National Police. In their joint thinking, establishment of a police service with power over life and death becomes a literal production line. Selection, training and deployment are mechanical processes requiring only dollars, bodies and infrastructure. Subsequent slides detail coordination and funding arrangements, but without mention of the 'mosaic' of police forces already present on the ground. An accompanying concept note asserted straightforwardly that the 'basic premise is that the [national police] is a comparatively more acceptable guarantor of law and order' than possible competitors. It followed that strategy discussions for stabilisation always 'revolved around the deployment of police' into the eastern provinces.[65]

This mentality led to some strikingly tone-deaf interventions. Sticking with the police sector, this was epitomised in a 2010 training programme aimed at recently integrated officers. The idea was to build a facility at a site named Mugunga; bring 500 cadres there for a six-month course of instruction; assign them to new posts around the province of North Kivu; and then repeat the process for two more tranches of 500.[66] All this work was to be shared between Congolese and international police.

The programme document is primarily about logistics. After a great deal of explanation of site plans and arrangements for feeding trainees it identifies five principal threats to success: (i) the security situation; (ii) price fluctuations in materials; (iii) transport and logistics; (iv) availability of land titles, and (v) local construction capacity. It is only deep in the technical annexe that one finds two rather more critical assumptions: 'Police from armed groups are prepared to participate actively in the process'; and 'Police are ready to be deployed in priority areas as defined by Inspectorate-General of the police'.[67] As assumptions go, these are heroic. What we found at the barricades in Masisi was that withdrawal of a police detachment, or its replacement, was invariably a hotly contested process. Was it really likely that local factions would simply hand over control and let the national police headquarters, one thousand miles away in Kinshasa, decide which of their cadres went where?

Hardly. Building comfort with the process was always going to be the hardest and most important part of the work. Yet there was no provision for discussion with affected communities or the armed groups that claimed to represent them; nor any staff or resources allocated to this end.[68] The programme document itself was agreed between the UN and national police headquarters in Kinshasa. The steering committee for stabilisation programmes in North Kivu likewise consisted of ministers of the provincial government, the Congolese security services, and international partners. On several occasions UN colleagues tried to encourage this group to reach out to affected communities. This was far from successful, with one record of meeting noting sharply: 'The police is national and it is not good to hear that they are linked to this or that other partner. This point is to be dropped.'[69] The resulting situation was well described by Oxfam in mid-2012:[70]

> Local government officials, traditional authorities, grassroots associations and local communities... have largely not been involved in defining a stabilisation strategy that would address their concerns and locally-relevant benchmarks against which to measure it. There has also not been an inclusive and broad local dialogue to identify local blockages to stability such as specific inter-community tensions and prejudices and to work together to find solutions to these problems.

From the UN side this status quo was more or less conceded and we found ourselves bystanders to 'purposefully opaque' processes that the central government held close to its chest.[71] In a debrief after the showdown of Zabuloni and Gilbert, the senior UN official on the scene noted lamely: 'It is not a question of meddling in internal Congolese affairs. It is rather a question of insisting that the free circulation of MONUSCO is guaranteed by the Congolese authorities'.[72] (How one could rebuild and extend 'state authority' while staying clear of internal Congolese affairs was not explained.)

Once the training facility was finally completed, the press release that accompanied the event spoke volumes. In frame in Figure 1.9 are a UN functionary, the Ambassador of Canada, the national Minister of Interior, and the national police Inspector-General.

The accompanying text quotes the chief of UN Police as 'assuring Congolese authorities of MONUSCO's support in order that police everywhere on Congolese territory could be trained' and notes that 'sensitisation work would be done to improve collaboration between police and their communities.' It is apposite to add that the Inspector-General of Police standing at right of frame is Charles Bisengimana, a Congolese Tutsi who had joined both the AFDL and RCD rebellions in the 1990s.[73] Both groups were ancestors to the present CNDP, the precise same movement that Colonel Gilbert feared was 'eating up the cake'.

Figure 1.9: Inauguration of the Mugunga training centre
Source: MONUSCO (2012) Press release, 18 June

For local factions suspicious of central government motives, the visual impression here was absolutely terrible (irrespective of Bisengimana's personal intentions and record). And uptake for training turned out to be minute. The infrastructure budget was scaled up and trainee numbers revised down to 284 police, or well under 10% of the *integrés* in North Kivu.[74]

This barely dented the overall caseload and local frustrations continued to grow. A March 2011 communiqué dropped off with the provincial governor and MONUSCO is illustrative. It was printed on home-made police letterhead, and authorship attributed to the 'coordination bureau of former armed groups of North Kivu'. Under the title 'Appeal to conscience: Are the Goma peace accords abrogated?', the signatories complained that integrated police were 'abandoned without any assistance' and that even where training had occurred the Government 'had not taken its responsibilities and deployed cadres with their [due] considerations'. [75] Meanwhile semi-autonomous local police forces and the *trafic d'influence* remained the realities on the ground.

On the UN side, the final report for the training programme claimed vaguely that 'in general the project attained its objectives, and the works done were received by national authorities who appreciated the quality'.[76] There is literally no comment on where trainees came from, who they were affiliated with, or where they went. Narrative reports for international stabilisation efforts were likewise limited to grandiose photos of the physical facility, and of a classroom of police being lectured on the ethical code of conduct.[77] In a burst of optimism the June 2011 instalment dressed up these modest achievements as necessary but not sufficient conditions for stabilisation of the East:[78]

> The [stabilisation strategy] has laid the groundwork to expand state presence in sensitive territories, but there is not yet durable change on the ground. In particular, completing planned deployments and training of officials will be a precondition for genuine impact.

In fact this was precisely backwards. Technical training and facilities were not the 'groundwork', but rather a superstructure that could be only as stable as its political foundations. As those foundations fell apart we penned the tragic coda to the story—the M23 rebels using the Mugunga facility to stage 'ideological briefings' for police after the capture of Goma in late 2012. This led to its own rather unfortunate photo opportunities.[79]

At the strategic level, we see the same error in stark clarity in Figure 1.10, below. This is a situation assessment for stabilisation programmes in 2011 (which I coordinated!), and which benchmarked 'state authority' for eighteen territories in eastern Congo. In it we see a simple linear scale, much as one might use for rainfall or temperature.

Empirically, as a map of government institutions' ability to arrest somebody or issue a land title, this was pretty accurate. But as a description of how Congolese civilians actually related to the national or provincial governments, it was worse than useless.

Figure 1.10: Evaluation of 'state authority'
Source: MONUC / Stabilisation Support Unit (2011)

Assessment criteria
(State authority)

| 5 | State can exercise core functions in all populated areas. |

| 4 | Exercises core functions in most populated areas; but significant groups or areas are excluded. |

| 3 | Exercises core functions for some major centres and axes; but large groups or areas are excluded. |

| 2 | Exercises core functions only in limited areas such as the territorial capital. |

| 1 | No effective presence. |

State authority
31 July 2011

Projection of authority outside territory capitals remains difficult
- Twelve territories: "effective presence only in limited areas".
- Four territories : "effective presence for some major areas"

ISSSS programs:
- "en cours" for five territories
- gaps in deployment mean we have not seen a level change yet.

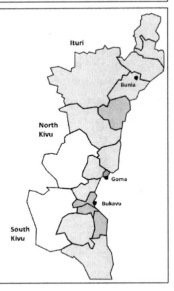

A similar, but even more reductive, approach was used for additional Government–UN assessments in 2011–12. The final reports were little more than inventories of facilities and personnel numbers across the eastern provinces, with MONUSCO's chief reporting back to the Security Council:[80]

> A common thread linking virtually all the areas, however, was the pressing need to secure adequate resources for State institutions and the national security forces in terms of sufficient numbers of adequately trained and equipped personnel, as well as the logistical support and suitable infrastructure to deliver State services.

The differences between this perspective and those that we saw in Masisi were unbridgeable. Stated simply, state institutions were conceived *purely* as 'infrastructure', the set of tools and techniques needed to implement decisions.[81] There was no account of what that infrastructure was used *for*. This ignored the long 'crisis of civic citizenship', and grievances regarding land and local governance where a widely accepted policy framework had never existed. It ignored equally a long history of factions co-opting the security forces and civilian institutions for their own benefit, which we encountered above in the guise of the *trafic d'influence*.

One lobby organisation summed up the approach as 'building on sand' and an 'extension of predatory behaviour'; another commented that work was premised on assumptions 'contrary to the abundant evidence of the character of the state'.[82] What is certain is that we were guilty of gross oversimplification. The political scientist and anthropologist James C Scott has called this *high modernist audacity*—the belief that complex political–social systems can be understood, mapped and re-engineered by understanding just a few variables.[83] That audacity left us extraordinarily ill-prepared when local communities started to resist and push back on the much-publicised front-line of 'state authority'.

Building on sand

The exit strategy in eastern Congo was premised on strikingly bold assumptions. Metaphors of 'decay' and the 'vacuum' gave way to their opposites: a strong and physically omnipresent state. This was translated into detailed assessments of the operational capabilities of police, prisons and decentralised administrators, accompanied by plans for rapid scale-up in chosen areas.

At a practical level we sold this approach more by symbolic association than by any evidence of effectiveness. Sprawling police stations and uniformed officers were taken for law and order; coloured squares on a map assumed away impossible logistical difficulties. In many cases, as on Stability Island in Figure 1.5, there was a literal raising of the Congolese flag to recognise the moment that state authority was 'restored'.[84]All this is what the organisational sociologists Paul DiMaggio and Walter Powell dubbed 'institutional isomorphism'—the attempt to gain legitimacy and support by *looking like* high-functioning organisations.[85]

As a tactic it was successful. From 2007–12 the statebuilding model dominated the conversation on exit strategy. The Security Council and most international partners bought into a vision of government institutions taking over the heavy lifting, and they found enough Congolese partners that programmes could go forward at significant scale. On the UN side we successfully raised funds for our Stability Islands, where police would deal with criminals and judges would calmly adjudicate disputes, and eventually delivered most of the work that we had promised.

As a strategy, of course, the approach failed. It proved extraordinarily difficult to create islands of effectiveness in otherwise weak institutions, as one after the another critical dependencies failed to materialise. We were also reminded of a fairly basic truth of government: that it depends on the consent of the governed. Before very long, our simple scale of 'How much?' had to yield to much messier questions of 'Who?', and 'How?', and 'To what ends?'. Absent answers to these questions, there was no great surge of confidence in police, judicial or administrative institutions. Passive and active resistance slowed programmes to a crawl, while disputes over land, taxes, migration and everything else that made up local politics continued to be resolved through violence or the threat thereof.

This pushes us towards an obvious question. These issues were known—conceptually if not always in the details. So why was there not a more serious push on institutional reform to accompany the 'statebuilding' project? We turn to this in the next chapter, on *policy without politics*.

2

Policy without politics

The security forces are the most maligned of all of Congo's institutions. In the press they are acknowledged only as malefactors—after the national army achieved a rare military victory, the British magazine *The Economist* sneered that it was 'not used to being feted with palm leaves and is unaccustomed to winning. Its men are better known for rape and pillage'.[1] In covering a mass atrocity the *New York Times* likewise dismissed the security forces with a single thumbnail photo, captioned 'the army is said to be in great disarray', and the offhand comment that police 'are often invisible or drunk'.[2] (How they achieved the former feat was not explained.)

More serious sources are not more charitable. The most widely read history of the Second Congo War describes the concluding peace process as 'botched and insufficient' in its military dimensions, with the approach to security institutions 'in a state of almost constant improvisation'.[3] The lobby organisation International Crisis Group declared that 'efforts to reform the Congo's military and police start from levels that were in many respects less than zero', in a turn of phrase often echoed by other analysts.[4]

In 2007, this problem jumped to the top of the (long) priority list. National elections had just been successfully completed, bringing a fragile transitional government to a close. Almost the second they were done, the Security Council acknowledged the 'milestone' and then turned in the same breath to the army and police. It emphasised the need to 'urgently' carry out reforms, to develop a security strategy for the eastern part of the country, and to bring individuals who had committed crimes to justice. It then implored international donors to provide 'urgent' assistance.[5] For its part, the new

Cabinet under Prime Minister Antoine Gizenga released a 'governance contract' almost immediately after taking office. The security sector was literally and metaphorically priority number one, with the preamble getting right to the point:[6]

> In this regard, the [Governance Contract] for 2007 concentrates on the domains judged fundamental to re-establishing stability in the DRC, such as the reform of the security sector (in the broad sense of the term, including the armed forces, the police and the judicial system).

Lest this be thought the mind-set of diplomats and a few politicians, let us triangulate with what the non-governmental sector was saying. Figure 2.1 comes from a selection of major policy briefs from 2007–12, each proposing priorities for peacebuilding in eastern Congo. The graphic pulls out the most frequently used words across this sample, with the size of individual words scaled by how often they appeared.

Figure 2.1: The 'priority of priorities', 2007–2012
Source: Panel of six policy briefs from non-governmental organisations[7]

Security everywhere dominates—factions (FARDC, CNDP, MONUC); institutions (army, armed groups, forces), consequences (security, violence, conflict, crisis). Or, as a joint statement of thirteen large non-governmental organisations was later to put it, 'the government's inability to protect its people or control its territory undermines progress on everything else'.[8]

The core of the problem was the national army, the *Forces Armées de la République Démocratique du Congo* (FARDC). The agreements that ended the Second Congo War had anticipated that the various belligerents would combine into a 'national, restructured and integrated army', but had been short on detail on how this might occur. High commands were allocated according to a crude power-sharing logic. For the lower ranks the process that ensued was dubbed *brassage*—literally 'brewing', one of many common words that have acquired a meaning peculiar to the Congo. The idea was to split up the factions that had fought each other during the war, provide brief retraining, and then re-mix individual combatants into integrated units. This would break up old command structures, prevent the concentration of military resources in any single pair of hands and, in time, encourage 'republican' allegiances.

In reality the process was far from comprehensive. It created eighteen integrated brigades that were reasonably cohesive, but around this considerable achievement all sides had gamed the system. Numbers were inflated; geographical deployments were manipulated; and informal/parallel command relationships persisted. [9] In assessing the results foreign commentators have struggled to out-do each other with clever quips, referring to the notionally unified institution as the 'beer that would not brew' and a 'half-cooked bouillabaisse'. Another titled his review article *Candide au Congo*, after Voltaire's satire on the death of optimism.[10]

On the ground the messy process 'produced many discontented commanders, who felt they had not received the positions and ranks they deserved'.[11] Many of them went back to the bush when it became clear they were not succeeding at the political game. Some of these *brassage* dodgers were formidable. We have already encountered the most dangerous: the National Congress for the Defence of the People (CNDP), boasting some 4,500 well-trained troops, an equally sophisticated media operation, and not-very-discrete support from Rwanda. Other factions were much more local. The militias that had mushroomed across eastern Congo during the war were particularly ill-equipped to succeed at politics, and suspicious that they would be hung out to dry as the command assignments that really mattered were partitioned among the major factions. Most never quite demobilised, prompting the Government and the UN to refer to them euphemistically as 'residual' combatants or *groupuscules armés* (micro armed groups).[12]

Against this background, where everybody was stressing urgency, it is striking that the period 2007–12 saw so little actual change. We noted in the Introduction that Congo actually *deteriorated* on widely used indexes of state fragility over this period—and if we unpack the underlying methodologies it was a lack of progress with security institutions that was largely responsible. Figure 2.2 extracts some of these more specialised indices for the period 2007–12. In each the trend is the same: stagnation for four years, followed by an obvious deterioration for another two.

Figure 2.2: Declining security capabilities of the state, 2007–12[13]

Higher numbers are worse, i.e. reflect more fragile institutions

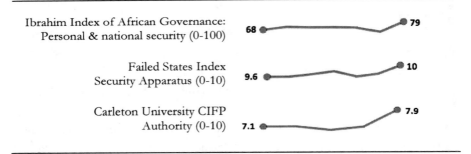

More prosaically, one review article summarised the period as 'revolving doors in a military mess (2007–09)' and 'accelerated integration and accelerated desertion (2010–12)'.[14] Supplementary peace deals were signed with some of the '*brassage* dodgers' in 2008 and 2009, but they didn't stick. Then in April 2012 the *Mouvement de 23 Mars* (M23) formed out of fragments of the CNDP. About eight months later, with Rwandan support, it drove the FARDC out of Goma. Both the Government and the UN peacekeeping mission were thoroughly humiliated—one representative photo essay from Al Jazeera recapitulated events with the M23 victory parade in Goma's stadium, its international press conference explaining plans for the city, and then a ceremony to collect oaths of allegiance from local police.[15]

In sum there is a contradiction here. On the one hand there were policy goals for security institutions that were regarded by all as extremely urgent;

and on the other hand there were very few effective measures to move towards them. This chapter seeks to explain why.

In the first section we look at Congolese efforts to reorganise the armed forces, with specific focus on the 10th Military Region in the province of South Kivu. This was a process characterised by fear, risk and uncertainty. Missteps frequently led to mutinies, and occasionally to grotesque violence against civilians. Then in the second section we shift focus to how *international* actors engaged with the same set of problems, invariably grouped together as 'security sector reform'. This was a process characterised by bold planning assumptions and repeated demands that the Congolese get their house in order. In effect, this meant scant interest in opening up the black box of policy and see why it wasn't working as desired.

Walking the high wire

In June 2011, Colonel Kifaru Niragiye deserted from the FARDC's Kananda military garrison with just under two hundred soldiers. His band marched west and north into the mountains, encamping in the towns of Abala and Nyakiele for several days. There they pillaged the local population and perpetrated quite extreme violence. International press attention was swift, with typical headlines reading 'Attackers rape more than 170 women in raids on Congo villages' and 'When rape becomes a game'; while Kifaru himself was frequently referred to simply as the 'DRC rape colonel'.[16] To this day there remain disputes over the exact number of victims, because the episode turned overnight into a political football. The possibility of objective fact-finding evaporated as provincial deputies started issuing public denunciations and local militias worked the incident into their recruiting pitches.[17]

International condemnation reached its height with the epilogue to the story: the 'reintegration' of Kifaru. Within four months he was accepted back into the army and assigned command of the 111th Regiment, a lateral move at worst and much closer to his home area. The lobby group Enough Project described the episode as a 'temper tantrum' that had been rewarded; Amnesty International declared that the Congolese army was marred by a 'culture of impunity, leading to attack after attack against civilians'. For its part, the UN peacekeeping mission commented blandly that 'the Government needed to do more to bring perpetrators to justice'. [18]

But what was going on from the point of view of Congolese decision-makers? How had they been held hostage by this sort of strong-arm tactic?

Early 2011 was a quiet moment by the standards of eastern Congo. A huge sweep against the bush guerrillas of the *Forces Démocratiques de Libération du Rwanda* (FDLR) was trailing off, and the Congolese army transferred its energies into a reorganisation process. (We return to the FDLR operations in Chapter 3.) Units were withdrawn from their deployments to regional centres, with the objective of reorganising scattered 'brigades' into larger 'regiments'. This was billed as a measure to increase operational effectiveness—quite plausibly since army brigades were chronically, sometimes ludicrously beneath their paper strength.

The process was referred to as 'regimentation' with this in mind but in reality it was an entry point for a different kind of restructuring. Specifically, key FARDC officials wanted to improve on the peace agreements of 2008 and 2009. These had been negotiated from a position of weakness and had abandoned the *brassage* principle elaborated during the 2004–06 political transition. The approach that had prevailed was instead called *mixage*, whereby significant chunks of armed groups were simply appended to the FARDC with their existing command structures largely intact. The high command viewed this arrangement as a stopgap, with the intent to 'integrate them, slowly wear down their chain of command, then deploy their officers elsewhere in the country'.[19] Senior officers had thus been testing the waters since late 2010 on reshuffling the assignments and deployment locations of their notional subordinates.[20]

The regimentation initiative had wide-ranging consequences all across eastern Congo, with security dynamics shifting significantly in places like Irumu and Shabunda (as we will see in Chapter 3). Down at the southern tip of South Kivu, Colonel Kifaru was watching the situation closely. He was the commander of the 43rd military sector, and a Rwandan-speaking Hutu whose last job had been with the *Coalition des patriotes résistants congolais* (PARECO). This was a multi-ethnic militia that had formed in North Kivu in 2007 to resist the CNDP; it had fought in alliance with the FARDC and staved off defeat for the latter on several occasions. Most of its personnel were then integrated into the army under the peace accords signed in March 2009.

Seen from Kifaru's standpoint, the regimentation process now seemed to be slipping out of control. The FARDC had concluded negotiations with the *Forces Républicaines Fédéralistes* (FRF) a few months earlier, a group based in the Banyamulenge community of South Kivu. In exchange for bringing most of their troops into the fold, FRF commanders had received control of a new military sector adjacent to the 43rd, a still more senior command appointment elsewhere, and guarantees they would not be redeployed outside their home area. All this had come to a head in May 2011, with the FRF's threats to pull out of the process securing the final concessions.[21] Now the word was that the commander of the 10th Military Region, General Pacifique Masunzu, intended to replace Kifaru with an FRF officer. Worse—Masunzu himself was Banyamulenge!

Kifaru stood to lose financially from the decision—his troops in the 43rd sector had been amply implicated in gold extraction and outright looting during his tenure.[22] But there was also considerable fear. PARECO's star had waned since 2009 as it split into rival factions, largely along ethnic lines, and Kifaru's own Hutu faction risked becoming isolated. The crude power-sharing calculus that dominated thinking at the time is perfectly captured in Figure 2.3 (overleaf), reproduced by the Congo-watcher Jason Stearns from FARDC records. Here, army command posts are listed down the left-hand side in order of seniority; and a rough list of factions across the top. The allocation of posts then becomes a means of keeping score over two phases (*vagues*) of reorganisation.

Commanders watched in alarm as their numbers changed—and PARECO's numbers seemed to be dropping rapidly. As a consequence, much of the Hutu wing had already been lured to the side of the CNDP with the promise of a powerful ally. (The fact that they had fought each other in 2007–09 apparently did not present a major obstacle, in what the Congolese wearily refer to as an *alliance contre nature*.)

Figure 2.3: Proposed division of posts for regimentation

Source: Stearns (2011) *Congo Siasa*[23]

FONCTIONS	NOMBRE DE POSTES		COMPOSANTES							
			GOV		CNDP		PARECO		FRF	
	1ère VAGUE	2ème VAGUE	1ère VAGUE	2ème VAGUE	1ère VAGUE	2ème VAGUE	1ère VAGUE	2ème VAGUE	1ère VAGUE	2ème VAGUE
Comd Regt	05	08	03	04	01	02	01	01	-	01
Comd 2ND Ops-Rens	05	08	02	05	02	01	01	01	-	-
Comd 2ND Adm-Log	05	08	03	04	01	02	01	01	-	01
Comd Bn	10	16	06	10	03	03	01	-	-	01
Comd 2ND Bn	10	16	08	12	01	02	01	02	-	-
S/Total	35	56	22	35	08	10	05	05	00	03
Total Gen	91		57		18		10		03	
% Par Composante			62,6%		19,7%		10,9%		3,4%	

Kifaru himself was reputedly courted by CNDP bigwig and International Criminal Court indictee Bosco Ntaganda in late 2010. The latter made dark intimations about Kinshasa's intentions, and gave promises of support in the army reorganisation process.[24] The pitch was no doubt that Kifaru's own Hutu community risked being left isolated. They had lived through a long history of serious inter-communal violence, along with repeated attempts to strip them of citizenship in the 1980s and 1990s.[25] Losing a strong role in the security forces was accordingly not to be taken lightly, and the high command *had* intimated it would move some integrated soldiers outside the Kivus. Moreover, was not Kifaru already a long way from home? Suspicion against Rwandan-speakers in the FARDC ran deep, no matter the services rendered in 2007–08. One can imagine Bosco Ntaganda echoing one of his junior officers, quoted by the researcher Judith Verweijen:[26]

> We are never safe in the army. Today they are your colleagues, but when something happens tomorrow, we are the first to get killed. We have seen this in 1998 in Kamina, in Kalemie, in Uvira, everywhere... and it can always happen again.

The crisis broke on 7 June when Masunzu ordered weapons at the Kananda site to be securely stockpiled. A standoff ensued; Kifaru deserted with his loyalists.

The bitter irony was that his group's rampage through Abala and Nyakiele affected the *Bembe* community, who had not been party to the dispute. It is unclear whether this was vindictive or simply pragmatic: Kifaru's own country lay to the north, and it would have been much riskier to foray into the FRF's heartland to the west. But either way the result was the same. There was further hardening of the Rwandan-speaking and 'native' (*autochtone*) factions within the FARDC, and Bosco Ntaganda's prophecy became self-fulfilling. The perception of many soldiers was that Hutu and Tutsi factions were struggling to parcel out choice posts without regard to the costs, a feeling only heightened by caustic press commentary on the 'feckless' and 'ill-disciplined' Congolese army. As one lieutenant put it:[27]

A Rwandophone can kill, assassinate, rape, and do whatever he wants. But if it were me, a Congolese, Moreno Ocampo [then-Prosecutor of the International Criminal Court] would be informed the same day.

The rest of 2011 saw considerable tit-for-tat fratricide within the army, including the murder of a Tutsi lieutenant-colonel and attempts on the commanders of the 82nd sector and the 1051st battalion by their Rwandan-speaking subordinates. From September onwards a document entitled 'Memorandum of FARDC military officers who are victims of discrimination' was circulated widely, complaining that 'all ranks in the FARDC are based on discriminatory and ethno-tribal criteria'.[28] There was clearly some truth to this, with the estimates in Figure 2.3 suggesting that 70% of command appointments were occupied by officers who had been integrated into the army from Rwandophone factions.

Down in Fizi territory, where Kifaru had been assigned, the fire was carefully stoked by local politicians and militia leaders. The latter included most notably William Amuri 'Yakutumba', who controlled (loosely) a few hundred men. He penned letters to local FARDC commanders declaring that 'we have a wide-ranging project to liberate our country with you the Congolese', as against President Kabila who had 'ceded the country to Rwanda'. This echoed a formal manifesto that decried capitulation to foreign interests and discrimination against 'natives' in the FARDC.[29] (In a fine example of Congolese politics, it was addressed to President Kabila but deposited at the local MONUSCO sub-office.) The self-proclaimed general was moderately successful in his appeals, with a steady trickle of arms and information from FARDC officers that allowed him to expand activities considerably over the course of 2011.[30]

Now, let us step back and look at this episode in wider focus. It concerned a single decision on command assignments for the FARDC in Fizi, perhaps one-tenth (by population) of one province of the Congo. The process by which it spiralled out of control illustrates two enduring truths of security policy in the DRC.

The first is that the commanders on the scene had *little effective control*. In key respects, the cohesion of the 10th Military Region depended on little more than the verbal agreement of its internal factions. Policy initiatives accordingly had to be premised on estimations of the relative strength and determination of those affected. In this case, General Masunzu and his superiors miscalculated. The attempt to contain the situation by collecting weapons instead provoked an outburst of incredible violence. Masunzu then had to back down and accept Kifaru for reintegration when his own superiors decided this was the more prudent course.

This was the half-cooked *bouillabaisse* seen close-up, and was the inevitable result of attempting reorganisation of the army while fighting several wars. The 'cold war' against the CNDP—the struggle for control over the FARDC in the East—was close to its peak in mid-2011. This gave minor factions like PARECO's Hutu wing and the FRF considerable bargaining leverage as they were courted by both sides and made frequent threats to withdraw back to the bush. (The FRF benefited from General Masunzu's presence, as he had spent many years trying to split the Banyamulenge community away from dependence on Rwanda and its proxies.) Meanwhile a 'hot war' was also on-going, with operations against illegal armed groups spread out over a very large geographic area. This provided ample opportunities for factions that were unhappy with trends in the FARDC. As discontent in the ranks increased, so did the flow of information, men and materiel to groups like Yakutumba's.

The second major theme of the Kifaru debacle was *mutual paranoia*. Reorganisation of security institutions was a serious business and nobody was about to trust in the paper roles and responsibilities of the FARDC.

Just to take one protagonist, the FRF agreed to put on army uniforms but only on the conditions that they would: (i) not be redeployed outside their home areas, and (ii) hold the important local commands. Then, even with these favourable conditions, several detachments still remained 'un-integrated' due to lack of trust in the process. Their reasons were simple enough. Within the very recent past, the troops in Kifaru's 43rd sector had been extraordinarily ill-behaved, ransacking the town of Fizi and engaging in ham-fisted counter-insurgency.[31] A longer history of violence by uniformed security forces against the local Banyamulenge population included: the Simba rebellion of 1964–7 and subsequent conflicts over administrative integration; spillover effects of the 1993 'Masisi war' that started in North Kivu; attempts in the mid-1990s to strip Rwandophone communities of citizenship; the division of ethnic groups across the battle lines in the First Congo War; and clumsy reprisals by RCD-G troops during the Second Congo War.[32] It is perhaps not a great stretch to understand why any 'reform' initiative would be thought a risky and uncertain proposition.

How did these dynamics play out on the larger stage? We can find some clues in Figure 2.4, on the next page. This is a mapping of armed groups active in South Kivu as at June 2011—or in other words the security environment which confronted the 'regimentation' process for the 10th Military Region of General Masunzu. (Note William Amuri's green 'Yak' bubbles at bottom right, on the edge of Lake Tanganyika.)

Some of the data underlying this map was rank guesswork. But the obvious reaction is also the right one—confusion. The FARDC was just one among many purveyors of violence, with the FDLR distributed over huge areas and eleven 'local' armed groups confined to smaller areas of operations.

The result was a rather delicate equilibrium. If a faction within the FARDC was confronted by a policy initiative that it disliked, it had no shortage of allies with whom to make common cause. Indeed most commanders in the field assiduously cultivated such outside connections. Congolese security forces had relied heavily on militias as force multipliers since the 1960s, when the Balukbakat party was supported to weaken the secessionist government of Katanga. Such collaboration was also the norm during the Second Congo War (1998-2003), when Government security forces had lost control of the terrain entirely and resorted to indiscriminate weapons drops to an array of militias. After a brief lull the industry picked up again during the showdown with the CNDP in 2007–08, with new armed groups spun out of whole cloth and encouraged to show up for peace negotiations to pump up the numbers on the 'Government' side.[33] As the rapprochement with the CNDP started to break down in 2011–12, the army went right back to the same old tricks, funnelling money and weaponry to a rogue's gallery of militias.[34]

Figure 2.4: Armed groups in South Kivu, June 2011
Source: MONUSCO / South Kivu (2011)

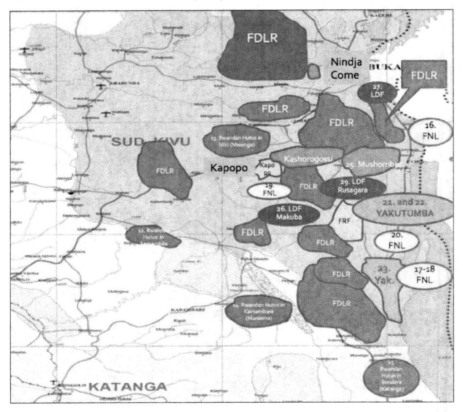

In extremis there was also the option of desertion, as Kifaru had demonstrated. Many of the groups in Figure 2.4 drew on deserters from the army and police, including micro-groups led by mid-level officers like Bede Rusagara and Nyerere Bunana (marked as 'LDF Rusagara' and 'Kashorogosi'

in Figure 2.4).[35] All through the regimentation process there was a bizarre merry-go-round as minnow factions like these made agreements to join the army, haggled over terms, 'deserted' and then re-started the game anew. Mai-Mai Kapopo, so small as to be barely visible in the diagram, entered into talks in February 2011. This was immediately interpreted in UN reports as the 'integration' or even 'surrender' of the group—until their demands emerged.[36] A weekly situation report explained with what can only be interpreted as dry under-statement:[37]

> Negotiations between FARDC and 'General' Kapopo ran into complications after Kapopo asked for money, a position of command in the 10th Mil Region, control over his territory in the Hauts Plateaux and two brigades composed of his units.

In fact such terms were preposterous. Kapopo's group numbered a few hundred poorly armed and ill-trained men—yet he was trying to carve an independent fiefdom within the FARDC, complete with a senior command appointment for himself. This reflects the same complete distrust of the army that we saw for the FRF, the belief that the only real guarantee of community security was physical control of the forces on the ground.

Another report, perhaps competing for ironic under-statement, added that Kapopo's demands did not 'bode well for full-fledged integration'.[38] In practice the process dragged on as FARDC officers and Kapopo traded competing offers, the former all the while trying to balance competing demands from heavy-hitters like Kifaru and the FRF commanders. By June 2011, it was clear that most of the Kapopo rank-and-file had already walked away from the process and were re-recruiting in their original haunts.[39]

A few months later, regimentation came to a close. The initiative was widely panned by external analysts as 'hijacked' by the CNDP and its allies, having strengthened rather than diminished their hold over the security forces.[40] Senior diplomats, including the Belgian Foreign Minister and the US Ambassador, complained that figures like Bosco Ntaganda remained in key positions, and pushed for his arrest.[41]

Government figures were either emboldened by this support or simply frustrated by the failure of the initiative. In either case they decided to play their hand more aggressively. A close aide to President Kabila tried to broker a deal with Kigali to break with key CNDP leaders, while many mid-level officers were brought to Kinshasa on generous allowances for indefinite 'seminars on security sector reform'.[42] The cold war rapidly heated up, with short-lived mutinies in January, February and March and threats of prosecution in return. Finally the *Mouvement de 23 Mars* announced itself in May 2011, with an initial force of just under a thousand deserters, and by November was marching into Goma.

This appeared to be the nightmare scenario—FARDC reform had fallen off the high wire. But what is interesting, and under-appreciated, is that all the scheming and side-deals largely worked. Kifaru Niragiye stayed with his new backers in the M23 and kept a chunk of the former PARECO alongside him. But he was an exception in the Hutu community, which largely ignored the new rebellion. The Banyamulenge community in South Kivu (and the FRF) mostly did the same. In the end the M23 was largely contained in North Kivu, and was forced to reach out to small and relatively unproven groups.[43] It was rather the presence of one specific ally that tipped the balance—Rwanda. Once it was removed from the equation in 2013 by massive international pressure the M23 found itself isolated and was defeated quite readily.

The myth of political will

A great deal of ink was spilled on the Congolese security sector throughout this period. The great recurring theme was to castigate the central government for a lack of drive and commitment, with lobbyists' policy briefs bearing titles like 'No will, no way' and 'Taking a stand on security sector reform'. The executive summary of one such report, from a coalition of local and foreign organisations, will give the drift:[44]

> The root of the failure to implement security sector reform (SSR) is a lack of political will at the highest levels of the Congolese Government. Rather than articulating a vision for Congolese security and marshalling assistance to achieve it, the Government has instead encouraged divisions among the international community and allowed corrupt networks within the security services to flourish, stealing the resources intended to pay basic salaries or profiting from exploitation of natural resources.

Note the grammar here: It is 'the' Government which lacks 'political will' and is 'stealing resources', and which 'allows' corrupt networks to exist. In another study we find the confident proclamation that 'the fundamental problem is with the will to do it rather than the means of doing it', along with advice to study 'the resistance and other strategies of avoidance' deployed by Government counterparts. [45] All this became elevated to the level of conventional wisdom, a chorus to the effect that the Congolese just didn't want security sector reform.

The problem is that it is rather difficult to square this with the story we have just read, where decisions were made in a context of considerable fear, risk and uncertainty. This is because identifying 'political will' as the binding constraint rather assumed the conclusion. The great sociologist Max Weber once identified the defining characteristic of *modern* bureaucracies as a capacity for 'goal-rational' (*zweckrational*) behaviour, meaning 'a high degree of calculability of results for the heads of the organization and for those acting in relation to it'.[46] At this point one sets policy rather than negotiating it; the institution is steered according to legally defined roles and responsibilities. His thesis, critically, was that this was the culmination of a long historical process of unifying institutions and eliminating competing centres of authority. In the security sector this process of 'bureaucratisation' inevitably unfolded by cautious steps: 'eliminating, subjugating, dividing, conquering, cajoling, buying as the occasions presented themselves'.[47]

The regimentation process was an all-too-real example of what such a process looks like. Congolese attempts to reorganise the FARDC ran into almost immediate resistance from internal factions and from stakeholders outside the organisation. This was because everybody recognised the risks of miscalculation—whether for the tiny hamlets of Abala and Nyakiele in the wake of Kifaru's desertion, or half of North and South Kivu when the M23 returned to the field. In this arena it was abundantly clear that 'all politics is real politics; people risk death when they make political mistakes'.[48] Any policy initiative had to rest on careful coalition-building and marginalisation of potential opposition. (It is with good cause that a 2013 survey of the Congolese security sector was entitled 'Untangling the Gordian knot!'[49])

The contradiction between this reality and the mechanics of international engagement are striking. From the second the elected government took office in 2007, foreign officials started to demand a big push. The Security

Council insisted on a 'comprehensive plan and timelines for the reform of the army'.[50] At country level, the head of the UN mission declared that there was 'a basic principle which must guide all our efforts in this sector, which is to have a national management plan'.[51] His team for security sector reform was configured accordingly, with just a few senior staff based in Kinshasa to lobby the central government. Budget documents identified their main performance indicator as 'adoption of comprehensive strategy and action plan for reform of the defence sector', alongside supplementary indicators related to meetings with Kinshasa-based partners.[52] For its part the European Union produced a working document on a 'comprehensive approach to SSR in DRC', while its support mission on the ground (EUSEC) was mandated to advise on 'national plans and policies' to 'integrate, restructure and rebuild the Congolese army'.[53]

All sides cited so-called best practices. A favourite point of reference was the Organisation for Economic Co-operation and Development's guidelines on security sector reform which declared:[54]

> The most critical task facing countries embarking on SSR processes is to build a nationally-owned and led vision of security. This is the foundation that countries require to develop appropriate security system policy frameworks and the required institutional mechanisms to implement them.

One report from Oxfam America carefully assessed Congolese practice against a list of eleven 'best practices' identified from its own advocacy work. These included 'a multi-national, multi-sectoral approach' (graded 'incomplete') and 'a comprehensive assessment of the range of security needs' (graded 'fail').[55]

At the end of the day, none of these objectives were attained. A high-level forum for partners working in the security sector came and went in February 2008 without much result. Successive Ministers of Defence presented reform plans that were widely derided by international partners as 'shopping lists'.[56] One NGO complained of the 2009 iteration that it 'involves reorganising and downsizing, but the plan is very general and has generated more questions than answers'.[57] (Ignoring that the Minister's vagueness was, perhaps, intended to aid in his own survival.)

Faced with this situation, the recurring international demand was for a counterpart on the Congolese side who could pin down unresolved issues and define what the country actually wanted. The EU had proposed a Steering Committee chaired by the Minister of Defence well before that office was even filled. Lobbyists asked for a technical working group with Congolese and international co-chairs.[58] Diplomats pondered whether it might be possible to appoint a security reform 'czar' reporting directly to President Kabila.[59] And MONUC was virtually obsessed with the issue. Virtually every periodic report to the Security Council from 2007 to 2012 opined on progress in establishing a decision-making group, pessimistically or hopefully but never with a concrete result. The instalment of May 2012, five years after efforts started, reported simply that 'only limited progress was made in this area, including regarding coordinating international partners' support to the Congolese government'.[60]

Throughout, it was never explained who a 'czar' might be or how they would exercise real authority over an utterly divided institution. This was apparently a matter for the Congolese themselves.

The mentality is well-illustrated by a MONUC-led training project that was workshopped extensively with government and international partners from 2008–10.[61] The idea was to withdraw fifteen battalions from the field, hundreds of kilometres from their deployment zones, for a twelve-week programme of individual and small-unit training. The summary presentation went through eighteen slides on camp preparation and training curricula before coming to a list of challenges that the Congolese army was facing, as reproduced in Figure 2.5 (on the next page).

The points it lists are all certainly true. But at the time this presentation was being written the CNDP rebellion was in the field. It had threatened Bukavu and faced off with the UN mission outside Goma in 2008, and was skirmishing with a good dozen other armed groups. At the time the presentation was being delivered to partners around eastern Congo, the ink was barely dry on the peace agreements of March 2009.

Figure 2.5: Evaluation of FARDC prior to military training
Source: MONUC / SSR-Mil (2009)

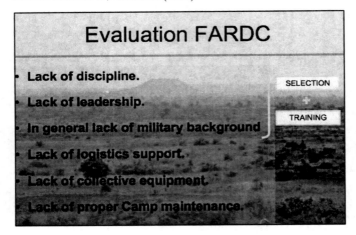

Against this background, it is nothing short of bizarre to omit factional divisions from the list of challenges facing the institution, and to fail to mention the conditions that newly 'integrated' contingents were known to have put on their deals. (Recall the FRF and Mai-Mai Kirichko in the previous section!) For this we have to wait until the very last slide, in the second-last bullet point. This is reproduced as Figure 2.6.

Figure 2.6: 'Conditions of success' for military training

This is an extreme example, but not an unfair one. A broader illustration of the same mentality can be found in an internal memorandum that circulated within MONUC in April 2009. (Again, this is just one month after those peace agreements were signed with the CNDP and a panoply of smaller armed groups.)

This document, entitled 'Proposal for a limited reform of the FARDC deployed in the Kivus', is quite remarkable.[62] It lists a series of fifteen extraordinarily sensitive tasks for newly integrated troops including reorganisation and restructuring of battalions 'according to the norm'; reorganisation of the command chain; selection of specific units for withdrawal to training sites (hundreds of kilometres away from their deployment locations); and prosecution of those accused of serious crimes. For item after item, the 'action' is for the FARDC headquarters. An international role is envisaged for only four tasks: screening and separation of children; logistical support (fuel and rations) to units in the field; and delivery of small-unit training at the designated regrouping sites; and construction of housing at garrison sites. Then under the heading 'political actions' we find just two points:

Announce publicly these measures and explain clearly that they were not a new reform but rather constitute emergency measures of the stabilization and reconstruction plan for the East, and the embryo for more general reform of the army.

Designate in the Ministry of Defence or the FARDC a focal point for the planning and implementation of this limited reform.

For lack of a better phrase, this is rather cold-blooded. In a more candid moment the envoy of the African Union to the March 2009 peace talks, former president of Nigeria Olusegun Obasanjo, commented that 'it did not matter how much will Kabila had if he had no means to exercise it... he was not well-served by the people around him'.[63] For his part, the chief of MONUC from 2007–10 explained to diplomats that President Kabila's 'agenda is survival... which is why he's never criticised the FARDC in public while criticizing other government institutions'.[64] He specified that removing CNDP kingpin Bosco Ntaganda from his post was 'one thing, but there are others around him; if the effort fails, the consequences could be disastrous'. In a retrospective published in late 2011 he then picked up the theme again:[65]

> Governments, especially the ones that are threatened, will be reluctant to allow their forces to be disarmed or cantoned unless they have strong guarantees that their own safety will not be jeopardized if their armed opponents do not disarm. They will not want to become hostage to the demands of opponents who remain armed. The question is: who would be willing to give such a guarantee?

Who indeed? Who would back a 'czar' or 'focal point' tasked with specifying who was to be relocated, demoted and downsized in Congo's fractious army?

At a political level, it was quite clear that Rwanda's hand was on the scales. Any solution was complicated by its support for proxy forces inside the DRC, and yet a strong message was complicated by Rwanda's status as a 'donor darling' for development assistance. Whatever private communications were made by Western ambassadors to Kigali, they were not accompanied by actual cuts in bilateral aid until the M23 was already in the field.[66]

On the ground, meanwhile, MONUSCO was the only international actor with military capabilities (in practice, about 18,000 infantry). However it is no accident that they were invisible in the first part of this chapter. The 'regimentation' initiative came as a near-total surprise to mission staff in South Kivu, with early reports noting curiously that a 'delegation of senior FARDC officials' had turned up regarding a 'proposed reorganization... to reportedly result in the creation of five regiments in the 10th Military Region'.[67]

Coming in early 2011, this was a lagging indication of just how far the mission had sunk into irrelevance from the point of view of the Congolese government. MONUC had not been able to deter the CNDP from abandoning the *mixage* process in 2007, nor the panoply of Mai-Mai groups that responded in kind, and President Kabila complained repeatedly about the UN's failure to set a red line.[68] Over the course of 2008, the President then lobbied unsuccessfully with both the EU and the Southern African Development Community for military contingents that could take a more active supporting role.[69] When that failed, the FARDC tried to force the point with a pre-emptive offensive against the CNDP in August 2008. The

UN again declined to play ball, limiting itself to ameliorating the consequences of the fighting for the civilian population. Kabila gave up and turned to direct negotiations with Rwanda that cut the UN out of the loop entirely, and to deals with local militias to shore up the balance of power.[70] Not long afterwards, he made a surprise demand that the UN mission should start to draw down in 2010.

The lack of interest from the UN side was not, of course, a matter of whim. It was a hotly debated question what a Security Council mandate to 'strengthen and reform security institutions' actually meant, given the ever-present threat of mutiny and desertion. But in the end policy-makers decided to limit MONUC's role to moral support for two reasons.

The first was that the countries represented on the Security Council were sending decidedly mixed messages. MONUC was mandated to consolidate government authority, but the Council nonetheless emphasised that 'the protection of civilians must be given priority in decisions about the use of available capacity'. [71] On the ground this was interpreted as physical protection in the face of imminent danger, meaning that troops were split into ninety-plus small detachments flung all over the Kivus.[72] This made for better tactical effectiveness in curbing day-to-day violence and looting, but also for strategic failure when the CNDP lunged for major population centres like Sake in 2006 and Rutshuru in 2008. The 'protection first' mandate also complicated any sort of collaboration with a Congolese army that was notorious for its poor human rights record. Pretty much any operation led to score-settling and pillage, and this in turn ignited a firestorm of criticism from the large and vocal contingent of relief agencies working in eastern DRC.[73]

The second factor was risk aversion. Intervening in the FARDC's internal struggle would embroil the UN mission in precisely the same uncertainties and dangers that marked decision-making on the Congolese side. Here is one head of UN peacekeeping looking back on 'robust' peace operations at the end of his tenure:[74]

> In the confusion of a civil war, the commitment of non-state actors to a peace agreement is never a solid guaranty; consent becomes a relative and evolving concept: it can be ambiguous, and it can be withdrawn. By definition, consent cannot be imposed. Peacekeepers cannot become a full-fledged counter-insurgency force chasing those who reject a peace agreement. The forces

deployed would have to be much larger than what the international community can provide.

The choice between the use of force and mediation will always be a difficult one, dependent on the dynamics of a particular situation. By a selective and politically savvy use of force—picking fights that it can win and thus discouraging others who would be tempted to use force—it can help create a political momentum that provides some limited protection to civilians, while a broader political strategy unfolds.

Rounding up the necessary support for the 'selective and politically savvy use of force' proved to be rather difficult. Any such orientation depended on agreement of the countries who contributed troops on the ground, as well as the permanent members of the Security Council. All these stakeholders were discouraged by the size and complexity of the operating environment. As one commentator put it, 'the danger of ratcheting up as crises get worse is that a mission's limit may be reached and the deterrent effect lost.'[75] MONUC contingents had already been pushed into direct confrontations with armed groups in Ituri in 2003; in Bukavu in 2004; and around Goma in 2006–07. This was already pretty much unprecedented for a UN operation, outside the first operation in Congo in the 1960s.

The reputational and probity risks of getting directly involved were no less significant. A massacre, or high-profile assassination, would have thrown the entire enterprise under close scrutiny. Moreover the central government had fading democratic credentials, with the controversial elections of 2011 the nail in the coffin. In these circumstances, the conclusion may well have been that the sin of omission was easier to bear than the risk of unintended consequences.

Taking politics seriously

Harry Truman, thirty-third President of the United States, once said of his military successor Eisenhower—'He'll sit here and say, "Do this! Do that!" And nothing will happen. He'll find it very frustrating.'[76]

President Kabila must have understood this in his bones. He headed civilian and military institutions that had been stitched together from rival factions at the end of a punishing conflict. All sides remained paranoid about the implications of reshuffling the deck. Periodic outbursts of horrific violence against civilians underlined that the game was still being played for real stakes, and initiatives to reorganise the armed forces ran almost immediately into resistance from those with something to lose. This remained true all the way down the chain of command, from senior officers who risked provoking a return to war to junior ones who faced frequent mutinies and occasional assassinations.

Against this background, international demands for 'comprehensive approaches' and 'czars' must have been rather infuriating. The better starting point has been suggested by no less an authority than Lakhdar Brahimi, probably the most accomplished of all UN trouble-shooters:[77]

It is easy to lose sight of the connection between mediation and peacekeeping, once attention shifts to the deployment of military, police and civilian personnel and the individual tasks they are expected to support... [but] one agreement is seldom enough. Most peace agreements that call for the deployment of peace operations to assist with their implementation only partially address the underlying political problems of the conflict.

He could well have been talking specifically about eastern Congo. The 2002–03 peace agreements had succeeded neither in unifying security institutions, nor in disarming all the remaining combatants. Subsequent agreements in 2008–09 did no more than return to that status quo. At this point, further progress depended not on the design of technically optimal institutions, but rather on Congolese perceptions of the likely winners and losers of reorganising the security sector. The Kifaru debacle and the merry-go-round of armed group integration had illustrated this at great cost, and international agencies would have been well-served to focus on the fears, incentives, and psychologies that lay behind such episodes.

In many ways, this is not a new observation. In fact it has become a common refrain over the last few years, or what one authority has called 'a long overdue wake-up call' to practices that are 'common in good policy-making anywhere'.[78] The common thread of this critical literature is the need for closer attention to local actors, their incentives, and how these factors combine to put problems and proposed solutions on the agenda.

The next chapter turns to the most basic question in this regard. In a country of Congo's immense size, what was the unit of analysis? Which political community were we talking about?

3

Geography denial

Distance has a peculiar weight in the Congo. The country is certainly vast—about 2.3 million square kilometres or 'as big as Western Europe' as foreign newspapers often put it. But it is more than this. Narrative accounts have always been obsessed with geography, with an unbroken string of travelogues stretching back to Henry Morton Stanley in the 1870s. The explorer's nickname Bula Matari ('rock-breaker') was allegedly attributable to his smashing a path across the country with dynamite and forced labour, and he loved this violent metaphor so much that he had it engraved on his tombstone.

The projection of authority over distance was to be a recurring theme. The Belgian king Leopold II commissioned Stanley to open up a permanent route to the interior. This was to be studded with trading stations, propagandised for international audiences as 'hospitable, scientific and pacification bases to be set up as a means of abolishing the slave trade, establishing peace among the chiefs, and procuring them just and impartial arbitration'.[1] This enterprise in turn gave rise to more travelogues, now by sundry administrators of the Congo Free State who were thoroughly preoccupied with their remoteness.[2] Joseph Conrad both plagiarised and pilloried these figures in *Heart of Darkness*, published at the turn of the century. His protagonist Marlow journeys languorously up the Congo River, musing on the progressive disintegration of social ties for the European officials he encounters, capped off by the trader Kurtz who 'knew no restraint, no faith, and no fear'.[3]

Marlow's trip became the model, and the journey assumed a peculiar salience in support of attacks and apologies alike for the Congo Free State (1885 to 1908) and *Le Congo belge* (1908 to 1960).[4] As the campaigner and politician Emile Vandervelde wrote in 1909: 'One can say much that is good and much that is evil about the late Congo Free State, whilst remaining vigorously truthful. All depends on the itinerary that one follows.'[5] Down to the present day this remains the case, with few authors able to resist a travel metaphor. Journalists walk 'in the footsteps of Mr Kurtz' or add the gratuitous subtitle 'a reporter's journey in the Congo'. The great VS Naipaul located his postcolonial story at 'a bend in the river'; biodiversity is documented via a 'journey into the heart of Congo'. Gendered violence, apparently, can only be understood by a 'journey into the worst place on Earth to be a woman'.[6]

Of course, there is a good deal of racism here. Editors like a touch of exoticism because they think this is what will sell books on central Africa. But there is also a banal fact. In fact it is so banal that I will cite the audit/consulting firm Pricewaterhouse Coopers, which recently described Congo as 'probably the most challenging transport infrastructure environment in Africa'.[7] In 2008 the World Bank's best estimate was that 5–10% of the 58,000km of major roads were passable with a normal vehicle, with just one provincial capital out of ten connected to Kinshasa.[8] In such a context, people working in the transport sector often seem overwhelmed. A recent exchange in the Congolese Senate had members haranguing the head of the national roads authority that his texts and budgets 'remained theoretical', against a reality of rutted walking tracks and roadside *calvaires* (memorial crosses).[9] International donors tend to fall into Conrad-esque prose, with one European Union project declaring that 'Congo is an ocean in which each town is an island, such that social and trade connections are rudimentary'.[10]

Against all this, policy-making for stabilisation had a remarkably casual attitude to geography. Plans were addressed to a mysterious entity called 'eastern Congo', which seemed to vary in size from person to person and moment to moment.[11] Perhaps the most absurd such fluctuation is captured in Figure 3.1, which comes from a presentation by the Prime Minister's office to explain the shift from the 2007–08 'Amani Program' to the new

Stabilization and Reconstruction Plan for Conflict-Affected Areas (STAREC).[12]

Figure 3.1: 'Enlargement of the field of action'
Source: GoDRC / Prime Minister's office, 2009

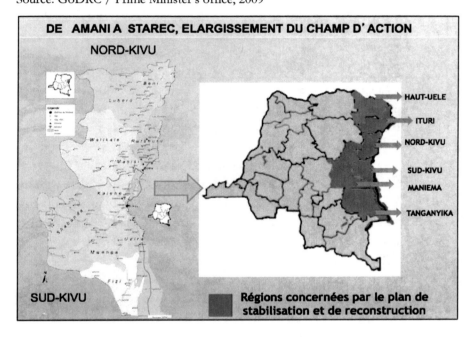

Here the target area was expanded by some 350% with a flick of the computer mouse: from the size of Eritrea to that of Mozambique, or in European terms from Iceland to Turkey.[13] The goals for this huge swathe of territory? Among others: completion of disarmament, demobilisation and reintegration for combatants; restoration of state authority through deployment of police, judicial, penitentiary and civil administrative personnel, and 're-establishment of conditions for viable economic activity'.[14]

Most of us working on stabilisation policy, from our various organisational niches, were flabbergasted. Nonetheless we wrote it off as political posturing. We did not know quite what to make of it when the UN Security Council kept doing the same thing.[15] From 2007–09 the UN peacekeeping mission (MONUC) was directed to give 'highest priority to addressing the crisis in the Kivus'. The implied area of operations was about

120,000 square kilometres, and eleven-to-twelve million people. But by 2010 ambitions had grown. The benchmarks for drawdown of MONUC were now 'minimizing the threat of armed groups and restoring stability in sensitive areas' in the Kivus *and* Orientale Province, and the 'consolidation of state authority through the territory'. In 2013 this broadened again to simply 'conflict-affected areas', with an earlier paragraph defining this to include the northern part of Katanga province.

Conservatively interpreted, the target area was now about 415,000 square kilometres and well over twenty million people.[16] But the core tasks, and the resources available to support them, remained the same. MONUC's budget changed only as supply costs fluctuated, while the numbers of military, police and civilian personnel held more or less constant. Nor was there any great influx of development aid, once we account for debt forgiveness, nor any significant rearrangement of Congolese budget priorities.

This pattern raises two rather pressing questions. The first is about *means and ends* for a country that is large by any measure—population, physical size, problems. How did blanket prescriptions to 'restore stability' and 'consolidate state authority' play out across a constantly expanding 'field of action'? What happened when the abstract entity of 'eastern Congo' collided with the actual topography and demography on the ground?

The second question concerns *differentiation*. Most of eastern Congo had lived through protracted violent conflict—all the targeted regions had this in common. But that similarity travelled together with enormous differences in operating conditions, culture and history, and political and administrative systems. Was it really valid to use the same basic formula notwithstanding those differences? To shed some light on this we turn to the difficult issue of local governance, including political participation and management of land, and compare how problems and solutions played out across different regions.

An 'ideal situation for the insurgent'

Congo's topography is perhaps the single best entry point to understand its recent political history. Figure 3.2 provides a snapshot for what the Belgians called Kivu province, comprising present-day North Kivu, South Kivu and

Maniema. Darker colours indicate higher elevation, while the grey area at right demarcates the international border. The lighter area at left is thus the Congolese interior, moving (ever-so-slightly) towards Kinshasa on the western edge of the country.

Figure 3.2: Terrain map for North Kivu, South Kivu and Maniema
Source: Maphill (2014)

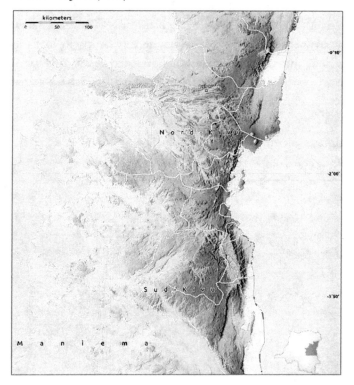

What we are seeing is the Albertine Rift which divides the Somali Plate from the rest of the African continent. The chain of volcanoes that sprung up along this line left a swathe of land, the Rift Valley, that is both stunningly fertile and heavily populated. The extreme eastern edge of the Congo shares these characteristics, and slopes down naturally into the compact markets of Rwanda, Uganda and Burundi. The crossings at all these borders are flat and easy, with gravelled roads passing across land that has been cleared of forest for a century or more. But going west into the hinterland feels very different.

The terrain is hard as one crosses the edge of the Rift, with an assessment team once describing our key road project in North Kivu as attacking a 'logistically nightmarish escarpment' where 'maintenance will be an on-going, hellish problem'.[17] (Again, Conrad-esque prose!)

Even more striking is the drop in population density as one leaves the Rift. In Figure 3.3 we draw an arrow westward from the point where Congo, Uganda and Rwanda touch. At the arrow's start there are 170 people per square kilometre, comparable to Switzerland or Italy. This drops to about 30 in the next territory over (Walikale). This is more like Peru or Brazil. Then at the tip of the arrow, in the province of Maniema, density drops to half this again. Now we are in company with desert nations like Saudi Arabia or Algeria, and from here it is still nearly a thousand miles to Kinshasa across similarly vacant space.[18]

Figure 3.3: Population density for the DRC
Source: CIESIN Gridded Population of the World v3, Columbia University

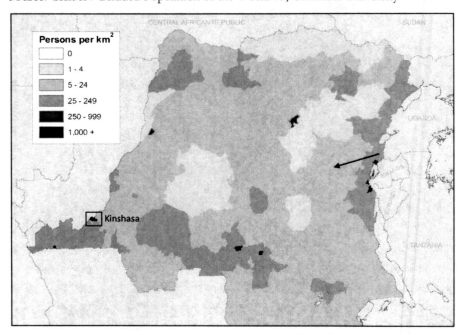

This situation is a limiting case for what the political scientist Jeffrey Herbst once called the fundamental problem of statebuilding in Africa: 'to project authority over inhospitable territories that contain relatively low densities of people'.[19] Stated another way, here is the celebrated French counter-insurgency theorist and practitioner David Galula:[20]

> To sum up, the ideal situation for the insurgent would be a large landlocked country shaped like a blunt-tipped star, with jungle-covered mountains along the borders and scattered swamps in the plains... with a large and dispersed rural population.

His point was that it is difficult to concentrate force in mountainous terrain, and fruitless to do so in vacant interior spaces. Local powers can thus sprout up without much surveillance or counter-pressure from the central government, or even from their nearest rivals. The added difficulty of being landlocked is that the neighbours end up providing deliberate or unwitting sanctuary for insurgents. For the last twenty years this last factor has been eastern Congo's biggest headache, with a constant struggle for influence among the 'three Ks': Kigali (Rwanda), Kampala (Uganda) and Kinshasa.[21] To give one indication, when the *Mouvement de 23 Mars* was defeated in 2013 one well-known commentator thought it notable primarily for 'being the first time since 1998 that Rwanda did not have a significant military ally on Congolese soil'.[22]

Historically this has put Congo's government in a strange position. As we noted in Chapter 1, Mobutu's Second Republic (1965–97) often struggled to implement policy in the East. But the central government also benefited from its isolation. Mobutu is said to have mocked his colleague Juvenal Habyarimana of Rwanda for building roads that simply allowed insurgents to 'drive down them to get you', and he was right on this every time but once.[23] His regime outlasted a string of minor rebellions in the 1960s and foreign incursions in the 1970s mainly by virtue of their geographic remoteness. Small armed groups ran off disorganised government security forces in a dozen locations, but proved unable to project force at anything like the distances needed to threaten Kinshasa.[24] (No less a source than Ernesto 'Ché' Guevara complained that there 'is no real lack of arms here—indeed there are too many armed men... [but] there are bands living in the forest, not connected to one another'.[25]) In the end it took an epic cross-country march for the Rwandan-backed AFDL to finally topple Mobutu in 1997, captioned the 'long walk into Kinshasa' and 'a thousand miles through the jungle' by two of the best-selling histories of the period.[26]

The AFDL's expedition was the exception that proved the rule, however. Geographic realities reasserted themselves in the Second Congo War (1997–2003) as the two major belligerents in the East—the Rwandan- and Ugandan-backed factions of the 'Rally for Congolese Democracy' (RCD)—grabbed huge swathes of territory but bogged down over distance. They reached a stalemate with Kinshasa and its foreign allies a few hundred miles into the interior, all parties struggling to bring much military power to bear at the notional front lines.

Meanwhile the vast intervening spaces proved impossible to control. Throughout the east, small local armed groups dug into a few especially inaccessible locations and spread throughout open spaces in many more. The Kinshasa government, pressed on multiple fronts, egged on these small groups with indiscriminate weapons drops. In response the two RCD factions focused their efforts on population centres close to the borders of their foreign backers and a few hinterland sites of special economic interest. Trade and transport networks grew along these lines, while those reaching to Kinshasa atrophied rapidly.[27] Elsewhere, the two RCDs didn't achieve much control over the terrain. They faced resistance from numerous small opponents and frequently resorted to massacres to intimidate the civilian population, engraving locations such as Kasika, Kilungutwe and Ilangi deep into local cultural memory.[28] When the major belligerents finally signed the Pretoria and Sun City Agreements in 2002-03, few of the small local factions that had troubled them had really been 'defeated' in a conventional sense.

It is this environment that confronted policy-makers a few years later when they began to speak of 'stabilising' eastern Congo and 'restoring state authority'. The practicalities are well-illustrated by Figure 3.4, a logistics planning map for North Kivu which can fairly stand in for neighbouring areas. The area shown is about equal to that of Lithuania or Ireland; roads marked in green boast an average travel speed of 40km/hour for a light vehicle; those in orange 20-40km/hour, and those in red less than 20km/hour (usually considerably less).

Figure 3.4: The road network of North Kivu

Source: World Food Programme / Logistics Cluster (2012)

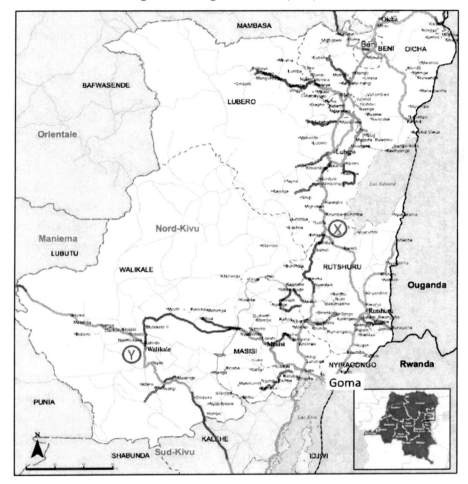

Note the patterns. (This is already *after* four years of road works by international agencies to improve operational mobility!) There is a small cluster of good roads extending maybe forty kilometres from the provincial capital of Goma and another cluster around the regional centre of Beni; both cities are also well-connected to the neighbouring countries to the East. But there is almost no access to the hinterland. Those roads capable of carrying traffic at all start in horrible condition and then trail off very rapidly. Kanyabayonga, marked X, is a hard day's drive from Goma in a good light vehicle. (Considerably more in a military truck, and usually impossible with an armoured vehicle.) Walikale, marked Y, can be reached only by motorbike, helicopter or light plane. Meanwhile there is no direct route whatsoever between those two points. A quick comparison with the topographic map (Figure 3.2) and population density map (Figure 3.3) will confirm that the intervening terrain is hilly and heavily forested with a dispersed rural population.

These are mundane facts, but the consequences for the 'state authority' project were profound. To explore them let us make a quick return visit to the police unit in Kinyandoni that we met in Chapter 1, deployed with the Tiger Battalion in early 2009. The Government and UN wanted these thirty officers to take over 'responsibility for public order' and support 'a fully functioning justice system' in the surrounding area. Instead they were attacked by a small detachment of the Democratic Forces for the Liberation of Rwanda (FDLR) not long after arriving, harassed for a while longer, and then fled back to the territorial capital of Rutshuru.

Their small police post (*sous-commissariat*) was located along the road from Rutshuru town up to Ishasha on the Ugandan border. Figure 3.5 (on the next page)) marks out the sixty kilometres of this route, with Kinyandoni town marked by a black square and MONUC peacekeeping deployments by red diamonds.

These were as favourable a set of circumstances as one was likely to find in eastern Congo. The road itself was good—flat gravel and a heavily trafficked trade route into Uganda. The areas abutting the road were flat and relatively clear due to high local population densities and intensive cultivation. Meanwhile the concentration of MONUC peacekeepers was as great as anywhere in the country, with perhaps one soldier per 1.5km^2 of populated area, or about 1 per 360 civilians. These detachments were a mere two to three hour drive from their forward logistics base in Goma, and not very much further from the rear logistics hub in Uganda.

And yet: the steep hills to the west belong to the thickly forested and (mostly) uninhabited Virunga National Park. The black line indicates distance to the park boundary which is about 5km at the point marked. The white jagged line to the east is the international border with Uganda, again hilly and forested on both sides and not permeable for military action without sparking a serious diplomatic incident.

Figure 3.5: Rutshuru–Ishasha priority axis, North Kivu
Source: Google Maps terrain layer, annotations by author

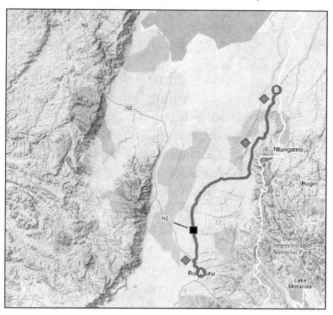

In this terrain it proved quite impossible to deny the FDLR freedom of movement. One consequence, as we saw in Chapter 1, was that the FDLR could concentrate itself at points where the central government was weak. Our police colleagues found this to their great cost just a few weeks after being dropped in place. By contrast, attempts to concentrate force against the FDLR were never very successful. The Umoja Wetu and Amani Leo operations in 2009–10 included massive sweeps of this area with tens of thousands of Congolese soldiers, buttressed by logistical support by MONUC and at one point a large detachment of the Rwandan army. These had little impact as the FDLR made orderly tactical retreats and the Congolese army, moving mostly on foot, proved unable to pin them down for significant engagements.[29] The cost of making the attempt was also very high for the civilian population, as the give and take of territory led both sides to intensify violence against 'collaborators'. Human Rights Watch summarised as follows:[30]

A comparison of the impact of military operations on the FDLR and the harm to civilians starkly conveys the suffering endured by the population. For every FDLR combatant that was repatriated to Rwanda during the first nine months of operations, at least one civilian was deliberately killed, seven women and girls raped, eight homes destroyed, and over 900 people forced to flee for their lives.

Pressure to scale back the operations mounted steadily, with international lobbyists virtually unanimous that the Congolese government was 'incapable of capitalising on its "victory" and holding the territory gained'.[31] They were ultimately proved right as the FDLR remains present in the area right up to date of writing in early 2015, and still a hot political issue.[32]

In short: reinforcement of 'state authority' in this seemingly best-case location faced very serious difficulties. Keeping this example in mind, let's pull out the lens a little further.

For the Rutshuru–Ishasha route depicted in Figure 3.5 was just one of six 'priority axes' for the International Security and Stabilization Support Strategy (ISSSS). This was a framework billing itself as 'the main vehicle for supporting the peace process through security, restoration of state authority and delivery of peace dividends', with MONUC and the larger UN agencies in the lead.[33] Each of these six routes passed through areas that were at best semi-permissive, with an active presence of the FDLR and/or other armed groups. Figure 3.6 (overleaf) is a PowerPoint slide that laid out this concept of operations, and became somewhat infamous as the 'explosion map'. Here the 'priority axes' are denoted by green arrows, with the Rutshuru–Ishasha road marked as #2.

What should jump out here is the enormous scale (the clue is the relative size of Rwanda). By road it is well over 1,000 kilometres from the top to the bottom of this map; the 'FDLR corridors' marked with thick grey arrows are up to 350km long. This is a colossal area for which to achieve the 'transfer of security to civilian police' who would 'uphold the rule of law and ensure public order', and the 're-establishment of decentralized administrative services'.[34]

Along the six 'strategic axes' (marked with numbers) all the problems that we saw in Kinyandoni increased with distance, akin to a weight held at arm's length. They weighed heaviest of all on axis #5—depicted as a straight line but in reality running a circuitous 360 kilometres from Bukavu, the capital of South Kivu, into Shabunda territory.

Figure 3.6: Concept of operations for stabilisation

Source: MONUC (2009) 'Security and stabilisation support strategy for eastern DRC'

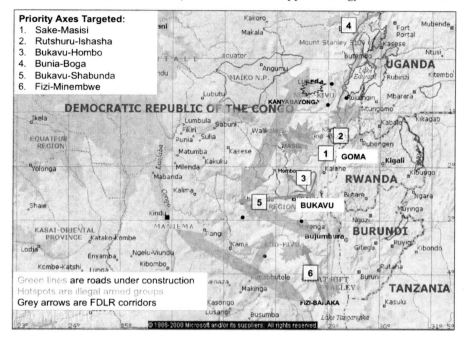

In 2011 a UN team drove this route #5 after two years of intensive road rehabilitation works. The press release that followed described the trip as intended to 'provide an insight to the need for restoring state authority'.[35] It did just that—on consecutive days the convoy managed to travel 22km, 34km and 44km, in some sections 'greeted by a population that had never seen a vehicle'. (It had been decades since anybody had managed to get a car all the way up the road.) A more detailed report counted 48 villages spread out along the thickly forested route. It went on to note that the FDLR and smaller armed groups preyed on these communities from time to time, walking several days each way from unknown locations in the bush.[36] Arrayed against them were a few small detachments of the Congolese army. Given the lack of road access they had no regular supplies, and were limited to day-patrols on foot. They survived off the civilian population and were viewed, at best, as a lesser evil than armed groups. A few civil servants were also present, but lacking salaries spent most of their time raising crops to survive.

In a detailed assessment of the security situation one finds yet again the metaphor of the island:[37]

> The population of Shabunda town is, for the moment, not directly affected by this menace. They rather suffer the indirect effects of attacks and predation of the FDLR in neighbouring localities, since the town is a zone of refuge. By contrast, the populations of collectivities neighbouring the town pay the price of FDLR predation.

Sweeping the jungle to completely dislodge the FDLR and other armed groups would have involved a physical area of close to ten thousand square kilometres. This was orders of magnitude larger than the territory depicted in Figure 3.5, for which the huge military operations of 2009–10 had proved fruitless. Just to curb attacks for the 48 villages close to the road would have required a security presence in nearly all of them, given the prevailing travel speeds. Each such detachment would have needed to be capable of resisting the type of harassment attacks that had chased the Tiger Battalion out of Kinyandoni. (To say nothing of ensuring 'the rule of law' by arresting the culprits!)

In reality, such deployment in force was hardly what was envisaged. The resources that were anticipated along the whole stretch were 120 Territorial Police split between four detachments, and six temporary deployments of Rapid Intervention Police. (The latter initially expected to last six months!) This was to be supplemented by reinforcements to the offices of three territorial administrators, senior officials who each covered jurisdictions of half a million or so people.

What appears as a solid arrow in Figure 3.6 was thus in reality a few dots, joined together only conceptually. These small detachments could well have had some localised effects. But the idea that all communities would benefit, or that the Government would have 'authority' over terrain beyond this, was pure fantasy. This was plainly demonstrated in 2010–11 by the spectacular growth of the local militias referred to as the Raia Mutomboki. This was a 'series of different armed groups, bound only by a name and a broad ideology of self-defence', that grew out of local frustrations with the FDLR and the Congolese security forces both.[38] They enjoyed startling success, pushing the FDLR out of an area it had inhabited for over a decade and essentially all the way out of Shabunda territory. Such aggressive expansion led inevitably to clashes with the Congolese army, and with armed groups in the neighbouring territories of Masisi and Kalehe.[39]

The reaction of those involved with Government–UN stabilisation efforts was telling. Official MONUSCO reports ignored the phenomenon, pretending that the Congolese army remained in the driver's seat, while works continued on each little dot on the 'priority axis' thanks to stepped-up security escorts. [40] In reviewing the situation, the UN Development Programme quoted the senior civil official for Shabunda territory that 'nearly all of the territory is controlled by armed groups', and the President of its court to the effect that 'we must organise sessions outside of town, but for the moment it is effectively impossible due to insecurity and the lack of roads'. UNDP's local head of office then drew the logical (?) conclusion that 're-establishment of state authority was an essential step' to improve quality of life throughout the territory.[41]

This was hand-waving at a map, not serious analysis. At its grandest scale it led to documents like the Government's Stabilisation and Reconstruction Plan, introduced at the top of the chapter. In Figure 3.1 the Prime Minister's office coloured in some 700,000km², declaring ambitions to 'assure and preserve a tolerable level of public security in the concerned zones' and 'prevent any threat of return of activities of armed groups'.[42] (Total cost: A one-off budget of $1.2bn over three years.)

International policy-makers were only slightly less exuberant. As UN peacekeepers shifted their focus to eastern Congo in 2007–08, strategic assessments asserted broadly that an exit strategy required 'completion of the disarmament and demobilization of former combatants' and that 'the State rapidly becomes visibly effective and accountable to people in areas where armed groups held sway'.[43] (Bear in mind the latter phrase covers all of eastern and northern Congo during the 1998–2003 war.) This language soon found its way into Security Council mandates referring vaguely to 'sensitive areas' or 'conflict-affected areas'. As we have seen, this was eventually interpreted to mean an area of well over 400,000km² and twenty million people.[44]

The growth in ambitions was fed by most international non-governmental organisations who interested themselves in the country. Their policy briefs were typically addressed to 'eastern Congo' as a whole; their local representatives angrily declared that they could not support 'stabilisation for some' but only 'stabilisation for all'.[45] One open letter from Oxfam complained that 'whatever stabilising effects the Islands [of Stability] may have will not be felt around them: protection of and assistance to civilian populations could be neglected'.[46] Human Rights Watch chimed in, virtually the second after one group was finally subdued:[47]

> In the wake of defeating the M23, the Congolese government and the U.N. must address the threat posed by groups like the FDLR, the Raia Mutomboki, and Sheka's militia. This should include efforts to encourage combatants to disarm voluntarily, restore state authority in areas controlled by armed groups, and arrest leaders wanted for war crimes and crimes against humanity.

The practical implications of action at this scale will perhaps be clear by now, but can illustrated with one final example—imposing civilian regulatory control over Congo's mining sector. This was pushed by a number of NGOs as a potential 'big win', with the Enough Project arguing that it would 'change the incentive structure away from violence and illegality towards security and rule of law', and make mining 'the main engine for economic development'.[48] Intensive lobbying and advocacy led to several major initiatives to ensure attention to a 'clean' supply chain, including the Dodd-Frank Act in the United States, OECD due diligence guidelines on responsible sourcing and voluntary efforts from major buyers such as Intel and Apple. For its part the UN Security Council dabbled with a few measures, directing the establishment of 'Mineral Trading Counters' in remote areas.

But ambitions to regulate the entire sector ignored a basic geographic fact. The vast majority of mining in conflict-affected areas in Congo is artisanal, with individually small sites scattered across a huge area. A subsequent OECD evaluation explained the practicalities for even relatively large and well-known sites:[49]

> Since Bisië is located in a remote corner of the province, the validation team would have had to walk more than 50 km in the forest, facing the risk of encountering Mayi Mayi rebels en route. It was suggested to replace this long hike with a helicopter flight, yet this option would negate the purpose of the validation mission, which is not simply concerned with a spot-check of mine sites, but also with thorough controls of trading routes.

As far as mine sites in Masisi are concerned, the issue of concessions titles, coupled with the lack of stability due to the presence of Mayi Mayi Nyatura and the inaccessibility of mine sites in Ngungu, make it unlikely that a validation mission to sites not previously validated will be deployed any time soon.

Another review summarised that the Congolese government was being asked to 'supervise the artisanal mining sector over a vast area with an insufficient number of personnel, few vehicles, and a lack of technical training' and (moreover) formalise 'a sector that involves an estimated 500,000 to two million people, for a limited financial return, especially when considering the taxes that can be taken from the industrial mining sector'.[50]

The gap between the notional policy regime and realities on the ground became enormous, and the results for the Congolese were hardly impressive. Many international purchasers simply stopped buying from the country, going 'Congo-free' to avoid regulatory and public pressure. Armed groups continued to exploit mineral resources, shifting focus from exploitation on-site to taxation further down the supply chain and from tantalum/tungsten to gold. The few real exceptions were 'closed pipelines', where unusual geographic and security situations permitted end-to-end surveillance of extraction, transport and wholesaling.[51] Even an enthusiastic advocate of tracing requirements was quickly forced to concede that 'positive developments in eastern Congo's mining areas tend to be fragile and localised, and opportunities must be acted upon quickly'.[52]

Broad-brush approaches remained, nonetheless, more the norm than the exception. Let us now turn to how they were seen from local perspectives.

Congo 'whack-a-mole'

In early June 2003 French paratroopers touched down at Bunia airport. They were the leading edge of Operation Artemis, the European Union's first-ever military intervention outside Europe. Such an extraordinary move was authorised because the national government and MONUC were overwhelmed.

Fighting over the previous few months had displaced some half a million people in the surrounding Ituri district. Thousands of civilians had been massacred in locations such as Nyakunde and Songolo, with the district quickly dubbed by Human Rights Watch the 'bloodiest corner of the Congo'.[53] In May 2003 the Union of Congolese Patriots (UPC) had seized control of Bunia, the district capital, after pushing out opposing militias in street-to-street fighting. The national government's response was timid and inadequate, as a deployment of Rapid Intervention Police 'rapidly disintegrated in the face of violence, with some seeking protection from MONUC in the makeshift camp that had sprung up around its headquarters'.[54] For their part, the peacekeepers' local detachment of 720 Uruguayan soldiers was huddled next to the airport. Their predicament has been accurately if painfully caricatured by David van Reybrouck:[55]

> In the offices of the peacekeeping mission, dispirited officials hung charts on the wall tracing the organization of the various militias: it made them only more dispirited. Every month a new militia came along, or the orderly chart had to be rearranged—more columns, more arrows, more acronyms, more additions to the rogue's gallery of photos beside them—until the chaos finally jibed with that in the field and lost all explanative value.

Over the course of a few months the European mission succeeded in establishing a secure zone around Bunia, then handed over to a full brigade of MONUC infantry in September 2003.[56] Ten years on, a French colleague, a development specialist and civilian to the bone, got very excited as he told the story: 'They used it as a training exercise—pow! Anyone tried to carry weapons, they just killed them! *Ce n'est pas grand chose, bof!*

But what is really striking about this episode is that it came two months *after* a transitional constitution had been agreed to 'end' the Second Congo War. At the same time as Operation Artemis was unfolding, the parties to the painstaking peace negotiations of the preceding few years were jockeying peacefully, if ungracefully, for positions in the new governmental institutions taking shape in Kinshasa.

The problem was that Ituri concerned a whole other set of interlocutors. The UPC had not bought into the national-level process, and had split into rival factions on how to proceed. A confusing array of smaller militias skirmished with the UPC factions and with each other, 'loosely organised on ethno-clanic lines and territorial origin, without any kind of unified command or even authority over their troops'.[57] Each sought support from its *patrons* in Kinshasa, Kigali or Kampala, while attempts to establish a local-level mechanism to deal with all the players had foundered. So when the Ugandan army declared 'the war' over with the formation of a national government, and pulled its troops from Ituri after a half-decade of operations, the situation simply exploded. Within a few weeks the UN Secretary-General was on the telephone with Jacques Chirac to outline the concept for Artemis. International agencies went into overdrive lobbying for attention and resources for the 'Ituri crisis', while MONUC treated it as 'a mission within the mission' with its own strategy and top priority in resource allocation.[58] Progressive military action successfully rolled back the militias, under an unusually able and forceful Force Commander.

Now flash forward to 2007. The UN was mentioning Ituri only as a success story, confidently labelling the remaining armed men 'a criminal, rather than a credible military threat'.[59] One also had to look carefully to find much attention to Ituri from anyone else. Figure 3.7 returns to the same sample of policy briefings that we reviewed in Chapter 2, coming from a cross-section of Congo analysts and lobbyists.

Figure 3.7: NGOs lose interest in Ituri, 2007–2012[60]

Here we see North Kivu, its capital Goma, the belligerents fighting there, and even one of the key personalities (Laurent Nkunda). There is no mention of Bunia, Ituri or any of the factions that were so prominent in 2003. For emergency relief agencies, Ituri now accounted for just 10% of total funding requirements for the 'Congo crisis'.[61] For Ituri residents themselves, 73% of respondents to one survey said that they felt safe or very safe sleeping at night compared with just 21% of respondents in North Kivu.[62]

The shift was dramatic and it illustrates a fundamentally important point—the 'Congo crisis' moves around. As Severine Autessere has summarised, 'after the national and regional settlements were reached, some local conflicts over land and power became increasingly self-sustaining and autonomous from the macro-level developments'.[63] Less artfully, diplomats sometimes call this 'Congo whack-a-mole'. Even as *Follies in Fragile States* was in progress there were new alarms about the surprise growth of the Raia Mutomboki movement in north-western South Kivu (2012–13); the 'triangle of death' in northern Katanga (2013–14); and a botched counter-insurgency against the armed group ADF in a previously quiet part of North Kivu (late 2014). Each of these crises led in its turn to forced displacement of hundreds of thousands of people, the occasional massacre, and re-prioritisation by UN peacekeepers and humanitarian agencies.

The existence of regional trends and threats like these should not have been surprising. The vast physical distances depicted in maps like Figures 3.1 and 3.6 also meant distances in culture and history, administrative and political systems, economics and local geography.[64] And the plain fact is that these variations have always made it very difficult to make useful generalisations about eastern Congo. An explanation that is true everywhere is radically inadequate in any one place; and a comprehensive explanation for any one place is misleading everywhere else.

One issue that straightforwardly illustrates this is inter-ethnic tension. The 'Congo crisis' is often interpreted around a cleavage between Rwandan-speaking (Rwandophone) and other ethnic groups, not least by Congolese themselves. Some analysts have elevated this to a master theory, arguing that a 'crisis of civic citizenship' for Rwandophones has been the primary driver of the crisis in the Kivus, if not eastern Congo more generally.[65] In Chapter 1 we saw that this divide was very real within Congolese National Police, and in Chapter 2 we encountered it in its starkest form within the Congolese Armed

Forces. There is also considerable support for the thesis at the level of mass politics. A large randomised survey in 2014 asked ordinary Congolese in North Kivu, South Kivu and Ituri which ethnic group they were uncomfortable with (if any). Some 41% indicated Tutsis and 30% Hutus, the two Rwandan-speaking ethnic groups, with the next most 'popular' choice at 14%.[66]

So this was an issue that policy-makers in the Congo clearly needed to take into account. But it is only one part of the story. Figure 3.8 reproduces results from the same survey for 18 territories in North Kivu, South Kivu and Ituri.

Figure 3.8: With which ethnic group are you uncomfortable, if any?
Source: Vinck and Pham (2014); author files

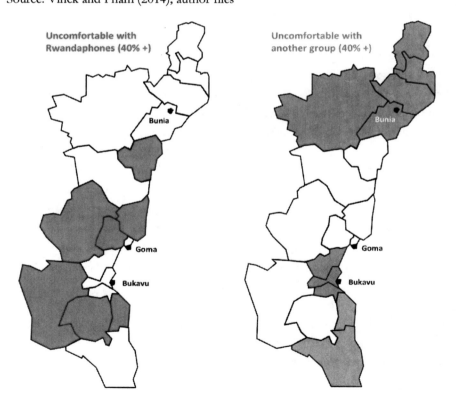

The territories highlighted at left are those where 40% or more of respondents indicated that they were uncomfortable with people of Hutu or

Tutsi ethnicity. Those highlighted at right are those where more than 40% of respondents nominated *another* specific ethnic group. What is immediately apparent is that the two maps are nearly mirror images of each other—where suspicions are not of Rwandophones they appear to settle readily enough on somebody else.

Of course, who that 'somebody else' was depended on where you were asking the question. There were no fewer than eleven ethnic groups nominated among the blue territories at right, with each response reflecting local social, political and historical circumstances.

In southern Ituri, around Bunia and the epicentre of the 2003–04 violence, it was the Hema and Lendu who nominated each other. And if one digs deeper and asks for the origins of these tensions, 'locals usually choose to begin with pre-colonial or colonial events'.[67] Eighteenth-century migration into the area had created immediate tensions between newcomers (Hema groups) and the pre-existing population (Lendu, and others). The fire was then fuelled by Belgian colonists in the nineteenth century. They recognised the 'traditional' authority of chiefs over broadly designated swathes of territory, making some rather arbitrary demarcations and re-enacting a familiar colonial drama in which 'the "customary" power... is defined mono-ethnically, but the population resident on the ground is multi-ethnic'.[68] Places like Nombe and Lakpa assumed outsized importance as the sites of these historical disputes. They were joined by many more contested areas after independence, as the Mobutu regime decreed large-scale commercialisation of land ownership without much regard for existing usages. Conflicts of claims based on customary entitlement versus those based on legal title mushroomed across the countryside. These often also mapped along Hema–Lendu ethnic lines due to different land-use patterns and approaches to tenure, alongside divisions within the Hema community itself.[69]

Throughout the Second Congo War and after its official 'end', these disputes became remarkably violent. All sides reached out for support where they could find it, with Uganda and Rwanda deeply entangled via proxy militias in-country. The snarl of competing interests became thoroughly confusing, with one brief overview of the period listing some twenty-three different factions with their associated acronyms, notable figures and political *patrons*.[70] Fighting displaced hundreds of thousands and further muddied the waters on pre-existing land disputes, while some factions simply grabbed large areas and created brand new problems. Meanwhile a third set of locations was engraved into memory. These were the sites of major massacres like Nyakunde (perhaps a thousand civilians dead) and Songolo (almost as many).[71]

None of these issues were resolved as fighting wound down after Operation Artemis—one history entitles this period 'Not with a bang, but with a whimper: the war's confused ending'.[72] But a sustainable reduction in violence required grappling with them. 'Disarmament and demobilisation' had to address small local militias still wary of land grabs and revenge killings, and still not averse to opportunistic robbery. And an 'effective and accountable State' had to mean an acceptable way forward on vicious disputes over land and the delineation of customary authority.

In other regions of eastern DRC these very generic phrases— 'disarmament and demobilisation', 'state authority'—ran into equally complex local histories. In the far south of the area shown in Figure 3.8, south of Bukavu city, it was the conflict between the Rwandan-speaking Banyamulenge community and its neighbours that soaked up most international attention. (We touched on this in Chapter 2, regarding the machinations of William Amuri Yakutumba to 'liberate our country with you the Congolese'.) There was certainly good cause for this. The 'Banyamulenge problem' was linked with a long and very violent history, and moreover one that had played a remarkably significant role at national level.

There were plenty of other inter-communal tensions in the same region, however. Perhaps the most serious was that in Uvira territory between historical immigrants from Burundi (known as Barundi) and longer-standing inhabitants (Bafulero, among others). The Belgian colonialists again contributed to the problem by establishing an arbitrarily demarcated chiefdom, this time for the entire Ruzizi plain. This chiefdom was controlled by the Barundi, thus enraging the Bafulero people who considered themselves traditional owners of large parts of the region. Post-independence fiddling with administrative boundaries then shifted the problem around without solving it.[73] This dysfunctional local political system 'turned land into an asset of economic and political power and marginalised large parts of the rural population'.[74] At one point even the basic political rights of the 'immigrant' Barundi came into direct question, with a notorious 1981 citizenship law stripping them of nationality.

Just as in Ituri, these local disputes mapped onto the larger divisions of the First and Second Congo Wars. The fighting was ugly. Then, as major combat wound down, the central government engineered a transfer of the Ruzizi chiefdom to the Bafulero without addressing the underlying problems with boundaries and 'traditional' land rights. The Bafulero, a clear numerical majority, then proceeded to establish a stranglehold on the new parliamentary institutions at provincial and national level.[75] Violence ebbed and flowed over the next few years, picking up in late 2012 when a compromise arrangement to transfer the chiefdom back to the Barundi was stymied by the assassination of the leader in question. An array of actors 'geared towards violent accumulation' of land augmented the chaos.[76] This included the Congolese national army, which was frequently implicated on one side or another. There was also a complicating factor unique to the area: a Burundian armed group, the *Forces Nationales de Libération*, which had established itself in the Congo in the mid-2000s and was not shy about renting out its services.

This is a complex story and many readers will complain that it is already grossly over-simplified. But the point is that there is little that unifies it with the story of southern Ituri, except at the most general conceptual level. Nor would it be easy to write a common history for the other sixteen territories marked in Figure 3.8. (Let alone the provinces not represented there!)

One consequence is that Congo analysts come across as rather cantankerous. They are forever castigating policy-makers for producing 'altogether feeble analysis' that misses the 'the multi-dimensionality and complexity of conflict dynamics'.[77] But no very compelling narrative can be offered in response. One recurring motif is that conflicts are about 'land, power and identity', which is certainly true but about as vague a statement as can possibly be made about politics in an agrarian society.[78] Another common theme is militarised or 'gangster-ised' contest over resources, equivalent to saying simply that political and security institutions for the pacific resolution of such disputes don't work.[79]

The truth in all the complaints, however, is that international agencies have long been intent on treating the 'Congo crisis' as a single unit. The political scientist Severine Autessere premised her entire account of intervention from 2003–07, entitled 'The Trouble with the Congo', on this insight. She noted that the habit was 'so ingrained that 'local' usually means national (in opposition to international), and not subprovincial'. Goals were almost invariably defined for the Congo (or later 'eastern Congo') as a whole, and senior expatriates 'spent their time mediating and, when necessary, pressuring the main Congolese, Rwandan and Ugandan political and military leaders'.[80] This meant that negotiations tended to exclude local strongmen, who lacked agreed representatives to interact with the diplomatic class in Kinshasa. Meanwhile national institutional reforms—notably for elections, the security sector and financial management—were important but did little to address the issues driving inter-communal conflict in places like Ituri and Uvira.

Autessere's criticism remained justified from 2007 onwards. The Security Council immediately insisted on 'comprehensive' security sector reform and a single 'national programme for disarmament, demobilization and reintegration'. Armed groups were requested to 'immediately lay down their arms... and present themselves without any further delay or preconditions to the Congolese authorities and MONUC for DDR'. State authority would then be re-established 'throughout the territory'.[81] Plans defined with bilateral aid providers were no less sweeping. The seventeen-donor Country Assistance Framework asserted simply that support would help 'finalize the Disarmament, Demobilization and Reintegration process' and that the police, army and intelligence services would be 'reformed and transformed into professional and unified structures, supported by coherent legal frameworks'.[82]

In none of these documents do we find reference to geographic sequencing, or much variation in objectives between areas.[83] The vision is rather of a 'big bang' in which everybody other than the central government would simultaneously surrender the means of violence, and the latter would become capable and effective everywhere.

This vision was faithfully reproduced at the operational level. One of the earliest forays into statebuilding in eastern Congo was the Programme for the Restoration of Justice in Eastern Congo (REJUSCO). This was a multi-donor initiative launched in 2006 and focused on Ituri, North Kivu and South Kivu. It focused on rehabilitation of infrastructure for civil/criminal justice and support to police, prosecutorial and judicial officers—broadly in line with the central government's draft Action Plan for Justice Reform.[84] From the outset the EU touted the approach as transformative for 'the eastern part of the country, in the areas affected by years of fighting'. A typical press release promised that:[85]

> Restoring justice will put an end to impunity and, in doing so, will make a decisive contribution to the return to peace, national reconciliation and state sovereignty. It will make a major contribution to stabilising the country in the post-electoral period.

As one observer pointed out, this split the country into just two categories—the East, marked by criminal 'impunity', and everywhere else.[86] Little scope was left to adapt the former problem statement to local needs. The REJUSCO programme's official counterpart agency was the Kinshasa-level Mixed Justice Committee, and successive evaluations criticised harshly the failure to work with provincial and lower-level officials. One slammed programme officials' 'paternalistic approach', quoting a provincial Minister of Justice to the effect that he had never been consulted. Others noted simply that there had been 'little appropriation' of the programme, with multiple facilities sitting unused years later.[87] A follow-up project then summarised the major lessons learned as 'working simultaneously at the centre and the periphery', 'involving authorities not only in decisions but in a material fashion', and 'involving civil society'.[88]

A few years later came the big 'stabilisation' plans for the East. We have already seen that the Government's Stabilisation and Reconstruction Plan (STAREC) covered some 700,000km². Across this vast area it proposed a uniform approach. For the justice sector this looked much like the 2007 Action Plan and REJUSCO: rehabilitation of courts and prisons, along with deployment and training of relevant officials. These activities were literally copied and pasted for the thirty-eight territories listed in planning documents, changing only the specific numbers of personnel.[89] For civil governance, plans were written in consultation between the national Minister of Interior, the various national ministries concerned with transport and mineral exploitation, the UN and the EU. They said nothing about the issues that were wracking Irumu and Uvira—legal versus customary title, land grabs during the war, and the configuration of 'traditional' authorities. Instead the list of actions was overwhelmingly generic: [90]

A.10 Redeploy civil and customary administration
A.10.9 ORIENTALE (axes Bunia-Boga, Dungu-Limayi)
Rehabilitate / construct infrastructure for 18 entities.
Provision of equipment for these 18 entities.
Sensitisation of the population in areas of deployment
Facilitation of transport for 180 agents to be deployed.
Evaluation of training needs for public officials and deployed agents.
Organisation of activities to update and reinforce the capacities of 180 deployed agents.

This list was, again, copied and pasted for the five target provinces and some 89 individual locations. Right at the end of the document, one then finds a single desultory reference to 'mixed structures for extra-judicial resolution of conflicts'. This is lumped in with de-mining, publication of laws on sexual violence and equipment for health treatment centres. All four points are budgeted together, and it is not identified which government entities might be involved.

On the international side, the core planning document for the International Security and Stabilisation Support Strategy devoted a total one-third of a page to region-specific analysis, with four bullet points for North and South Kivu together and one for Ituri.[91] Approaches to justice and local governance were described in common language, with boxes checked for the areas where the 'package' was to be delivered. The mental model was revealed most vividly in overview maps like Figure 3.9 (overleaf). These used standard iconography to represent the progressive roll-out of institutions, much as one might find in a computer strategy game.

There was considerable resistance as these programmes hit the provincial level in 2008-10, just as there had been for REJSUCO. It fell to UN colleagues to provide copies of the central government's planning documents to provincial-level officials, along with the already-finalised project documents.[92] The roll-out process slowed to a crawl as the provincial ministries pored over blueprints, site designs and equipment lists, seeing most of it for the first time.

Below this level, communication and engagement was even weaker. No government agency undertook organised public information work until mid-2011, some three years after the launch.[93] Up until then it fell to junior UN personnel, Congolese police officers and often the private contractors putting up facilities to explain the purposes and objectives of 'stabilisation' initiatives. One critical review concluded that plans were 'rightly regarded by many Congolese as a "top down" policy – one that was drawn up in Kinshasa with no input from the Congolese people, provinces and territories'.[94] Another noted flatly that provincial governments 'were uninformed about the plan and did not feel included in it'.[95]

Figure 3.9: Map of works under the Stabilisation Strategy
Source: MONUC / ODSRSG-RC-HC (2011)

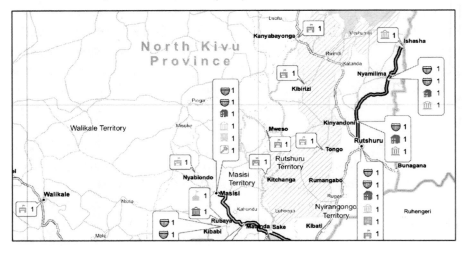

We return to all these process issues in detail in Chapter 5. For now they lead us to the urgent questions: 'How did generic approaches play out for the different permutations of the "Congo crisis"? How well did they address the differing causes of violence?'

Let us trace this in Irumu territory, southern Ituri. Here programme implementation more or less met specifications. Under REJUSCO, court and prison buildings were renovated in Bunia town, and new magistrates were deployed from outside the territory thanks to extraordinary financial incentives. The rate at which civil and criminal cases were heard increased, at least until 2010 when funding was abruptly cut off due to concerns about financial impropriety. Under STAREC, new police facilities were delivered in the chiefdoms of Bahema Sud, Walendu Bindi and Bahema Boga, along with some training for the staff of customary authorities in the same locations.

But there were two glaring limitations. Most strikingly, 'the silence of the State on land disputes in Ituri was deafening', despite near-unanimity that this was a major driver of violence.[96] The judicial mechanism was certainly used—one survey found that 50–60% of civil suits that came before local courts concerned land, and that judicial settlements accounted for 20% of all successfully resolved land conflicts.[97] However this still covered only some fifty disputes a year out of a total caseload numbering well into the thousands. Impact was particularly limited by the fact that most of the disputes concerned conflicts between legal and customary title. The President of the *Tribunal de Grande Instance* in Bunia town explained the resulting situation:[98]

> I've often had cases decided in favour of whoever holds the registration certificate, some of which are obtained without taking account of the rights of local communities. The Tribunal rules in their favour because legally, it is valid title... but I'm aware that executing the judgment will re-awaken war in Ituri.

Another interlocutor from the local confederation of civil society organisations explained that clarifying proper procedure for the award of land titles was, in the Ituri situation, a bit like describing preventive hygiene to someone who already had dysentery.[99]

However, support to alternative mechanisms was tentative at best. There was no sustained focus on land titles processing, nor did the District Commissioner take an active role.[100] A Land Commission had been launched in 2008 with a broad range of stakeholders but failed to garner significant support from the central government or international partners. By 2011 participants had to concede that 'the increasing number of cases and lack of rational organization of its work contribute to growing dissatisfaction... the credibility of the institution and its legitimacy are imperilled if a solution is not found in the short term'.[101] The stopgap was a trickle of support to informal mediation services delivered by non-governmental institutions. These employed a few dozen staff members on the ground, who through unending toil secured agreement on a few hundred disputes by the end of 2012.[102] Guidelines prepared by one such organisation listed rather forlornly the 'practical difficulties' that they confronted: lack of an adequate legal framework to reconcile legal and customary title, widespread problems with the process behind existing legal titles, disputes over demarcation of traditional authority, and complex patterns of displacement and land grabs during the war. [103] Another more critical source noted the obvious implication: these structural issues meant 'extreme fragility' for mediated settlements when the personalities changed.[104]

By 2011–12, one had to concede that the prevalence and intensity of land disputes had hardly decreased. [105] Meanwhile work under the 'civil governance' rubric did little to rebuild trust between communities, or between them and higher levels of government. There was no serious attempt at the level of central or provincial governments to address that long list of 'practical difficulties', nor to review the demarcation of traditional authorities and how they exercised their responsibilities. Inter-communal reconciliation remained the purview of small non-governmental organisations, with no mechanism to link discussions with district and provincial-level political institutions.[106]

In some cases, programmes to reinforce local-level authorities were so tone-deaf as to aggravate the situation. New road works passed from the district capital Bunia into the Hema-dominated chiefdom of Bahema Sud, but then stopped at the border of the adjoining (Lendu) chiefdom of Walendu Bindi. Rehabilitation of administrative facilities followed the same pattern, with new buildings completed in Babiase-Bogoro (Bahema-Sud) but kept 'on hold' in Gety (Walendu-Bindi).[107] The reasons given were insecurity due to the activities of small armed groups in the Walendu Bindi area, along with rationing of programmes due to lack of funding at country level. Both were true enough, but one could hardly imagine a more counter-productive result. Lendu figures complained almost immediately about international bias.[108] Over the course of 2010–11 this escalated into an orchestrated campaign of dissent against the UN mission, which was accused from various quarters of supplying ammunition to armed groups and facilitating their movements.[109] Several interlocutors complained of deliberate discrimination reaching all the way back to Henry Morton Stanley, who had broad-brushed the Hema as 'amiable, quiet and friendly' and Lendu clans as 'abrasive and violent'.[110]

All this combined with erratic counter-insurgency by the Congolese army to create fertile ground for a resurgence of violence. A nearly-dormant armed group, the FRPI, surged back into prominence on the back of serious divisions in the Lendu community and widespread frustration with the central government. This led to a crisis in late 2011 and early 2012 as the

FRPI seized control of much of Walendu Bindi, followed by a major FARDC mutiny at Marabo. This, in turn, was accompanied by increased mobilisation of Hema combatants under the slightly ludicrous title, 'Coalition of Ituri's Armed Groups' (COGAI).[111] By 2012, most observers concluded simply that the international community had dropped the ball on Irumu and Ituri, allowing it to creep back to a state of semi-crisis.[112]

Dealing with difference

'Stabilisation' in Congo was a generic product that the international community tried to sell in very different markets. It failed as it fell foul of major differences in physical geography, history and socio-political systems. Operational concepts that were optimistic in a best-case scenario like Rutshuru looked downright fantastical in remote areas that had stubbornly resisted state administration since the colonial period. Meanwhile the fact that these locations had experienced violent conflict did not mean they had much else in common. Generic concepts of the 'rule of law' and 'state authority' had either to adjust to local needs and expectations or to lapse into irrelevance, and in places like Irumu they typically did the latter.

These results should not be surprising. In the first instance: a government monopoly on the use of force from border to border 'is, in a world historical perspective, highly abnormal', a fact which has given rise to an entire literature on 'quasi-sovereignty' and 'internal frontiers'.[113] Even among specialists in peacebuilding it is now widely accepted that institutional solutions require 'sustained and long-term international political, financial and technical support.'[114] It defies logic that this could or should happen everywhere at once. Cost–benefit calculations have resulted in geographically differentiated approaches to governance for millennia—from the Byzantines and the Celestial Empire, through the colonial period, down to countries in the present-day that govern some territories with an exceedingly light grasp.[115] This last group includes many countries with much greater economic and organisational resources than the Congo. The real curiosity is thus why the point of reference has been Western states unified in the seventeenth to nineteenth centuries rather than Nigeria, Uganda or Pakistan.

A second point that bears emphasis is the breakdown of political engagement. It is also now the conventional wisdom that stabilisation depends on 'local ownership' and 'inclusive' political systems. But Severine Autessere, quoted above, was right in asserting that 'local' has too often been equated with 'the national government' in the Congo. This choice of interlocutors led directly to a quite different version of priorities from those articulated locally. It also biased intervention towards 'common denominator' approaches that made sense to ministers thinking at national scale, rather than reflecting the issues that dominated in any one area.

All this directs us to an obvious question: why did a coincidence of interests emerge among national and international policy-makers around a 'common denominator' solution, and such a limited set of interlocutors? We turn to this subject in the final two chapters, on the Coordination Fixation and the Iron Triangle.

4

The coordination fixation

The Congo is an actual poster child for the incoherence of foreign engagement in fragile states. From 2008 onwards its Finance Minister Olivier Kamitatu Etsu helped found and lead the g7+, a group of countries lumped together as 'fragile' by their donors. They joined forces to lobby for better treatment, with a brochure and manifesto stating that:[1]

> We believe that aid delivery, interventions and programs instigated by international actors are often inapplicable, unsustainable and incompatible with our in-country national agendas. As a result they are often not conducive to addressing the immediate or long-term needs of our countries and regions.

For once there was broad agreement on the side of international partners. The OECD, the club of rich-country donors, backed a global survey chaired by Kamitatu. For the Congo it found that only 20% of aid passed through the regular government budget, with donors instead setting up some 140 different 'project implementation units' to manage spending of their funds. [2] The EU found that mechanisms set up for policy dialogue around its aid choices 'had no clear mission, objectives, responsibilities, budget or timetable'.[3] Along the same lines a group of six bilateral donors and five UN agencies were told by their own evaluation team that:[4]

It is an approach by project that prevails... fundamentally, it is difficult to define the progresses achieved by the interventions towards conflict resolution and peacebuilding, as the contextual analysis is defective.

Donor programming must be founded on definitions of value-added of the different sector towards a broad and comprehensive peacebuilding and conflict prevention strategy adopted by all intervening actors.

Previous chapters of this book have made similar arguments. They can be summarised by saying that efforts to 'stabilise' eastern Congo were marked by substantial over-supply of certain types of work and under-supply of others. Chapter 1 documented a striking preoccupation with 'how much' government—personnel, equipment, buildings—at the expense of more basic questions of 'who', and 'how', and 'to what ends'. This left pressing questions of institutional representativeness and legitimacy largely undiscussed, let alone resolved to the satisfaction of local interlocutors. In Chapter 2 we saw an 'international community' willing to provide money and technical advice for security sector reform, but not to take sides by sanctioning deserters or insubordinate units. Its risk aversion was matched by that of Congolese policy-makers, who insisted on retaining control even when mediation or good offices could well have proved useful. In Chapter 3, we encountered issues that simply faded from view when they could not be slotted into national policy frameworks. Dysfunctional systems of local governance and land management staggered on without much attention, even in regions that had made world headlines just a few years prior.

In short, everybody was busy but essential work slipped readily through the cracks. This poses a problem to be explained, because it was concurrent with serious, high-level initiatives to avoid exactly that result.

Olivier Kamitatu's work with the g7+ in 2008–09 led directly to the International Dialogue on Peacebuilding and Statebuilding. Pretty much every major donor signed up to this process, with the main outcome document using the acronym 'FOCUS' to summarise their 'core commitments'. For individual countries these included a joint fragility assessment, a joined-up plan and compact of mutual commitments, a monitoring scheme to shift attention to overall progress rather than individual projects, and 'credible and inclusive processes of political dialogue'.[5]

The Security Council for its part had asked the peacekeeping mission (MONUC) successively for 'benchmarks and an indicative timetable' for drawdown of international peacekeepers; a 'strategic workplan' to the same effect; and a 'national oversight mechanism' to keep track of key reform issues.[6] Meanwhile, the Secretary-General had been attempting the same trick for planning amongst the agencies of the United Nations system. A first sally in 2000 had tasked the head of MONUC with ensuring 'a coordinated and coherent approach', and shifted reporting lines around with this in mind. Subsequent initiatives in 2006 and 2008 added on detailed procedures for assessment and planning, aimed at a 'maximising the individual and collective impact of the UN's response, focusing on those activities required to consolidate peace'.[7] On the ground these led to a sustained push for an 'Integrated Strategic Framework', but it lingered in unofficial drafts for several years before being quietly abandoned.

This chapter explores why all these initiatives never succeeded in closing the gaps. We shift our focus from Congolese institutions and communities to those of international agencies and ask—Where did policy come from? How were priorities formulated, and how much scope did executives have to steer them towards emerging issues?

The first section looks at the sprawling UN peacekeeping mission. We examine where its work streams came from, and how they evolved over time, taking us from the ground up to the great-power politics and influential lobby groups of the Security Council. In the second part we map what happened when this decentralised, highly political process encountered the standard tools of 'coordination': joined-up planning, policy dialogue, and evaluation.

Le Roy gets ambushed

In March 2010 the head of UN Peacekeeping walked into a meeting with President Joseph Kabila. Alain Le Roy had flown in for the last few days of a strategic assessment requested by the Security Council, which had put special emphasis on criteria to guide reconfiguration and eventual drawdown of MONUC.[8] His advance team had accordingly prepared a briefing kit with status updates and proposed benchmarks across a dozen different domain areas: protection of civilians, justice and corrections, repatriation of foreign combatants, and so on. The meeting was a final check-in—a formality before reporting back to the Council.

Instead, Le Roy was met with an abrupt demand. President Kabila informed him that MONUC should start drawing down its twenty thousand uniformed personnel within three months, with all of them to be gone by 30 June 2011.

Pretty much everybody was taken by surprise. Le Roy was reportedly furious at the lack of advance warning (and at his own embarrassment). Independent analysts and the international press were mostly incredulous, with one posting the sarcastic alternate-universe headline 'As peace returns to the Congo, the UN leaves'.[9] The UN's official report solved the problem by ignoring it, explaining that:[10]

> The President noted that there was no divergence of views between the United Nations and the Government on the proposals that the Under-Secretary-General had presented to the Government, with the exception of two issues only: (a) the final withdrawal of the MONUC military component, which the Government said should be completed in 2011; and (b) the proposals of the technical assessment mission regarding the contribution of MONUC to building the capacity of FARDC.

Of course, the very same report identified MONUC military support to operations against armed groups as the first 'critical task' before drawdown; and support to FARDC reform as the second.

The bureaucracy consequently went into crisis-management mode. Le Roy and the head of MONUC, Alan Doss, appealed directly for support to the member states of the Security Council.[11] On the ground, MONUC's satellite offices entertained a steady flow of representatives from provincial governments, civil society groups and armed factions who were alarmed or (in a few cases) delighted by the prospect of drawdown.[12] Meanwhile, many agencies working in eastern Congo prepared contingency plans, having grown reliant on logistical and security support from the peacekeepers after a full decade of their presence.[13]

The conclusion to the story was less dramatic. The DRC's international interlocutors pushed back against Kabila from the foreign minister and head-of-state level, as he had certainly known they would.[14] The Security Council made minor concessions, with a token drawdown of 2,000 troops and provision for 'joint assessment' exercises to assess conditions going forward. The mission was also rebranded from MONUC as MONUSCO, the UN *Stabilisation* Mission in the Congo, 'in view of the new phase that had been reached'.[15]

Nonetheless, there is something very interesting here. Le Roy's advance team comprised several dozen staff members. They had flown to a half-dozen far-flung locations across the country and held hundreds of meetings with interlocutors in international agencies, the Congolese government and (to a much lesser extent) other actors. How could he have been blind-sided by a breakdown in the most basic pre-requisite to achieve MONUC's objectives, the consent of the host country?

The answers can tell us a lot about how priorities are actually formulated in these environments. Four months earlier, the Security Council had instructed the UN Secretariat to propose 'the modalities of a reconfiguration of the mandate of MONUC, in particular the critical tasks that need to be accomplished before MONUC can envisage its drawdown without triggering a relapse into instability'.[16] But getting clear recommendations implied an awful lot of stakeholders, because the existing mandate consisted of an almost unbelievable array of tasks. The assessment team summarised as follows:[17]

> Several of the tasks mandated to MONUC over the years are on-going, including the protection of civilians; the monitoring, protection and promotion of human rights; the development of a transitional justice strategy; facilitation of the delivery of humanitarian assistance; implementation of disarmament, demobilization, repatriation, resettlement or reintegration and support to the Government's disarmament, demobilization and reintegration processes; coordination of international efforts in security sector reform; coordination and implementation of mine action activities; supporting the building of the capacity of national institutions, including FARDC, police capacities and strengthening the judicial and correctional systems; strengthening democratic institutions and the rule of law; and addressing the illegal exploitation of natural resources.

In-country this meant that MONUC boasted some sixteen separate 'substantive' offices, four infantry brigades of different nationalities, several more specialised military detachments, a thousand-plus UN police, and the support functions associated with all of these.[18] Each had their own set of interlocutors, dealing with different national and provincial ministries, local authorities, international agencies, non-governmental organisations and often also armed factions.

Unsurprisingly it proved difficult to weave together a coherent story about all these different sectors of work. So the report on the Le Roy visit simply 'factored' the problem and proceeded sector-by-sector, without significant comment on their inter-relationships or relative priority.[19]

For the first priority listed above, 'protection of civilians', the authors start from 'the continuing high level of human rights violations throughout the country'. This is linked with significant population movements, albeit somewhat below the levels recorded over the previous few years. Against this background they note approvingly that 88% of MONUC's 18,000 military personnel were deployed in 'must-protect' localities, a rating based on perceived severity of threat, and recommended 'that this high correlation be maintained'. They go on to stress the need for still more resources, including allocation of more civilian personnel and helicopters that had been budgeted but had not yet arrived in-theatre. The other major concern is the poor human rights record of the national army. We get a great deal of detail on types and kinds of violations, and then a long overview of a 'conditionality' policy for MONUC support to upcoming operations. The gist is that MONUC will support only activities that are 'jointly planned and commanded by officers not previously involved in serious human rights violations'.

If we go down the list, to the section on the Congolese National Police, we get a rather different angle. Here the authors' main concern is the 'legacy of integration of armed groups which has contributed to a lack of cohesion and significant differences in, or the absence of, vetting and training'. This requires thorough-going institutional-level reform, and it is mentioned approvingly that the police service has just adopted a fifteen-year strategic plan and three-year action plan. The job is now for MONUC and its partners to 'support the effective implementation' of these reforms. The second major finding is that police operating capacities remain 'greatly constrained', including problems with equipment, logistical support to the field, and payroll. The authors note that MONUC has already supported training to 8,625 regular officers and 210 judicial police. The recommendation is then to 'continue to focus on building the capacities of the Congolese police to respond to crises' and in particular support targeted deployments to 'critical areas' in eastern Congo. In practice this means more policy work, training of police trainers and perhaps support for a 'core force' around which further reforms might develop.

These are strikingly different perspectives. The first is focused on direct action, viewing Congolese institutions mostly as a threat to be managed, and looks only a few months into the future. It also contemplates physically risky deployments into the deep bush, including expensive and scarce military assets. By contrast the second section contemplates action *only* through Congolese institutions, with this work situated on a three- (or fifteen-) year timeline. UN personnel are needed for headquarters-led advice and assistance rather than field operations, with concomitantly lower levels of risk and logistical expense.

The same extreme heterogeneity runs all the way through the document. There are nine more capsule assessments like these—each with its distinctive criteria for what a good outcome in Congo would look like and its specific resource requirements. The attempt to pull all this together into the 'critical tasks' that would enable MONUC to withdraw (per the Security Council's original request) gets broader and vaguer by the sentence:

The first critical task should be to neutralize the threat posed by FDLR, LRA and residual Congolese armed groups.

The second critical task should be to build a professional FARDC core force, which the mission considered could be up to 20 battalions.

The third critical task is the establishment of effective State authority in the areas freed from armed groups... in this regard, the capacity of the public administration, policing, judicial and correctional systems in the Democratic Republic of the Congo needs to be developed to a sustainable level to allow the independent monitoring of human rights, contribute to ending impunity and allow the establishment of an effective prison system fully respecting international standards.

The other critical tasks identified by the technical assessment mission were full implementation of the Agreements of 23 March; addressing the illegal exploitation of natural resources; establishment of effective community-based mechanisms for resolving land-related and other inter-communal disputes associated with returns of internally displaced persons and refugees, including a transitional justice process; completion of the voluntary repatriation of the Congolese refugees from neighbouring countries who wish to return to the eastern Democratic Republic of the Congo; and the conduct, by the Congolese authorities, of credible and peaceful national elections in 2011.

The common joke in the UN is that this is 'integration by stapler'.[20] The binder was the only thing holding together a list of tasks in obvious competition with each other for resources and political attention. With it in hand, Le Roy was ill-prepared to meet the President. The latter had been agitating since 2007 for a plan to draw down MONUC, an operation that was after all justified with reference to 'a threat to international peace and security'. But there was hardly a compelling storyline for why this could or could not happen. Instead many of the critical tasks seemed open-ended, 'more like receding horizons than fixed targets'.[21] It was not clear whether all would be needed, or in what combinations. Nor was there much effort to map the Congolese government's ideas on the subject, notwithstanding the hyperactive diplomacy of Olivier Kamitatu and the g7+ over the two years leading up to the assessment.

An additional aggravation—for all concerned—was that this was hardly the first time this had happened. MONUC had promised to develop 'benchmarks' in 2007, a 'strategic workplan' in 2008, and an 'integrated strategic framework' in 2009–10.[22] Yet the array of tasks had only grown more daunting. To give a sense of this, Figure 4.1 totals the headings in MONUC's periodic reports from 2007–12. The bottom line counts the number of geographic areas; the top line counts thematic headings like those we saw above.

Bear in mind that these reports are not long documents. On average, Figure 4.1 thus suggests four paragraphs per heading, each as broad as 'rule of law and judicial institutions', or 'North Kivu, South Kivu, Maniema and Katanga Provinces'. (Recall from Chapter 3 that the latter is a combined area of 400,000 square kilometres.) The consequence, as practitioners will readily admit, is that one approached MONUC reports a lot like a newspaper. You didn't expect a coherent narrative but rather small, self-contained stories. Most of the time, you read the front two pages and then skipped to the sections that interested you due to some personal or professional interest.

Figure 4.1: Proliferating peacekeeping tasks, 2007–2012
Source: Reports of the Secretary-General on MONUC / MONUSCO[23]

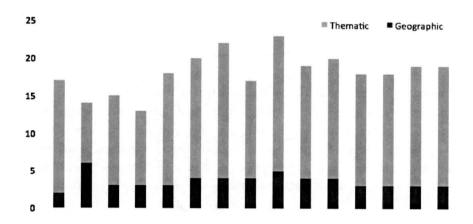

The same analogy holds quite well on the production side. MONUC's Political Affairs Division acted as managing editor, and allocated a fixed number of paragraphs to each sector of work. Arguments inevitably ensued about how your number compared to those of rival teams, and the order in which issue areas would appear in the document. All sides tried to read the political mood in New York and cite it in their own favour. In mid-2011, my own team for stabilisation coordination considered it a major coup to move from dead last in the sequence to third, and to have increased our real estate from one to two paragraphs.[24] (I shudder to recall the amount of lobbying and manoeuvring that this entailed.)

But the key point is that these were minor course adjustments. For anyone trying to steer the ship, the reality was that the international public sector 'is something that exists. It is the end product of a long process of development and the changes that can be made are subject to pretty severe restraints and limitations'.[25] To understand how policy really changes, we thus need to turn our attention to that long historical process. In MONUC's case, it is perhaps best illustrated by the first task noted above—the protection of civilians 'under imminent threat of physical violence'.

Peacekeeping 911

In 1999, Secretary-General Kofi Annan argued forcefully that UN peace operations needed to change. The principle that force could be used only in self-defence had to be left behind, for the 'plight of civilians is no longer something which can be neglected, or made secondary because it complicates political negotiations or interests'. Henceforth, he suggested, the Security Council should authorise violent means to prevent abuses in those situations where the 'United Nations is the only international organisation with the reach and authority to end these practices'.[26] The Council obliged almost immediately, mandating the mission in Sierra Leone 'to afford protection to civilians under imminent threat of physical violence'. It then added similar language to MONUC's mandate in 2000.[27]

In the Congo, with its enormous geography and multiple intersecting conflicts, the practical difficulties proved immense. MONUC's limits were shown by massacres in Kisangani (2002) and Ituri (2003), and then the capture of Bukavu (2004). In response the Council ramped up military personnel on the ground from an initial 5,500 to 16,500, and needled troop contributors to adopt a more aggressive posture.[28] (It also welcomed in the EU's Operation Artemis in Ituri, as we saw in Chapter 3). National elections and the wind-up of the transitional government provided a brief distraction, but violence against civilians surged in prominence again in 2007–08. Army integration broke down in North Kivu, hundreds of thousands of people were again displaced, and the Security Council became very vocal indeed. During one indicative debate the Belgian ambassador declared vehemently that 'where MONUC is present, where it can be deployed in time and where civilian lives are endangered, it must act'. His French counterpart jumped in to add that 'the testimony of non-governmental organisations was overwhelming', and that 'everything must be done to put an end' to atrocities.[29] In the end the Council gave MONUC unambiguous instructions: protecting civilians had to be 'given priority in decisions about the use of available capacity and resources'.[30] On the ground the mission interpreted this task as follows:[31]

> This 'safety-oriented' definition of protection primarily entails direct 'responsive' actions, aimed at preventing and stopping violence. MONUC is requested to 'contribute to the improvement of the security conditions in which humanitarian

assistance is provided'. This focus on security gives clear immediate protection goals – reducing the number of attacks, recorded human rights violations and violations of the international humanitarian law, as well as creating security conditions that facilitate the delivery of humanitarian assistance; and allows to measure progress [sic] against them.

The overall idea is well-summarised by Figure 4.2. This is the cover photo for a retrospective by the mission's senior civilian specialist in this area, entitled simply 'The protection of civilians in the Democratic Republic of the Congo'.[32] We see foreign military personnel; the tools of combat; and Congolese women and children.

Figure 4.2: The face of the UN in the Congo
Source: Martin (2012) 'The protection of civilians in the DRC'

The article includes four more photos along the same lines; just one Congolese soldier is present in the margins of one of them. This is not by chance. From 2007 onwards MONUC split its 18,000 military personnel across ninety-some locations to provide a local deterrent and facilitate an immediate tactical response to violence. In many long-standing trouble spots these detachments developed Community Alert Networks, distributing free cell phones and radios to underwrite a sort of 'UN 911' service.[33] At the strategic level, there were extensive discussions with troop-contributing countries to coax them to take on greater risk. In parallel, training modules on the 'new protection' were developed by a variety of institutions and actively marketed to troop contributors to MONUC and other UN operations.[34]

All this sounds rather different from the first and second 'critical tasks' identified by Le Roy's assessment mission: to neutralise armed groups, and build a 'core force' for the Congolese army. In fact, working documents refer but rarely to Government security forces, except as a target for oversight. In the review article cited above, the first reference is on the second-last page, noting:

> Establishing a protective environment requires a wide range of complementary activities. These vary from support for political processes and governance, security sector reform and the extension of State authority to areas formerly under the control of armed groups.

There follows a total of two paragraphs on such 'complementary' activities. One finds the same pattern in other specialist literature, written almost exclusively in the peculiar dialect of the UN bureaucracy rather than the normal language of government.[35] On the ground the 'Protection Cluster' grouped together several dozen relief agencies aiming to reduce violence through monitoring and advocacy. The latter was directed primarily at a 'rapid and appropriate reaction by MONUSCO', while a 'possible link with the armed forces... must be decided locally according to the wishes of the civilian population'.[36]

We can summarise: the measure of excellence for the 'protection' sector was smart prioritisation, in a situation where peacekeepers could 'never have the full complement of resources and capabilities that may be required to protect civilians in the extremely challenging circumstances in which they are deployed'.[37] In this regard practitioners sometimes cited MONUC as a strong performer, perhaps even best-of-breed. One paper declared that Congo enjoyed 'undoubtedly the most proactive protection-of-civilians strategy of any DPKO peace operation'.[38] Others commended 'best practices' such as the

Alert Networks ('UN 911') and coordination with the Protection Cluster, with the Security Council itself endorsing such 'innovations'.[39]

Much more often, as Congo-watchers are well-aware, MONUC was harshly criticised. We have already seen that violence and displacement of civilians continued unabated throughout 2007–12, with the lobby group International Crisis Group writing that the UN had 'strikingly little success at fulfilling its primary objective to protect civilians, though some of its innovative operational improvements should be acknowledged'.[40] In the wake of high-profile acts of violence, press and lobbyist reports invariably reviewed and broke down what MONUC had done or not done.[41] Frequently this extended right down to the tactical level. In the aftermath of the 2008 Kiwanja massacre, Human Rights Watch issued a lengthy report examining who knew what when, when patrols left the base and when they returned, and which parts of the town were prioritised.[42] One passage is enough to give the flavour:

> In Kiwanja a week later, assuring the security of humanitarian workers, a foreign journalist, and a group of military observers became the priority. In a situation where resources were inadequate, virtually none were devoted to protecting Congolese civilians.
>
> The Indian troops had four Russian BMP (Bronevaya Maschina Piekhota) fighting vehicles, more effective vehicles than the armored personnel carriers available to the Uruguayan troops. But when the CNDP attacked, two of the four BMPs had been sent to Kalengera (some 7 kilometers south of Rutshuru) and were unable to return to town. The other two BMPs were initially sent south to block the CNDP advance but then had to divert to assist in rescuing humanitarian workers whose convoy out of town had been stoned by local people angry at their departure. The Uruguayans had brought the humanitarian workers to the UN refugee agency (UNHCR)'s base, located between Kiwanja and Rutshuru, but the base was soon fired on by retreating Congolese army soldiers. The Indian BMPs were needed to extricate the workers and bring them safely back to the MONUC base in Kiwanja.

On the ground the large and vocal Protection Cluster (a group of emergency relief agencies) gave itself a similar role, 'holding the force to account for effective implementation of its protection mandate' as one participant termed it.[43] Members critiqued action or inaction in specific cases and produced detailed trend analyses by region and perpetrator. These were used to lobby for MONUC deployments here or there, with much of eastern Congo classified into 'must-protect', 'should-protect' and 'could-protect' areas.[44]

All this scrutiny amounted to powerful reinforcing feedback for the initial policy choice for 'direct responsive action'. The UN became progressively more sensitive on protection issues, commissioning major internal and independent reviews over the course of 2008–09.[45] In-country, any major incident was followed immediately by a Headquarters code cable requesting details of who did what, where and when. One internal audit report demanded precise annual estimates of the number of civilian casualties and incidences of sexual violence in order to gauge the mission's effectiveness. Another reviewed every historical incident it could find to assess MONUC's role and whether there was 'appropriate' (in the audit unit's retrospective judgement) use of force.[46] Seeing which way the wind was blowing, MONUC officials gave the lion's share of its internal situation reports to cataloguing individual incidents and the mission's response thereto.[47] (Read daily, they became rather depressing litanies of robberies, rapes and murders.)

Throughout this story, there are two features that are critical. The first is the existence of *parallel problem definitions*. From 2000 to 2012 the 'Congo crisis' was addressed in succession by peace agreements, elections and 'stabilisation'—but savage violence against civilians was a constant. The conviction accordingly grew that that whatever else it did, 'where MONUC was present it must act'. The rationale was not that this would contribute to an exit strategy for peacekeepers, or that Congolese priorities had been re-assessed. It was rather explicitly moral, with roots in much older humanitarian appeals to 'spare civilians the agony of war'.[48] The measure of success was thus very simple: reduced violence, by the most direct means available.

The problem, for coordinators and 'integrators', is that this competed with a good dozen other answers to the question 'What is to be done?' The advocates for army reform who we met in Chapter 2 believed that a security dilemma lay at the heart of Congo's woes. They painted the situation as a Hobbesian 'war of all against all' where the only protection was self-protection.[49] Elsewhere, the natural-resource zealots introduced in Chapter 3 argued that redoubled efforts would 'change the incentive structure away from violence and illegality towards security and rule of law'.[50] Still others believed that addressing land disputes, or criminal impunity, held the keys to a better life for the Congolese. Each defined 'success' in their own way and lobbied hard for resources. And all of them were at least a little bit successful, as we saw above. Coalitions formed for work in each sector, bringing in like-minded Congolese interlocutors, operational agencies on the ground and financial contributors in foreign capitals.

The second feature that I want to stress is *organisational specialisation.* Reconfiguring MONUC to focus on protecting civilians was no minor undertaking. The Security Council had only gradually increased troop levels from 2000–05, with considerable equivocation from member states who feared escalating expectations and costs.[51] The countries which provided those troops had to be continually prodded to adopt a riskier posture and make corresponding changes to training and standard procedures. At the operational level, MONUC's military contingent was then split into small detachments and scattered over eastern Congo, while much of its civilian workforce was dedicated to analysis and reporting. This in turn became the new normal. Any attempt to reallocate resources was scrutinised by half a hundred organisations eager to 'hold the force to account'; while major changes would have had to navigate the same political obstacle course at the highest levels.

Other organisations were no less hard-wired for selective attention. To work on issues like security sector reform, or regulation of natural resources, requires specialised capabilities. Virtually all agencies try to build these at global scale and this means developing funding relationships with like-minded donors, recruiting experienced staff, and building complex transnational systems for procurement and financial management. By the time any officials hit the ground in Congo, they were thoroughly bound by this chain of adaptations, often stretching back decades. Changes could be only at the margins.

Together these two conditions made 'coordination' initiatives uniquely suited for a dialogue of the deaf. In the next section we dig into just such an exercise—a two-day inter-agency workshop on 'stabilisation' of eastern Congo that was held in June 2011. (After insurgencies, mutinies and vicious land conflicts we are now into the really grim subject matter.)

'We can't fix this at the Hotel Venus'

There were sixty-three people in the room, representing thirty-four different institutions. They came from every branch of the sprawling UN system, a scattering of non-governmental agencies, and the more active international donors in Congo. The conference space at the improbably-named Hotel Venus was jammed with tables, flip charts and projection equipment. From the window you could see a forest of little flags in the parking lot, with heavily branded 4WD vehicles filling every space and spilling down the street for two blocks.

The objectives were to stock-take international efforts to 'stabilise' eastern Congo, and to define common priorities going forward. Both tasks were urgent, because the problems discussed in previous chapters had become impossible to ignore.

Perhaps most crucial was the security sector, as we saw in Chapter 2. The central government's latest army reorganisation ('regimentation') initiative was a train wreck in slow motion, with Colonel Kifaru rampaging through the mountains of South Kivu even as we sat in that conference room. The 'cold war' with the CNDP was at its peak, with its senior figures working furiously to solidify allies and marginalise enemies. It was clear that 'the government's inability to protect its people or control its territory undermined progress on everything else'.[52] Yet there was little constructive engagement. International support was confined to small infrastructure projects, some work on the army's administrative systems, and demobilisation packages for fighters who showed up of their own accord. (Even the latter had recently been suspended as it became clear that fighters were 'recycling' back into armed groups.)

Everyone had the feeling that something must be done, although opinions on what this might be were varied. Among international agencies debate had become heated and at times violent. (I vividly recall one colleague screaming that another agency's representative was 'the devil' during one such exchange.) The refrain had become that such issues would be addressed 'at the workshop'. The agenda was then put together as if cribbed from a textbook on how agencies are supposed to work together. Item number one was a shared assessment of progress against overall objectives. This would be informed by free-form discussion in groups for the three main work-streams: security, state authority, and return / reintegration / recovery. Agenda item number two was to define priorities for a planned 'phase two' of stabilisation efforts. We would define strategic orientations and then (item number three) procedures to work with the Congolese government at both central and provincial levels.[53]

All this was supported by a facilitation team (my own unit), not affiliated with any individual agency. After two days it became apparent that we had made no progress whatsoever on the core outstanding issues. In fact— more than this—that it was fruitless trying to do so in the room.

To understand why, let us take a short walking tour. In Figure 4.3 we see the working group for 'return, reintegration and recovery'. This was shorthand for the safe return to their home areas of people displaced by violence, along with rebuilding agricultural livelihoods and local social services.

Figure 4.3: Within the comfort zone: return and recovery
Source: MONUSCO / ODSRG-RC-HC (2011)

Sitting around the table is a microcosm of the aid business. The uniform is short-sleeved shirts, rumpled blazers, cardigans. The organisations represented include the UN Development Programme, UNICEF, UN Women and assorted other bits and pieces of the UN system. Alongside them are the few non-governmental organisations who interested themselves in 'stabilisation' work, notably International Alert and Oxfam. A few representatives of MONUC look out of place in police uniform and suit, relegated to the back-right of the table.

These organisations had long-established offices and programmes in eastern Congo. They overwhelmingly used a 'direct execution' approach, meaning they delivered services through agency staff or sub-contractors rather than passing funds to Government institutions. This means the people pictured were project managers for the most part. In discussions leading up to the workshop they had developed a mishmash of thirty-six proposed new activities, costed at USD 144m.[54] These now needed to be organised and presented to international donors as a coherent package. This meant lively arguments around the table as everybody insisted on their various priorities. The UN Refugee Agency stressed orderly assistance to cross-border movements and people displaced by fighting; UN Women opined on support to female heads of household and women's political empowerment; Oxfam lobbied for community-led development and support to agricultural livelihoods; and so forth.

Ultimately, the work was divided under three headings: resolution of local-level conflicts; re-establishment of basic services; and agricultural and economic recovery. This list was broad enough to bring everybody into the tent. Collectively, there was also agreement on how to measure success. Each priority area was associated with a few high-level measures of effectiveness, each 'owned' by a single agency with an established methodology to measure it.[55] The points of biggest contention were rather *where* to work, given a turbulent security landscape, and how to coordinate dealings with financial donors. (The latter point entailed a lot of back-and-forth on who should present, in what sequence, and with what comments on priorities.)

In the language of political science, this is a self-contained policy sub-system. There were severe problems in the security sector—in fact signs of an incipient collapse—but life went on for relief and development agencies. They continued to plan, fundraise and implement their normal lines of work, simply adjusting geographic targeting to work around the worst violence. As one review article put it, 'an observer would not be able to distinguish it from any "normal" intervention to support reintegration and a transition to longer-term development'.[56]

Standing in the room it was hard to argue that this was perverse, or misguided. The famous figure of 5.4 million deaths in the Congo wars was after all due to interruption of livelihoods and basic services, not battle deaths.[57] Social indicators had improved considerably since this nadir but remained bad by any measure. It was also pretty clear that modest economic growth since the end of the Second Congo War had been concentrated in Kinshasa and a few regional centres. Anything that delivered concrete benefits to people on the ground thus had a strong presumption in its favour. (Leaving aside the many questions of how to design programmes that were actually effective.)

The problem rather came when one walked to the opposite side of the room, as we see in Figure 4.4. Here the working group for 'Security and Political Processes' was subdued and distracted. Participants frankly admitted they had no idea what success looked like. No one had data on levels of public trust in the armed forces or the effective integration of factions that had been recently brought into the fold, with the main suggestion instead that MONUC should create a 'protective environment' for other work. There was also little jockeying for priority. While humanitarian and development agencies had been churning out proposals to work around deteriorating security, there were zero concrete proposals to address the problem itself. The fastest way to see why is a quick glance at who was represented.

Figure 4.4: Orphan problems: the security sector
Source: MONUSCO / ODSRSG-RC-HC (2011)

What is striking is not that the group looks very different. Quite the opposite—the cast of characters is the same. Jeans and casual shirts predominate, albeit with slightly more central African flavour. There are no diplomats in suits and just one man in military uniform, almost invisible at top right as if to downplay his presence.

The cosmetic similarities are not by chance, for we are looking at very similar interlocutors. Seen around the table here are more civilian agencies of the UN: the Development Programme, Office for Human Settlements, and Mine Action Service. There is a United States government contractor working on community development, and a magistrate working on judicial reform. The single military specialist is a colonel from the Plans department of MONUC's military headquarters.

The plain fact was none of these actors had capacity to do much for the most urgent issues. MONUC was the only one with any coercive capacity—but we have already seen that its troops were fully committed under the protection mandate, splintered into a hundred small detachments across the East. That was not on the table for renegotiation, at least not without an explicit directive from the Security Council. Pending that, there was no available capacity to deter two-bit deserters like Colonel Kifaru, let alone large factions like the CNDP. Nor were MONUC's numbers sufficient to provide much comfort to militias who baulked at disarming in a still-volatile security environment.

The civilians, for their part, had few entry points into policy-making for the security sector. MONUC's small Political Affairs department was made up of foreign ex-diplomats and included no former Congolese military personnel or militia leaders with insight into the inner workings of these organisations.[58] Its team for Security Sector Reform, as we saw in Chapter 2, comprised a few foreign staff members based in Kinshasa and fixated on a 'national management plan' and 'reform czar' at this level. And other agencies deployed project managers, not fixers. Even the biggest, the UN Development Programme, had no full-time political specialists at all deployed in the East. Per normal operating procedure this was part of the duties of the local head of office, who also had oversight responsibility for a hundred million dollars of programmes.[59]

There was little to be done about this around the table. At the best of times, telling an agency about gaps and unmet priorities felt a bit like lecturing a nurse that the police were under-funded. ('I may agree with you, but it is not my problem'.) More often, it was met with a return lecture. As one global review of efforts to 'integrate' UN activities put it:[60]

> Repeatedly, the Study Team found that some individual agencies argued that their 'mandates' were based upon international obligations that transcended Security Council mandates, or the original resolution establishing their agency. Not all agencies or UNCT members saw the adoption of a Security Council mandate authorising a UN mission into their country of operation as actually affecting the nature of their own job.

Sitting at the Venus this sounded like: 'We are not that type of agency. Our staff aren't trained for it, our Board hasn't authorised it, and our donors won't pay for it. There is, moreover, a compelling argument for what we are already doing with our time.' The result was that little changed. As the report following the workshop put it, critical issues in the security sector 'remained "context"—external success factors—rather than programme targets'.[61] To add insult to injury, some donors had put funds into a funding facility for flexible response to emerging priorities. It had promptly been disbursed to a demonstration centre for organic farming, and a centre for treatment of victims of sexual violence.[62]

In this fashion, 'coordination' in eastern Congo ran into some unyielding realities of the larger international system. In 2009 the UN Secretary-General echoed a string of blue-ribbon panels and strategic evaluations in asserting that priorities must come to 'reflect the unique conditions and needs of the country rather than be driven by what international actors can or want to supply'.[63] This was a polite way of saying that this was not presently happening. Blunter reviews concluded that 'strategy-resistant' interventions were the norm, and that 'many of the civilian capacities most needed by conflict-affected communities were not to be found within the United Nations'.[64] Many of them specifically highlighted difficulties in engaging with politically sensitive policy processes like that in the Congolese security sector. One recent think-tank review summarised this state-of-play perfectly:[65]

> Donors seeking to influence policy-making as outsiders need to make deliberate efforts to be politically informed and to prioritise local leadership. They have not often done so because aid and relationships with countries dependent on aid

have traditionally given them some leverage, encouraging false assumptions that they can bypass local politics and policy-making processes. In that sense, the appeal for donors to adopt politically smart, locally led approaches is a long overdue wake-up call.

At country-level, the result was that the scene at the Hotel Venus was re-enacted again and again, with different actors stepping into the same roles. The purpose of the International Security and Stabilisation Strategy was to address 'limited and urgent priorities', with sequencing to be 'tailored to realities at the provincial, district or territorial levels'.[66] But this proved elusive and the conclusion of the Strategy's first major evaluation was both devastating and familiar: the strategy remained a 'patchwork of activities' without means of 'prioritizing among the various priorities of the different actors'.[67]

Several critics illustrated the point by simply reproducing the pattern of spending that emerged after a few years, with Figure 4.5 an example from mid-2011. They pointed out that the priorities seemed more or less backwards. The years 2007-11 had seen aggressive fundraising for programme areas that fit within agencies' existing preferences and capabilities, but few new ideas on how to unblock the security sector and political processes.[68] In short, orphan issues had not found a home.

Figure 4.5: Backwards priorities?
Source: MONUSCO / ODSRSG-RC-HC (2011)

Other initiatives to improve coordination met much the same fate. Within the UN system the biggest push, and the most spectacular failure, was the attempt at an 'integrated strategic framework' from 2009 to 2011. The motivating idea was to organise activities under a 'single coherent framework outlining a shared vision and common objectives' for a three-year period.[69] It was endorsed at the highest levels with a direct request from the Secretary-General's Policy Committee in June 2009, and the Security Council following suit shortly afterwards. Both were concerned about an eventual drawdown of MONUSCO, whose cumulative budget was just about to pass the ten billion dollar mark. The specific goals will by now sound all-too-familiar: concentration on 'critical tasks' and 'activities required to consolidate peace'; smooth 'transition' from security actors to civilian development agencies; 'coherent and mutually supportive' action by the different parts of the system.[70]

On the ground MONUC's coordination team prepared a draft assessment, and then organised discussions around a table much like that in Figure 4.3. To their credit, the first draft waded right into battle. It stated bluntly that MONUC 'needs the support of [the UN's civilian agencies] to strengthen national capacities in such areas as security, governance and the administration of essential services, so that it can initiate a responsible drawdown'. Achieving this would require 'recalibration' of interventions, and above all 'coordination of spending priorities' such that 'savings in one area can be directed to others'.[71] Specifically singled out for 'recalibration' were large emergency relief programmes in eastern Congo, by this point running continuously for a half-decade, and the large 'direct execution' programmes for local recovery. These were explicitly labelled as stop-gap measures, to be phased out within the three-year timeframe in favour of work on the policy and institutional environment.

The proposed language met a frosty reaction. Indeed for many in the specialised agencies, this was just finger-pointing. MONUC personnel had the mandate for restoring peace and security and an operational budget of one-and-a-half billion dollars per year; why didn't *they* do this work? Besides, what about all the concrete benefits of those programmes on the ground? Were they just to be yanked away from the Congolese population?

Both sides scrambled to mobilise their allies. MONUC's leadership went directly to its paymasters in New York, presenting the draft ISF to the Security Council and troop-contributing countries in February 2010. The Secretary-General then touted the framework as defining 'agreed results, timelines and responsibilities'.[72] The UN's other agencies went instead to their Congolese interlocutors, with copies of the supposedly confidential document landing on ministers' desks within weeks. Their grievances dovetailed nicely with President Kabila's position that the situation had 'normalised' in the East and no longer necessitated international peacekeepers. In his showdown with Alain Le Roy in March 2010 he accordingly indicated in no uncertain terms that the Congolese government did not want UN activities 'subordinated' to conflict prevention objectives, let alone under the strategic direction of the head of MONUC.[73] And there the battle ended. The ISF staggered on for a few months to demonstrate the UN's independence and was then quietly dropped. It was not mentioned in subsequent Security Council resolutions or reports on MONUSCO; as at mid-2015 it is hard even to find reference to it online.

A subsequent 'transition framework' was a much more anodyne document. It aimed merely to identify the 'common areas of joint activities and collaboration' in the *existing* planning frameworks of the UN system in-country.[74] The summary diagram that followed was almost too perfect an illustration of 'integration by stapler', as we see in Figure 4.6.

Figure 4.6: 'Let's keep doing what we're doing'
Source: MONUSCO / ODSRSG-RC-HC (2011)

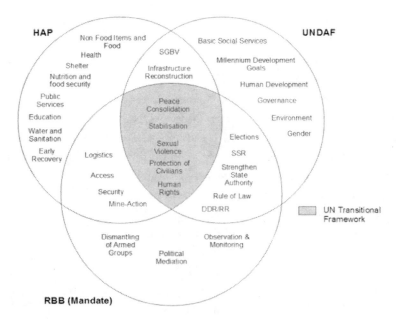

Here UN strategy in the Congo is simply the arithmetical combination of planning frameworks for emergency service delivery (the Humanitarian Action Plan or HAP); development assistance (UNDAF); and MONUSCO's operations budget (RBB). Each is formulated and proceeds in parallel, with separate reporting lines and criteria for success. The idea of a 'broad and comprehensive strategy' lay where it had fallen.

Finding the storyline

In Pirandello's play *Six Characters in Search of an Author*, a family arrives on the set of another play, complete with already-formed storylines.[75] The director is informed that he has become an author, a 'task made much easier by the fact that we are all here alive before you'. He is perturbed but agrees to stage scenes that seem to fit his new characters. In response they critique his direction and the available actors, and then take over themselves. By way of explanation they inform the director of a harsh reality:

> When the characters are really alive before their author, the latter does nothing but follow them in their action, in their words, in the situations which they suggest to him; and he has to will them the way they will themselves—for there's trouble if he doesn't.

This captures rather well the experience of 'coordinating' international engagement in the Congo. Calls for better analysis and planning ignored a basic limitation: we could only stage a story with the characters that were available. Ninety per cent of what foreign officials could do and say was decided before they ever set foot in-country, as country-level priorities flowed inexorably from global strategic plans, mandates and capabilities. This meant that tools were simply not available to fill the gaps explored in Chapters 1-3.

This fact was most striking for the biggest asset in-country: MONUSCO's 20,000 troops. For half a decade MONUC had struggled to operationalise the idea of protecting civilians 'at imminent risk of violence' in a country the size of the Congo. But by 2007–08 any confusion had cleared. The Security Council had specified unambiguously that this task had first call on

MONUC's military assets, and the countries who contributed troops had begrudgingly adapted their expectations and training. On the ground this was complemented by dozens of agencies that collected data, scrutinised performance and lobbied frenetically. The result was a complex and increasingly well-structured policy system with its own jargon, permanent bureaucracy and measures of success.

But the choice necessarily left other areas much worse-served. At the same time as MONUC was splitting its forces into a hundred small pieces to protect civilians 'under imminent threat of physical violence', it was watching the Congolese security forces implode. But there was neither political will nor (available) capability to coerce recalcitrant factions. Nor was there much effort to influence Congolese security policy by more indirect means. Few agencies were willing or able to swim in the murky waters of Congolese policy-making, preferring instead to work on projects they could control and implement themselves. The UN's peacekeeping and development arms thus engaged in mutual finger-pointing over who was responsible for four years, before adopting a Transition Framework that declared nobody was and that existing strategic frameworks were just fine.

None of this is to say that a division of labour is unwise. The range of tasks that was being attempted in the Congo was comparable in complexity to a full cabinet of ministries, and attempting to oversee everything at once would have paralysed both overseer and operators. The protection sector is thus hardly an aberration; it was entirely appropriate that 'most issues, most of the time, were treated within such a community'.[76] The table of development agencies at the Hotel Venus also functioned well enough, in difficult conditions, if measured on their own terms.

The problem rather came when the link to the general public interest was broken—when these specialised logics became the *only* logics. As Herbert Simon once put it:[77]

Administrative man recognizes that the world he perceives is a drastically simplified model of the buzzing, blooming confusion that constitutes the real world. He is content with the gross simplification because he believes that the real world is mostly empty—that most of the facts of the real world have no great relevance to any particular situation he is facing and that most significant chains of causes and consequences are short and simple.

This was the compartmentalised mentality that declared MONUC best-in-class at 'protecting civilians' right before the largest city in the conflict theatre was over-run by insurgents.[78] It was also the mentality illustrated by Figure 4.5, where interventions to reduce conflict were drastically under-subscribed by international donors and those to 'recover' from it drastically over-subscribed. The administrative women and men working away on the latter were rudely reminded of bigger 'chains of causes and consequences' when a rapid escalation in violence wiped out most of their hard-won achievements in the course of a few months.

This takes us to the final question posed by *Follies in Fragile States*. What was it about the politics of international stabilisation that allowed this situation to persist? There was ample evidence that public priorities in eastern Congo didn't line up very well with the plans as written. Why did this fact not intrude more forcefully into the policy-making process?

5

The iron triangle

The marketing for 'stabilisation' efforts in the Congo promised a remarkable metamorphosis. The larval state was a sort of shared governance, whereby national authorities cohabited with a UN peacekeeping force to underwrite public security, and international relief agencies to provide many social services. The mature state was a government 'capable of sustaining the vital sovereign functions required to preserve national unity'.[1] The pupal stage in between was increased Congolese oversight and direction of international support, or what development workers call 'national ownership;.

The first draft of MONUC's stabilisation plan thus called it simply a 'support package' for Congolese institutions. Later versions elaborated that the 'overall objective... is to support national efforts to promote a secure and stable environment'.[2] Press and fundraising materials then hammered the point. It became internal policy to use the awkward formula 'the International Security and Stabilisation Support Strategy, in support of the Government stabilisation and reconstruction plan'.[3] Even more awkward in-house graphics adorned the front covers of key documents. Unusually, these featured police officers, frontline administrators and even the much-maligned Congolese army—rather than the more usual fare of smiling school teachers and health workers. Inside one found prominent headings like 'Planning and implementing together' and graphics like that in Figure 5.1, depicting all international efforts pointing inwards to the Congolese government at the centre.

Figure 5.1: The government in the centre

Source: MONUSCO (2011) 'International security and stabilisation support strategy for eastern DRC'

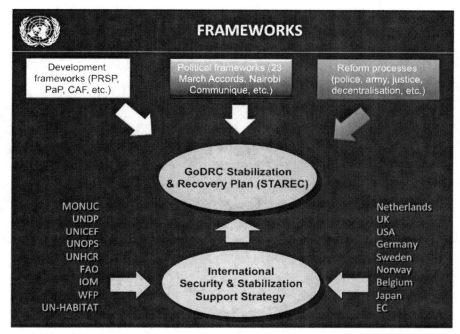

This sounds like aid-speak one would hear anywhere, but for eastern Congo it already implied significant behaviour change. International donors and their in-country partners were well-accustomed to a half-decade of operating independently. Within MONUC, one introductory briefing picked out the novel features of the mission's stabilisation activities as 'governments' and 'partnerships'—and then rhetorically asked what UN support to Government efforts meant for those present.[4] Briefings back to the Department of Peacekeeping in New York invariably emphasised the 'joint leadership' of the strategy.[5] Outside MONUC, in the chaotic melee of international fundraising, there was a rush to claim the moral high ground. The Terms of Reference for a new funding mechanism for stabilisation efforts strained to offer a distinctive product:[6]

> The SRFF is designed to support a transition in Eastern DRC from donor-driven (and essentially humanitarian) forms of international assistance to a

GoDRC-led stabilization and recovery process. Accordingly, the SRFF will emphasize national involvement, partnerships with national and local actors, synergies with longer-term national strategies and programmes, and the need to mainstream development of national and local capacities in all programmes and projects.

All this drew on the spirit of the times. By 2007–08, 'national ownership' was the respectable thing in the aid business. The idea had reached peak momentum with the 2005 Paris Declaration on Aid Effectiveness, produced at a forum of all the major international donors. Among its commitments, #1 was to 'respect partner country leadership and help strengthen their capacity to exercise it', and #2 to 'base their overall support on partner countries' national development strategies'.[7] The same parties had reaffirmed the same principles in 2008's Accra Agenda for Action. In parallel, as we saw in Chapter 4, Congo's energetic Minister of Finance had grabbed the ball and started running. Right as stabilisation programmes were being formulated, the g7+ forum of fragile and conflict-affected states was lobbying hard that 'true assistance should promote ownership of policies by the recipient country'. This should include, they insisted, nationally led plans with which international donors would align their programmes.[8]

At this point a simple question arises: 'Was there a gap between the rhetoric and the reality?' For we have already seen reasons to think that Congolese priorities were not always well-represented in 'stabilisation' policy-making. In Chapters 1 and 3 we saw a series of issues that were critical for people on the ground but simply omitted from national-level frameworks. In Chapter 2 there were immense difficulties in formulating any widely accepted policy direction at all amongst stakeholders in the security sector. And in Chapter 4, international aid responded to agency 'mandates' and global strategic priorities rather than being 'nationally led' (by the nose?) to where it was needed.

This chapter accordingly explores the nature and limits of 'national ownership' of the policy process. I argue that it was misidentified with a small clique of central government officials, whose interests coincided with donors and agencies who were keen to limit the kinds of feedback they had to receive. In homage to the large literature on how well-meaning social legislation is often 'captured' by narrow interests, I call this an *iron triangle*.

We accordingly proceed in three contrasting scenes. The first is a steering meeting at the stylish, if slightly faded, Hotel Karibu in Goma. Here we meet the *patrons* of stabilisation—an array of central government ministers, chiefs of aid cooperation and country directors for international agencies. Most arrived by specially arranged flight from Kinshasa, and were shuttled by helicopter to inaugurate a police station the next day with much pomp and ceremony. The second scene is a rather-less choreographed performance in the office of the Governor of South Kivu. Here, provincial officials tried to catch up with a machine that was already fully in motion, and carve out a role in a policy process centred overwhelmingly in Kinshasa. Our final stop is then a sweltering municipal government building in the town of Kinyandoni, North Kivu. Here mid-level bureaucrats 'sensitised' an assortment of local people on the whats, hows and where-tos of stabilisation, lecturing from desks set up as if for a teacher and their pupils.

At the table

MONUC's Canadair jet touched down in Goma around noon. It carried a full complement of officials from Kinshasa: seven heads of cooperation from international embassies, a half-dozen members of MONUC's senior management team, and heads of assorted other UN agencies. They were joined by the national Minister of Defence Charles Mwando Simba; the national Minister of Social Affairs; the national police Inspector-General; three provincial governors and two deputy governors.

All were swept across town to the sprawling Hotel Karibu, a green expanse described in Congo's few guidebooks as boasting an 'Old Zaire feel'.[9] The setting was a 'Partners meeting' for stabilisation efforts in eastern Congo. The invitations promised a review of progress in 2010 and discussion of priorities for 2011. This would be followed by an inauguration ceremony for police, prison and administrative facilities in the town of Rutshuru, and it was carefully noted that the Netherlands had paid for the first two, and the United States for the latter.[10]

All told there were about fifty people in the room, but the agenda organised proceedings neatly into a three-character play. First to speak was the United Nations, represented by MONUC's Deputy Special Representative. Next came the donor countries, represented by the head of office for the US Agency for International Development. Last in sequence was the coordinator of the government's Resource Mobilisation Cell for stabilisation, the Abbé Malu Malu.[11] Others got their chance to speak during a one-hour plenary of 'conclusions and recommendations'. The next day a specially arranged helicopter took all the VIPs to Rutshuru. Proceedings there featured much the same cast, as we see in Figure 5.2. This is a promotional shot that featured from left to right: the Ambassador of the Netherlands; MONUC's Deputy Special Representative of the Secretary-General and its head of office for North Kivu; and the Congolese National Police's Inspector-General and Provincial Inspector for North Kivu. (Plus a security guard lurking suspiciously behind.)

Figure 5.2: The *patrons* of stabilisation in the East
MONUSCO (2011) 'ISSSS quarterly report, January to March 2011'

Seated around the table at the Karibu, the UN's narrative was straightforward. The Deputy Representative Fidèle Sarassoro was a careful career bureaucrat who was acutely sensitive to the need to keep the government on-side. He asked for a presentation focusing on concrete achievements. Of twenty slides there were eighteen on projects already implemented by international agencies, including twenty-four photos of physical works, and just one slide on 'strategic challenges'.[12] For the former he was particularly interested to know if we could cite a figure of 25% reduction in the price of beer in one town, Bunyakiri, due to road works. (We were uncertain about the reliability of the figure, so as a compromise it ended up in the 'notes' section rather than on the slide itself.)

The aim was to demonstrate momentum and build 'buy-in' of national officials, as reinforced by the elaborate theatre of the inauguration ceremony. Afterwards he tabled a cautious list of issues to 'unblock I4S programme activities', as the follow-up report put it.[13] These related primarily to the administrative and logistical support of officials deployed into new facilities like that in Figure 5.2, along with upkeep of the works themselves. These ran for several pages. A few non-sequitur bullet points then listed out 'problems of a generic nature', including 'the presence of a parallel administration' in certain areas; 'areas falling back under the control of armed groups', and 'growing insecurity' in the highest-priority areas. None of the latter 'problems' were raised at the meeting itself.

For the international donors, the USAID representative laid out two concerns in slightly halting French. The first was consolidating gains to date, including attention to the 'software' that had to go along with 'hardware' like the new police *commissariat*. The second theme was extending the same approach to new geographic areas in 'logical and coordinated' fashion, meaning where security and political conditions permitted. Both were to be supported by reinforcement of the UN's coordination team on the ground.[14]

These remarks had been thoroughly pre-cooked with the international agencies who handled project execution and reflected increasing concern, even paranoia, that investments to date would be wasted. Successive dossiers had been prepared for the Prime Minister and Minister of Justice setting out personnel and budgetary requirements in great detail, but with little effect.[15] Even public reports were now littered with warnings that 'focus must be shifted to deployment and support of state officials as more and more facilities come online', and that 'the shortfall is particularly grave for the judicial and corrections sectors where no completed facilities are yet in use'.[16]

Finally it was the turn of the Government's representative, the Abbé Malu Malu. He gave a short PowerPoint presentation on road-rehabilitation priorities, and handed out a thick book of provincial road maps and proposed works. Much vaguer were ideas for a youth employment scheme and an 'inter-provincial solidarity fund', a sort of mutual savings association for Congo's provinces. (Neither proposal ever came to much.) Chairing the meeting, the Minister of Defence weighed in to complain that garrison facilities built for the army were not up to standard, and that his staff had not been adequately involved in the selection of the construction agencies. The Paris Declaration on Aid Effectiveness meant, he insisted, that these sorts of tasks should be handed over to the FARDC's own engineering staff. Moreover the funds provided were inadequate, and this issue should be the highest priority for those looking to support 'stabilisation' of eastern Congo. And that was it from his side.

Afterwards the chief of MONUC's political division came over for a chat. He was a wiry Austrian with frenetic energy, usually contained behind a diplomatic exterior but right now peeking out around the edges. 'That was a weird meeting,' he noted. 'I didn't expect it to go like that.'

In some respects, I had to agree. These were exactly the kind of conversations we were *not* supposed to be having at this late date—in fact we had just heard the first four Follies reeled off in rapid succession. The Minister of Defence chairing proceedings added a particular air of unreality. We saw in Chapter 2 that the security situation was firmly acknowledged as problem number one by this time. The 'cold war' within the FARDC was more and more prominent, and the merry go-round of integration and desertion of armed groups was running at full speed. Yet all this was kept out of the discussion. The UN's written list of issues asked lamely for 'the presence of FARDC units on priority axes to permit police and administrative deployment', while USAID's chief noted blandly that donors were 'hopeful of finding ways to promote human rights and improve accountability' for the force. Meanwhile the Minister himself intervened quite ferociously on even the innocuous issue of garrison construction.

From another perspective, however, the scene at the Karibu was anything but surprising. We were focusing on the same issues because we were dealing with the same interlocutors—the narrow circle of officials that had first defined stabilisation problems and solutions back in 2007–08. A review by Oxford University's Refugee Studies Centre summarised these origins scathingly but fairly:[17]

As activities under the rubric of stabilisation have increased, disagreement over the policy's legitimacy and the process of its development have come to the fore. The stabilisation framework was formulated in the mission's integrated office and was far from an inclusive process. What little consultation there was took place in Kinshasa with Prime Minister Adolphe Muzito, and Apollinaire Malu Malu... As such, ISSSS and STAREC are rightly regarded by many Congolese as a 'top down' policy – one that was drawn up in Kinshasa with no input from the Congolese people, provinces and territories.

Once the stabilisation plans were already up and running, an ordinance laid out the steering system summarised in Figure 5.3 (on the next page). At the summit was a national-level steering committee, chaired by the Prime Minister, as 'the organ for decisions and evaluations relating to matters exclusively within the competence of the central government, and those where both the central government and provinces have competence'.[18] This would include the Vice-Prime Ministers, an array of national ministers; the governors of affected provinces; and the UN's top two officials. Beneath this level provincial committees chaired by the governors were then charged with 'validation and follow-up of projects' determined at national level, and setting priorities for those subject areas exclusively within provincial competence under the Constitution.

On paper this was already a highly centralised arrangement. There is no provision for involvement of the Congolese parliament, let alone specific reference to opposition parties. Meanwhile for the provinces, the job of the *Comités Techniques Conjoints* (Joint Technical Committees) was essentially to be 'validation and follow-up' of priorities decided elsewhere. From a constitutional standpoint almost no issues fitted within their exclusive competence and those that did, such as the issue of land titles and running the provincial civil service, were explicitly subject to national legislation.[19]

Figure 5.3: Stabilisation planning, from the top-down and centre-out

GoDRC (2009) 'Programme de Stabilisation et de Reconstruction'

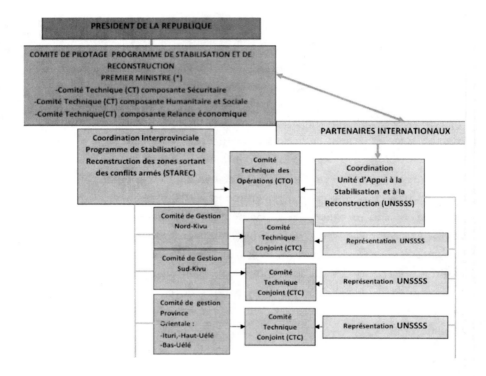

In practice the circle of decision-makers became smaller still. The Prime Minister convened the Steering Committee just four times from 2009 to 2012, and never chaired it himself. Of these four meetings provincial governors were invited to participate only once. Meanwhile a supporting 'follow-up committee' that was supposed to include one representative each of civil society and the private sector was simply never convened.[20] The net effect was that the 'smoke-filled room' became the norm. The prevailing lines of communication were between international agencies and a small group of national ministries: planning, interior, defence and justice, in that order.

International agencies enabled these tendencies—in fact set them in concrete—through two habits. The first was the project funding model. As we noted in Chapter 4, virtually all aid destined for eastern Congo was spent via a 'direct execution' approach. This meant that international agencies delivered schools, police stations and everything else through local sub-contractors rather than passing funds through government institutions. Government 'ownership' in this scenario meant sign-off on individual projects by a counterpart agency, almost without exception a national ministry or the police Inspectorate-General. Reports and project briefings were then prepared along the same lines. International agencies wrote narrative documents for thirty-plus individual projects, discussed each briefly with the relevant 'counterpart' in Kinshasa, and then sent them off to donors in The Hague, Washington DC or Stockholm. These were largely treated as confidential documents and there was no publicly available, consolidated report on 'stabilisation' in eastern Congo until Quarter 3 of 2010. (Even this was not distributed very widely, with no systematic printing or distribution effort.[21])

To put it mildly, this process left many officials in the dark. Some major programmes even bypassed the affected ministries at national level, with the Minister of Planning signing as overall coordinator for stabilisation programmes.[22] Many of these officials indicated in private conversation that they had been blind-sided and humiliated by decisions taken over their heads.[23] The result, as one internal memo noted drily, was that it 'proved difficult to ensure engagement of governmental stakeholders who feel they have not been consulted during planning or implementation'.[24] At the provincial level, North Kivu's Minister of Planning spoke for many when he complained publicly that 'the dysfunctions of the structure are evident... there are no exchanges of information, much less discussion and challenge'.[25]

Parliamentary institutions were not better informed. The best ballpark estimate for total funds committed through the government budget, up to the end of 2012, was just USD 320,000.[26] This meant that the annual appropriations process provided no entry points for the National Assembly or the Senate to review priorities. Their oversight role in any event had received no outside support since the end of war, and remained moribund through the end of 2012.[27]

Alongside project aid, there was a second habit that helped to close the circle of decision-makers: the heavy centralisation of foreign officials in Kinshasa. From the day the Kabila regime entered office after the 2006 elections, it made it clear that it did not welcome a diplomatic presence in the East, and those few diplomats working there were junior and administratively fudged to look like they were based in the capital.[28] The UN followed the same logic. Despite MONUC's military forces being overwhelmingly concentrated in the eastern provinces, fully 80% of staff at the director level and above were based in Kinshasa, along with the entire military and civilian intelligence teams.[29] The pattern for the UN's smaller civilian agencies was much the same, with management and analytic personnel in the capital and project management staff in the provinces. On all sides the problem was compounded by recruitment practices, a point rightly highlighted by Severine Autessere:[30]

> The consequence of these various recruitment processes is that, of the hundreds of expatriate peacebuilders I have met during my career—and of the thousands of interveners that the Listening Project teams encountered in other conflict zones... very few had pre-existing knowledge of their countries of deployment. All had been hired based on their substantive and technical capacities.

MONUC took this tendency to its logical extreme. Most of its civilian personnel were recruited from global rosters of candidates structured into generic 'job families', and interviewed according to generic requirements. The consequence was that very few staff members had personal networks of any kind in Congo, let alone spanning the politically and ethnically diverse regions of the East. One major evaluation for stabilisation programmes concluded bluntly that 'MONUC and the UN system are not organised to regularly and systematically analyse local, shifting realities and to assess the implications.' It added that there was a pressing need to redeploy analysts from Kinshasa to the peripheries where implementation was taking place.[31]

It was very difficult under such conditions for other voices to be heard in the policy debate. In the next section we look at one effort to expand the circle, a sustained push from 2010–2012 to bring provincial governments into the conversation.

In the back row

The Governor's office was crowded, but the mood was optimistic. South Kivu had just passed peacefully through a period of deep political uncertainty. The previous office-holder had been forced out by a parliamentary mutiny and widespread strikes by public officials, then succeeded by an 'outsider' close to President Kabila. The incoming Marcellin Cishambo had briefly tussled for position with the incumbent and very popular Vice-Governor, but they had ultimately found an accommodation. Now the resuscitation of the Joint Technical Committee for stabilisation programmes attracted a relatively large crowd. The Vice-Governor chaired, with a half-dozen ministers and a variety of senior officials in attendance. On the other side of the table sat a confusing array of UN agencies and the various departments of MONUSCO, along with a few intrepid non-governmental organisations.[32]

Of course, one doesn't get a big turnout at an interminable coordination meeting by accident. The UN's provincial stabilisation adviser had done the rounds to encourage attendance—for there was exciting news. During South Kivu's inter-regnum period the national government and foreign donors had agreed on a new way of doing things for stabilisation programmes. A Stabilisation and Recovery Fund would fund initiatives going forward. The provincial Joint Technical Committees were to develop and approve project proposals, and then send them up to the national level for prioritisation and funding.[33] Around the table in the Governor's office it was agreed to set up 'sub-commissions' to do just this for each of the three pillars of the government's Stabilisation and Reconstruction plan. In public remarks, Governor Cishambo deplored that stabilisation efforts 'had not attained take-off speed' prior to his arrival, and encouraged his ministers to henceforth 'resolutely commit themselves'.[34]

The process quickly took on a life of its own. The lack of consultation during 2008–10 meant that there was considerable pent-up demand and the first meeting was followed up by 'how-to' notes, templates for project proposals, and briefings.[35] By mid-2011 South Kivu's Joint Technical Committee had approved a list of 26 project proposals, costed at some USD 58 million. All had to be shepherded through the 'sub-commission' process by senior advisers, and discussed with the ministers themselves and the Governor in plenary. The UN's coordination team provided updates each week on the process, with early notes slightly panicky about the low frequency of meetings and later ones optimistic that 'project concepts are now in place for many of the top priorities'.[36] Throughout, they worked hard with provincial counterparts to build their ability to organise the process. Reaching back to UN headquarters in New York they found scarce 'un-earmarked' funds that could be used to underwrite training, equipment and travel for the chronically cash-strapped provincial ministries.[37]

Publicity for stabilisation initiatives switched provincial officials to the centre of attention. The next quarterly report on international stabilisation efforts featured a photo of Cishambo solemnly speaking to camera, one arm raised. The accompanying blurb was a rare acknowledgement of the everyday language of Congolese politics:[38]

> In his remarks, Governor Marcellin Cishambo emphasized that it is time to move on from *débrouillez-vous* – a Congolese expression meaning to make do, to get it done on your own – to *appropriez-vous*, public ownership of local governance and increased civic engagement.

Press and partner briefings were equally reworked. In place of Figure 5.1, with all efforts pointing inwards to 'the government', the new briefings featured a jauntily coloured bottom-up process. In Figure 5.4 we see project ideas originating locally and passing through the provincial Joint Technical Committee en route to the national steering committee.

Figure 5.4: Letting the provinces decide?
MONUSCO (2010) 'Le financement de projets ISSSS'

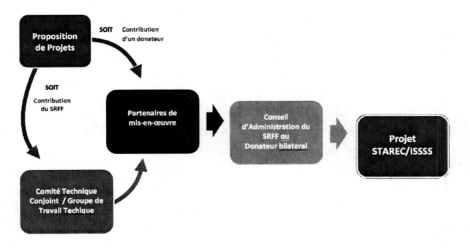

In other provincial capitals a similar process was unfolding. North Kivu's Joint Technical Committee developed a similar number of funding requests to those from South Kivu, costed slightly higher at USD 75 million. The province of Maniema, up to that time ignored by stabilisation programmes, tabled USD 46 million in project proposals with a strong slant towards roads and administrative infrastructure.[39] In the latter case, the Governor told me repeatedly he was eager to get the process moving 'in fact and not on paper' and pushed his cabinet hard for concrete projects. Maniema must, he stressed, organise itself even better than other provinces because it was not usually a priority for foreign donors.[40] Right up to the Partners Meeting of February 2011 he was pressing forward, calling his ministers into his office on the Saturday to make sure he would have the dossier in hand for travel on the Monday.[41]

This will all seem rather dry to the casual reader—coordination and project development are not the stuff of high drama. Nonetheless it was a moment of considerable optimism. Engaging the provincial governments was hardly a panacea, but would go some way to address criticism of the 'top-down' formulation of stabilisation plans. At a practical level, we also hoped to re-emphasise some neglected priorities. Day-to-day, provincial officials were much closer than national officials to some problems, among them the co-option of state institutions (the *trafic d'influence*) that we saw in Chapter 1, and the malfunctioning systems for local governance that we encountered in Chapter 3. The theory was that adding their voices to policy discussions would add their pain to the agenda, a tactic that political scientists call conflict expansion.[42]

Ultimately, optimism was dashed. Through to the end of 2012 the Stabilisation and Recovery Fund channelled funding of just USD 16 million—less than 5% of overall spending on stabilisation projects.[43] To add insult to injury, even these allocations went to pet donor priorities. The first project approved was for a centre to treat victims of sexual violence (noble, but hardly germane to stabilisation), and the second was a demonstration centre for organic farming.[44] Provincial-level officials continued to wait in vain for good news. Meeting minutes record slightly forlorn 'hopes that advocacy work would continue with international donors', and slightly mendacious responses that 'donors have integrated priorities in their planning, but the amounts are yet to be determined'.[45] Meanwhile the project machine rolled on. Over the same period, foreign donors approximately doubled the funds committed through bilateral agreements with national ministries.[46] Soon the provincial-level process more or less petered out.

We are faced, then, with an attempt to expand the circle of policy-makers that failed badly. Why? What 'defence mechanisms' killed off the attempt, and kept the policy process as it was?

First was the role of the Prime Minister's office. The most apposite term for this—sandbagging—comes from carnival wrestling. It means being in the same ring but providing minimal cooperation, in essence being pulled along as dead weight. The co-performer is made to look as bad as possible.

In practice, of the four meetings of the stabilisation Steering Committee from 2009 to 2012, none included an agenda slot for provincial governors to speak on their own behalf. Only one—the last one—included a presentation of the prioritisation process that had unfolded so laboriously at provincial level. This was included under pressure from MONUSCO's Deputy Representative Fidèle Sarassoro, who tentatively commended back to national officials 'this impressive work, on which our future interventions could now be based'.[47] Beneath this level, the 'inter-provincial coordination team' envisaged in Figure 5.3 remained largely inactive. Provincial ministers stressed privately and publicly that they had received no guidance on terms of reference, working procedures or what kinds of programme support might be available.[48]

Concurrently, the central government made heavy use of its convening power to ensure that international support went to pet priorities. The Security Council was petitioned directly for equipment for no fewer than 23 police battalions and vehicles for 145 territorial administrators.[49] On the military side, a new army reform plan was presented to bilateral partners in January 2010. This was heavily criticised for 'reading like a long shopping list to the value of $686 million, mainly for military equipment'.[50] Still, it received some support given the acute pressure to do something—anything—in the security sector. Several garrison facilities went ahead in South Kivu at the exorbitant cost of USD 25 million for two of the hundred-plus battalions stationed in the East, and there were live conversations for another USD 25 million.[51] For the transport sector, the banner headline of the first government newsletter on the STAREC declared 'Launch of STAREC: Priority for roads', and we have already encountered the thick book of proposed works that was thumped onto the table at the Hotel Karibu. For international partners these became the single biggest line item for 'stabilisation' spending, accounting for a bit over 20% of overall spending.[52]

In retrospect this pattern should not have been surprising. The reality was that pushing decision-making to the provincial level went directly against the grain of Congolese politics at this time.[53] President Kabila had declared his intent clearly enough in 2009: 'to first of all, consolidate the authority of a state that has only just been restored, in a context where centrifugal tensions could yet reassert themselves'.[54] He followed up by engineering the election of members of his Alliance for a Presidential Majority as governors of all eleven provinces. Were this to prove inadequate, an unpopular constitutional revision in 2011 accorded him power to remove them, along with the provincial assemblies. From a fiscal perspective the trend was even more obvious. One commentator summarised: [55]

> Hardly any of the financial measures for decentralisation in the Constitution, or in subsequent organic laws, have been implemented. Contrary to article 171, the finances of the central government and those of the provinces are not separated. Contrary to article 175, the government does not allocate 40% of revenues at national level to the provinces, and the little that it does allocate are not retained at the source but rather passed back after collection by national fiscal authorities. And contrary to article 181, the government has not created the *Caisse Nationale de Péréquation* for which the objective is to redistribute 10% of national revenues into public investments in the provinces.

On the ground it was a rare conversation with a provincial-level official that omitted the problem of a crippling lack of money, and the consequences for the province's ability to self-govern. During one 'puff' interview for the official STAREC newsletter, Jean Ruyange, the provincial Minister of Finance for North Kivu, interjected to retort 'I didn't speak of keeping 40% at the source in my own name. It is the Constitution which said that'.[56] This is mild in comparison with other occasions on which governors accused Kinshasa of 'asphyxiating' the provinces and demanded the latter 'reclaim their rights'.[57]

An additional factor for the district of Ituri, in which we spent some time in Chapter 3, was the issue of 'status'. The 2006 Constitution envisaged dividing the 500,000km^2 Orientale province into four parts, which would entail Ituri getting its own governor and provincial assembly. But the issue had gone in circles at the national level and progress any time soon appeared unlikely. This left the district 'united by an immense frustration with the Congolese government', if little else.[58] For stabilisation programmes this rapidly manifested in tensions between the Governor in Kisangani and the district administration in Bunia. One internal assessment noted drily that 'autonomist tendencies and the intent to convert the district into a province... have meant that programme activities were led with little collaboration with the Province'.[59] These 'tendencies' were rapidly reined in, with the Governor insisting on final sign-off on projects formulated in Ituri and that he speak for the district with donors.

In short, it was naïve to think that regional government could be shoe-horned so easily into the policy conversation. A 2012 evaluation of EU assistance to administrative decentralisation put the matter bluntly, but fairly:[60]

> The current Presidency is in a phase of trying to consolidate power. Decentralisation requires the sharing of power, which the President is reluctant to do at this time. In these circumstances, the sustainability of any results that both programmes might achieve is very questionable unless there is a major change in the political context.

But what of international partners? What drove their reluctance to attach greater weight to provincial-level voices?

Here we must recall the situation outlined in Chapter 4. Concurrent with the launch of the Fund, the biggest single evaluation of conflict prevention projects in the Congo was blasting 'a multiplicity of strategic frameworks and policy initiatives, funding sources, programming guidelines, complex projects, which has resulted in a scattering of efforts'.[61] At the inter-governmental level the g7+ group of fragile states had just issued the Dili Declaration. This complained of 'too many overlapping plans', 'lack of shared vision', and a predilection for funding specific projects rather than more flexible arrangements. In mid-2010 a donor-commissioned review team for stabilisation projects cited this text back to their employers, adding tartly that: 'Donors supporting the ISSSS should move from basing their involvement in the ISSSS on only some of the above principles to taking all of them into serious account'.[62]

There was, in other words, a coincidence of interests between the government and its international partners. Each of the latter arrived in the DRC with idiosyncratic organisational preferences, or 'in the place of a unified strategic vision... a welter of competing white papers and policy statements'.[63] With a project-aid model they had the freedom to focus where they wanted to focus. With un-earmarked funds passing through the Stabilisation and Recovery Fund, they would have lost that level of control.

It is an abiding irony that the few contributions to the Fund, set up to 'transition from donor-driven forms of international assistance to a GoDRC-led stabilisation and recovery process', were earmarked for specific purposes. Sweden specified that its money should be used for economic recovery; and Norway, Belgium and the Netherlands that theirs was intended for action against sexual violence. These restrictions led to highly peculiar meetings of the national-level Funding Board. The minutes record preamble remarks on the importance of 'coherent national and international efforts'; a discussion on priorities established through the STAREC governance structure; and then financial allocation decisions which pertain to absolutely none of those priorities.[64] In private conversations donors indicated that they wanted to help... but did not want their money to end up with police or administrative programmes that were both politically sensitive and more likely to fail. Thus, they cherry-picked some elements and left others behind.[65] One country director explained apologetically that he 'received a fixed envelope for sexual violence, and there was nothing that could be done about it from country level'. In other cases there was an 'underlying expectation, among some donors at least, that assistance to basic services will promote peace'.[66] As has been pointed out in many other contexts, this approach flowed from headquarters-level policies to attempt it rather than empirical research that it was true in the DRC's particular circumstances.[67]

Whatever the reasons, the net effect was evident. Budgeting remained the same three-way conversation that we saw at the Hotel Karibu—finding common ground between a few national officials, foreign donors and the international agencies.

In the next section, we look at how this was seen from ground level. To do so, let us return to where we started way back in Chapter 1, in the town of Kinyandoni in Rutshuru territory, North Kivu. We last visited in mid-2009, just after a police deployment had been driven off by an ambush. Now it is June 2011, and the scene looks a little different.

Outside the tent

The hand-painted banner was pinned awkwardly to the exterior of Kinyandoni's small new administrative building. It advertised a 'Sensitisation Campaign on the Restoration and Extension of State Authority', with a trio of little logos crammed in above the text for the provincial government, MONUSCO and the UN Development Programme. All around, the building's paintwork had been touched up for the occasion, courtesy of an advance team who had visited a few days before.

Inside, a hundred people were squeezed onto four rows of folding chairs and into the standing room behind. At the front, facing the crowd, were the visiting dignitaries. They included two officials from the provincial minister of interior, the Governor's adviser on the Stabilisation and Reconstruction Plan, the Administrator for Rutshuru territory, and a smattering of UN personnel. Figure 6.5 captures the scene, with the photos making up in authenticity what they lack in quality.

Figure 5.5: 'Sensitisation on the restoration of state authority'
Source: UNDP (2011) 'Compagne de sensibilisation de la population'[68]

The officials' brief was to explain the roles and responsibilities of public servants deployed under the Stabilisation and Reconstruction Plan. They had been whisked to the site in a UN convoy, with foreign donor money paying for refreshments and an international consultant to organise proceedings. The UN Development Programme's supporting grant agreement explained the logic:[69]

> The durable return of legal authorities and the deployment of public administrators in zones emerging from armed conflict can only succeed if the population accept and recognize these authorities and cooperate with legally re-established customary and civil administration.

Each official spoke for about twenty minutes. This was already optimistically brief, given that it was the first real attempt to exchange perspectives with the local population in about three years of activity. Back in 2008, a UN assessment team had visited the town and noted that it was under FARDC control but 'militarily menaced by the CNDP'. It recommended project support to civil administration, given its position on the main road to Uganda and significance as headquarters of the Bukoma *groupement*.[70] More than a year later, in late 2009, UN contractors based in Goma started works on new offices. These were finished in September 2010 and the fifteen officials that were to occupy them given a week's training, on topics including the basics of financial management, procedures for issuing civil documents and the workings of Congo's convoluted planning processes.[71]

This 'town hall' meeting in early 2011 was accordingly the very last step in the process. One UN report noted slyly that we 'hoped [it] will be a starting point for frequent and visible presence of provincial officials in these formerly isolated localities'.[72]

A question-and-answer session followed all the prepared remarks. It proved a bit incongruous as local interlocutors jumped right to their main concern. They itemised in detail the exploits of bandits active in the area and the Democratic Forces for the Liberation of Rwanda (FDLR). What use, they wondered, was talk about taxes and local development planning when the government did not have control on the ground?

For those in the room, it was difficult to argue with this line of reasoning. The security environment around Kinyandoni had not improved since the Tiger Battalion was driven away back in May 2009. In fact the months just prior to the meeting had seen a serious deterioration. A string of attacks on ordinary people had been punctuated by the nearby ambush of a convoy carrying the national Minister of Education.[73] This had kicked off swirling rumours about the politics of the attack, with some local journalists claiming that the Nande community was behind it. The Governor of North Kivu had been forced to hold crisis meetings in Rutshuru town, a dozen kilometres to the south. He had also been forced to switch up personnel, and the territorial administrator sitting at the front of the room had arrived just a month before to replace the incumbent. A communiqué from North Kivu's confederation of civil society organisations captured something of the prevailing mood:[74]

> The silence of the international community faced with the slide of the peace process and of security in this part of the country disquiets each and everyone, which is why the Civil Society declares …
> - that all the Civil Society calls on the International Community to take greater responsibility and change strategies against the FDLR and the ADF/NALU, in order that the Congolese can set themselves to the necessary steps for a real democratic transformation of the country.
> - that the Government begins frank discussions with the international community to liberate the population of the East from the toll of the FDLR and the ADF/NALU before the general elections. For, each will be judged according to his acts.

Such declarations from 'civil society' must always be taken with a pinch of salt in the Congo, but this was not a minority position. The preceding few weeks had seen significant protests in the provincial capital of Goma; the territorial capital of Rutshuru; and the Bunagana crossing point to Uganda (the last chosen because of its economic significance).[75]

Given all this, the banner waving from Kinyandoni's new building seemed rather beside the point. Moreover the mood was not improved by ham-fisted publicity. Official government publications captioned a photo of sleepy-looking administrators with the promise 'the training started here will equip the DRC with a high-performing administration'. A UN team, going one better, reported back up the line that the 'responses were given to the satisfaction of all... the population declared themselves very moved by the different interventions'.[76]

This form of engagement—much too late and much too patronising—became one of the key targets for criticism of stabilisation efforts. Civil society figures complained from the outset that it was unclear 'who does what, with whom and how'. Many went further to allege co-option of the process by specific ethnic or political groups.[77] One report from Oxfam Great Britain, based on community research, elaborated the point in more polite terms:[78]

[Civil society organisations] have limited knowledge of the stabilisation plans and involvement in defining what stabilisation entails... The same is also true of many local government officials, traditional authorities, grassroots associations and local communities.

While many individuals have received trainings or benefitted from projects, they have largely not been involved in defining a stabilisation strategy that would address their concerns and locally-relevant benchmarks against which to measure it. There has also not been an inclusive and broad local dialogue to identify local blockages to stability such as specific inter-community tensions and prejudices and to work together to find solutions to these problems.

The author went on to quote a local government official to the effect that 'When a doctor treats an adult, he asks them what is wrong. When he treats a young child, he does not ask. We are not children.' Other research reports contain litanies of similarly unflattering assessments in non-governmental interlocutors' own words, up to and including the UN's own strategic review of stabilisation programmes in mid-2012.[79]

All were speaking to a hard truth, which is that public frustration with 'stabilisation' efforts was very high. It has also been a common thread throughout *Follies in Fragile States*. In Chapter 1, for example, we met citizens and street-level bureaucrats who were acutely aware that the 'restoration and extension of state authority' was more theatre than reality. When asked, they readily pointed out weak support systems and an inability to control the security environment. (One strategic review summarised simply that 'no observer contacted suggested that these officers were contributing in any important way to stabilization in their areas of deployment'.[80]) When pressed, once a little trust had been built, the same observers would also explain that basic concerns about the *nature* of government institutions had simply not been addressed. The brute fact was that some of the people in that meeting room in Kinyandoni had collaborated in the 2009 attack—and were not particularly repentant about it afterwards.[81]

Thinking more systematically, we can pin down some clear divergences between stabilisation priorities as defined in venues like the Hotel Karibu, and broader public priorities. A useful tool here is a 2014 poll conducted by the Harvard Humanitarian Initiative, already briefly mentioned in Chapter 3. This solicited the opinions of 5,200 randomly selected adults in North Kivu, South Kivu and Ituri—enough for statistically representative answers according to the science of such exercises.[82]

In answer to the question, 'What should be the government's top priority?', the top five survey responses were 'peace' (35%); 'security' (22%); 'employment' (11%); 'payment of salaries' (11%); and 'education' (9%). Among the subjects that didn't register at all: 'justice' (1%), and 'roads' (1%). This list is already strikingly different from the presentations at the Hotel Karibu, with their endless slides on 'rule of law' infrastructure and the thick book of road-building priorities. It is also very distant from the workshop for international agencies that we spied on in Chapter 4, which produced fulsome recommendations on 'return and recovery' and nothing at all on the security sector.

When we turn to ways and means, the gap between public and elite perspectives becomes even more apparent. Below we see the top five answers to the open-ended question, 'How can security be achieved?' (The figures sum to over 100% as respondents were not limited to one answer.)

Fight armed groups	29%
Pay the army	27%
Pay the police	26%
Education	22%
More jobs	19%

One striking fact is that the second and third priorities here—paying security forces at the 'point of the spear' in eastern Congo—were pre-emptively ruled out. International partners considered only the two 'equally unpalatable options of pushing the government towards politically dangerous comprehensive civil service reform or doing nothing', and ultimately opted for the latter.[83] By contrast, less than one in five people mentioned more police deployments as a high-impact approach to achieve security, despite this being arguably the centrepiece of stabilisation efforts. Indeed, in some high-priority territories that had been targeted for accelerated deployments only 10% of respondents thought more police should be a priority.[84]

There are equally striking disagreements with the stabilisation policy mix when things are turned around to enquire after the causes of violence. When asked, 'What were the origins of the conflict?', the responses were as follows:

Exploitation of natural resources	46%
Fighting for power	34%
Ethnic divisions	32%
Land / access to land	30%
Poverty	22%

This is as plain an indictment of political institutions in an agrarian society as can be imagined. In Irumu territory, for example, more than 50% of those surveyed identified land disputes as the primary driver of violence. Along the boundaries of Rwandan-speaking areas in North and South Kivu, similar proportions felt that 'ethnic divisions' were the biggest single factor.[85] Yet there was little sustained attention to either issue. As we saw in Chapters 1 and 3, questions of institutional design and national policy gave way to a preoccupation with 'restoration and extension' of the government's physical footprint.

It is a pressing question why these concerns did not intrude into the policy process. And the short answer must be that there was no direct way for them to do so. 'Joint' steering mechanisms at national and provincial levels included the executive branch of government on the one hand, and international agencies on the other. This was occasionally supplemented by donor country representatives but not by citizen representatives, trade associations or even parliamentarians.[86] Where efforts were made to include 'civil society' institutions, this was in their capacity as delivery partners for project aid: an 'indicator species', as Arundhati Roy has put it, 'accountable to their funders and not the people they work among'.[87] One indicative discussion note on 'NGO / civil society participation' that was circulated among UN partners in December 2010 listed twelve organisations—every one of them international agencies engaged in relief and 'peacebuilding' programming using foreign donor funds. The 'outreach' meetings and briefings that followed over the course of 2011 likewise focused on how NGOs could ask for funding support via the process underway in the provincial Joint Technical Committees.[88]

There were also few serious attempts to gauge public opinion. It is a remarkable fact that the survey data recapped above was the *first* statistically representative investigation of public priorities for stabilisation. A single concept note had raised the point plaintively in mid-2010:[89]

> One year after the launch of the STAREC, significant outputs have been delivered: police infrastructure, roads, rehabilitation of basic services, etc. However, it is time to start asking the question: Is this making a difference from the perspective of the population? Have there been real changes in security, state authority, and pacific co-existence?

It landed with a thud, or rather without any noise at all. After brief discussions, the idea was dropped from funding proposals for stabilisation coordination support, and not resuscitated until well after the fall of Goma at the end of 2012.[90]

For informal 'back-channels' the situation was not much better. Here we can quickly check back in with Severine Autesserre's research on the 'everyday practices' of conflict resolution in eastern Congo. Her chapter on information gathering is entitled 'Fumbling in the dark', and concludes simply that 'on the whole, the average local inhabitant has no voice'.[91] The most important reason was that, most of the time, there was nobody there to listen.

For the corollary of the heavy centralisation of decision-making in Kinshasa was a limited civilian presence in the provincial and district capitals, and almost none at all elsewhere. MONUSCO's military contingents were usually the only permanent presence in rural areas, but until 2009 they hosted no civilian staff and had no facility to communicate in local languages. It took the 2008 Kiwanja massacre to create adequate momentum for the recruitment of local interpreters, finally reaching a ratio of one per one military detachment near the end of 2012.[92] These personnel were soon rebranded as 'liaison assistants' as troops inevitably relied upon them to interpret local conditions and political currents. However, the job remained marginal and, under the UN's elaborate system of personnel classifications, was placed at the level of an administrative or medical assistant.[93] Attempts to put more seasoned, civilian–police 'joint monitoring teams' (JMTs) on the ground in priority areas sputtered along from 2009 to 2011, then died as the major financial donor gave up and pulled their funding. That donor's evaluation can stand in for a series of intensely frustrating internal conversations:[94]

> The JMTs have been described as a potentially very useful source to provide information on the situation on the ground. Unfortunately, however, the distribution of JMT reports is irregular... positive examples in most cases can be related to the efforts of committed individuals. There is no system established to actually ensure that reports and recommendations therein are reviewed, discussed and acted upon.

With such little demand from top management, there was simply no appetite to deal with the logistical, security and organisational challenges involved in getting these personnel out into communities. The two field-based teams in North Kivu were operational well-under 50% of the time, while their two counterparts in South Kivu failed to deploy at all.[95]

Faced with this situation, MONUSCO's fall-back mechanism was the rapid assessment. From 2009 onwards this was almost invariably through 'joint protection teams': one-off deployments of civilian staff into a remote location for two to five days. One major limitation is already evident from the terminology—areas were selected based on an imminent threat of violence, or to investigate violence that had already occurred.[96] That urgency left little opportunity to collect views on broader socio-political issues. When combined with the one-off, reactive nature of visits, the resulting analysis was often crashingly banal. After two days in the Uvira territory of South Kivu, one team concluded that:[97]

> The Head of Office should use their good offices to support Civil / Political Affairs in convincing the provincial authorities and the South Kivu Traditional Rulers Association to address all major customary conflicts in remote areas like Kikozi in order to install State authority.

Another team, after four days in Kalembe in North Kivu, noted that there were serious disputes at this line of fracture between the Hutu and Hunde communities. It concluded that the local detachment of MONUSCO troops should 'bring all the partners together for the inaugural meeting of the inter-community committee, or *Baraza intercommunautaire,* to mediate on the land and inter-community disputes'.[98] There was only one small problem— the local detachment was commanded by a South African infantry lieutenant, and the nearby company operating base by his superior officer. Neither spoke any local language or had any civilian advisers, and they had access to one locally recruited interpreter between them.

In addition to a lack of obvious entry points, local people also had to overcome a lack of transparency. The same 2014 survey referenced above found that 85% of respondents 'never' read newspapers, and 95% 'never' used the Internet.[99] Yet the main tools of public communication were written reports, or more rarely newsletters, circulated online.

On the government side a planned public communications cell was limited to a few staff members working out of the office of the UN Development Programme. They produced a four-page weekly newsletter with feature-type stories on individual projects and clumsy headlines such as: 'STAREC: Things are moving!'; 'One year more... still more hope!'[100] Over time this improved to include some of the basic legal documents for the government's Stabilisation and Recovery Plan, and coverage of major initiatives around the sensitive topics of land and refugee returns. But the more fundamental problem remained circulation. There was no budget for distribution of hard copies or adaptation for radio until 2011, with the result that the Kinyandoni 'town hall meeting' was the first official communication of any kind for most of the participants. The few previous sessions had been confined to urban audiences in North Kivu, notably the vocal student populations of Goma and Beni.[101]

The performance of the UN and international donors in this area was even worse. As those readers who pay close attention to end notes will by now be well aware, there was little effort to make documentation publicly available. Most project documents, reports and evaluations remained confidential between implementing agencies and the foreign donors who bankrolled them (and were in any event written in impenetrable aid jargon). There were no efforts to produce a generally comprehensible report on stabilisation activities until late 2010, and no public engagement plan until late 2011.[102]As one telling indication: Radio Okapi, the news agency with the biggest reach and moreover heavily supported by MONUSCO, recorded just eighteen mentions of the government's Stabilisation and Reconstruction Plan from 2009 to 2012. Of these, eleven mentions were simply reworded press releases for the inauguration of buildings.[103]

The need for feedback

James C. Scott's *Seeing Like a State* reviewed social engineering disasters across the twentieth century, and identified four common ingredients. The first three were: a bad model; confidence that it was nonetheless the right model; and an authoritarian regime. The fourth was a 'prostrate civil society that lacks the capacity to resist those plans', usually splintered by war or economic collapse. He added that:[104]

> High-modernist ideology thus tends to devalue or banish politics. Political interests can only frustrate the social solutions devised by specialists with scientific tools adequate to their analysis. As individuals, high modernists might well hold democratic views... but such convictions are external to, and often at war with, their high-modernist convictions.

For practitioners working in contexts like the Congo, this is a troubling thought. For there is always urgency. Early stabilisation concepts were filled with references to a brief 'window of opportunity' and the payoffs for 'early and effective implementation'.[105] In one heartbreaking passage, a colleague who strained and bled to get efforts off the ground recalled 'a period of unprecedented optimism among Congolese and international actors... many hoped that the brutal and bloody conflict that had consumed the country from 1996 to 2003 was finally behind them.'[106]

The choice was made to go ahead with a small group of decision-makers based in Kinshasa. Over time this entrenched itself. The executive branch of the national government insisted on its prerogatives, a copy of the Paris Declaration held in one hand. International donors and operational agencies insisted on project aid that allowed them to work on what they wanted, and with whom they wanted. Mutual accommodations were found, and the Iron Triangle snapped shut.

The consequence was an ever-widening gap between the concerns of the Congolese public, and those articulated in forums like that at the Hotel Karibu. It is for this reason that the Iron Triangle is the last of the Five Follies. Chapters 1-4 argued at length that the model was bad; but it was the lack of feedback and resistance which ensured that it would not be corrected.

There is increasing acknowledgement of this risk in the fragile states business. The (inter-governmental) International Dialogue on Peacebuilding and Statebuilding has put the focus squarely on 'new ways of engaging', with twin imperatives of being 'country-led' but also driven by 'credible and inclusive processes of political dialogue'. [107] Within the UN the same tendency is apparent. A 2014 Security Council debate on peacebuilding saw the word 'inclusive' used some 57 times in 2.5 hours; this has also become a favoured theme of the technical people in the UN Secretariat.[108]

The difficulty, as always, is in the execution. Looking beyond, within and below the government of the day poses a tough challenge for the international aid architecture. It means finding a new middle ground between the two extremes contemplated in the UN Charter—the default position of non-intervention in the internal affairs of member states, and the exceptional case of Security Council action to meet a threat to international peace and security.[109] This in turn means revisiting institutional designs entrenched by decades of repetition and standard procedure.

It is on this rather introspective note that we turn to the Epilogue, to try and weave the various strands of *Follies in Fragile States* together.

Epilogue

There is a well-known primer on policy studies whose first sentence reads 'The task of analysis is to create problems, preferences tempered by possibilities, which are worth solving'.[1] This description does not apply to the bare fact of human suffering in the Congo. The target presents too clear a field: every line of attack seems exactly as justifiable as all the others. This has led to a 'talking points' mentality where international agencies jockey in policy forums for greater visibility and funding of their pet priorities. With no obvious means to resolve the paper fight, policy then becomes the sum of the disagreements.

The limiting case for this tendency was the 2013 'Framework of Hope' signed by the government of the Congo and no fewer than ten countries in the region. In purporting to 'address the root causes of the conflict and foster trust between neighbours' this document essentially just reproduced the Congolese constitution, already quite progressive on paper.[2] In response the magazine *Politico* blared that the US special envoy Russell Feingold had just 'ended a war'; the UN downgraded its own Special Envoy from a former president to a former deputy ambassador.[3] The incoming head of the UN peacekeeping mission adopted 'momentum' as his unofficial watchword, declaring on Twitter that 'our robust protection stance and the hard won stability are the foundation to build peace'.[4]

As I write, in early 2015, it is two years on from that Framework. There are headlines screaming of massacres in areas 'previously thought quiet' in North Kivu, supplanting those screaming of massacres in areas 'previously thought quiet' in Katanga.[5] The international community is again at loggerheads with the Congolese government over the security sector. In a recent televised meeting President Kabila berated a gaggle of uncomfortable-looking ambassadors that 'to preserve the DRC's sovereignty he must renounce MONUSCO's support for operations against the FDLR', and that all those present must 'respect Congolese institutions and not intervene in internal politics'.[6] Not long before, he had kicked the senior UN human rights official out of the country, citing 'self-promotion through systematically hostile performances against Congolese institutions'.[7] Faced with all this, the top few UN officials will shortly depart to give way for a new team and fresh 'momentum'. Small wonder that a colleague who stayed throughout this period, long past my own departure date, has just sent me a draft manuscript entitled 'Going around in circles: The complexities of UN peacekeeping in the DR Congo'.

Follies in Fragile States maps out the behaviours that have led us to this impasse, as a list of problems 'worth solving'. They are deliberately not formulated as policy recommendations because the issue is not with individual initiatives or decision-makers. Indeed, this would be a serious misreading of the situation. As John Dewey has written of public institutions in general:[8]

> Were actual dishonesty the only, or even chief, foe, the problem would be much easier. The ease of routine, the difficulty of ascertaining public needs, the intensity of the glare which attends the seat of the mighty, the desire for immediate and visible results, play the larger part.

Such pressures, and their results, are well-documented in the wider aid sector. International agencies are organised at global scale around values and aspirations that can motivate staff and entice funding partners. They have few incentives to take on the most difficult and uncertain types of work. National authorities, for their part, do not want to lose control of decision-making in deeply fraught political environments. In situations of dire need they are loathe to proffer only the 'small bets' and 'co-evolving and learning processes' currently in vogue at development think-tanks.[9] The combined result is that work in the Congo fits squarely into the most uncomfortable and unsettled areas of international aid. If this industry is 'detached from everyday reality', as some influential voices have recently asserted, it is certainly most detached when everyday reality looks like the places we have visited in eastern Congo.[10]

It is for this reason that the failure of ambitions in the DRC poses an adaptive challenge, to return to the language used in the Introduction. This book's first few dozen pages could really have been boiled down to the following: 'Here are the issues that we do not know how to address, where we really do not know how to do well.'[11]

So what do we do with the challenge? Now that we have climbed back up to the balcony and answered that painful question 'How did we get here?', what next?

In my day-job as a management consultant, we say that clients walk in the door with a 'presenting problem'. Much as for a physician, they just tell us they're in pain; that something isn't working as it should. It's then our job to diagnose the condition lying behind the pain, and from there hopefully identify a treatment.[12]

From this standpoint, I would caution a client presenting any one of the Follies that they had picked a doozy. Defining what we want—catchy phrases like 'good-enough governance', or 'politically smart, locally led development'—is just a small piece of the work.[13] It is still necessary to change over a good deal of the operating software that enables complex international organisations to function. This includes: planning, budgeting and procurement systems; longer-term capital investments; security management protocols; recruitment and training; and a half-dozen other moving parts. For any public organisation, it is also necessary to bring an array of outside stakeholders into the picture. Executive boards and oversight committees have to be convinced that the new direction is consistent with founding charters and comparative advantages in a crowded marketplace. Funding partners must agree to redirect their (wholly voluntary) contributions to new priorities—perhaps with greater fiduciary risks and the prospect of indirect association with unsavoury individuals sitting high on sanctions lists.

The twin nature of the challenge is why the Prologue was addressed first of all to the engaged member of the public. To you I say: create demand for what matters. Don't accept the insidious message, 'Give us your support, and more importantly your money, and we'll take care of this.'[14]

This is a tough ask for a sector that is both complex and unaccustomed to transparency, but there are some positive signals of late. A recent review by the United Kingdom's Independent Commission for Aid Impact (ICAI) pored over efforts from 2011 to 2015 to roughly double the share of government development assistance allotted to fragile states. ICAI found that results on the ground had been poor. It criticised engagement in the Congo, specifically, for 'an unstructured "umbrella" programme... with goals so general that it is impossible to identify impact or roll out on a wider scale'.[15] But the more interesting takeaway was the report's insistence that transformative goals of the type bandied about in strategy documents 'will take a generation to achieve', and its prodding for 'smaller, more reactive or opportunistic programming or greater inbuilt flexibility'. What is even more striking is that the British parliamentary opposition ran with this to criticise a 'target-driven culture' in official aid, and a failure 'to focus on the long term processes of peacebuilding and nation-building'.[16]

At around the same time, the International Broadcasting Trust published a research report on how journalists engage with the aid sector. The author noted that polemics like *Dead Aid* and *The Tyranny of Experts* had fed into increased scrutiny of 'grandiloquent objectives', and quoted an editorial emphasising that 'just like any other industry, the aid industry must be examined, 'not just financially as is current practice, but also in how it operates from headquarter level to field level'.[17] The Congo, with its unbroken decade of peacekeeping and 'emergency' humanitarian relief, is surely an appropriate subject for such scrutiny. And the UN and non-governmental agencies suggesting (grandiloquently) they can deliver 'state authority', prosecution of 'warlords' and comprehensive regulation of trade in minerals across that vast territory should surely be subject to such examination.

Now let me speak to my second intended audience, the Critical Practitioner. Here the request is simple: forget strategic goals for a moment. Consider instead how your organisation (research initiative, freelance consultancy, etc) *behaves* day-to-day and month-to-month. Did some of the Follies make you nod your head, even if others prompted shouts of denial?

If you've nodded once or twice, find who's willing to work with you to make small progress. As Ben Ramalingam has put it, 'put out probes in complex settings and learn tirelessly—fearlessly, even—from the outcomes'.[18] For those charged with strategic direction, orchestrate that debate. Raise the temperature enough that differences, passions and conflicts can surface, albeit not so much that they become paralysing.[19]

Such a process is invariably disorienting. In my consulting work with one client, the focus was on service delivery to vulnerable populations. There were decades of distinguished history of the agency 'taking care of it', and getting better and better at very difficult field-level operations. However, times had changed. A combination of diminishing resources and shifts in norms for how international aid is supposed to work meant that a high-performing 'shadow state' was no longer sustainable. There was tremendous pressure for faster hand-off to national governments, and tremendous frustration that those officials seemed to be resisting their 'responsibilities'.

After discussions with hundreds of stakeholders, the final report was entitled *Grasping the Nettle*. This was because getting out of service delivery meant bending the course of organisational history. Senior staff just didn't 'do' lobbying with line ministries, or horse-trading with their counterparts in development agencies. They were doers and implementers: public health specialists and camp managers rather than diplomats and policy analysts. Policy Without Politics was thus, in a very real sense, built into the DNA. Evolving the organisation meant building a new cadre of staff members who could do politically smart work, but who often possessed few of the traditional credentials. It also meant relaxing 'minimum standards' that applied in every country around the world, a proud and hard-won guarantee of organisational competence, in favour of locally led political processes with unpredictable results. All this created a lot of friction. It meant directly clashing visions for what a 'good sub-office' or a 'good country operation' looked like, a debate that became very heated with such mission-driven people.

In helping to articulate what's at stake in these types of discussion, the question invariably comes: 'So what? You've given us your diagnosis; now what's the treatment?'

The unhelpful answer is: 'It depends'. *Follies in Fragile States* has probed deeply into banal topics like budgeting, human resources and situation reports. This is because these are the building blocks of the design problem. Doing better means long arguments about which blocks should be moved, and which should stay where they are. But the result, ironically, is that my facts are already out of date for organisations working in the Congo, let alone anywhere else. There is no point proposing specific changes for institutions that have already moved on unless one is interested in the stock-standard answer to defuse a critical outside evaluation: 'Acknowledged and already acted upon'.

The better answer is accordingly: 'Let's find out'. The plain fact is that alternative ways of thinking and acting must originate with individuals, a constituency for change, long before they can infiltrate the official policies of large institutions like the UN and the major bilateral donors. Since 2012, the Rethink Fragility listening project has collected such perspectives. We have asked what 'good' looks like, with respect to both country-level operations and the 'supply-side' factors that constrain what happens before anyone ever gets on a plane. Over time, these small testimonies have mounted up.

In a 2014 blog post I pulled together the common threads and the optimism as the Five Virtues. This is the flipside of the Five Follies: instead of maladaptations they are ideal capabilities for foreign organisations trying to create public value.[20] They are addressed to both the operational agencies who execute the work; and the political and financial stakeholders who set them in motion.

THE FIVE VIRTUES:
For better policy-making in the Congo, and places like it.

Pragmatic goals

Ambition	Be 'demand-driven', and work backwards from policy problems that can be articulated in everyday language.
Stakeholders	Allow priorities to emerge, rather than working from ideal templates. They aim for improvements realisable in a realistic political timeframe of 3–5 years.
Operators	Have the expertise to understand historical governance failures, or can manage those who do. Use mentoring and embedded advisory positions to build deep understanding of *how* things go wrong.

Getting the politics right

Ambition	No gap between the way that development/peacekeeping personnel think that public policy works, and the way that everybody else does.
Stakeholders	Make bets on promising policy initiatives rather than hoping for one-and-done comprehensive solutions. Balance the need to 'do something' with the need for change to be locally-led.

| Operators | Search out local reform entrepreneurs who would be active with or without international assistance. Flexibly deploy resources to boost the incentives for reform and reduce its perceived risks. |

Thinking local (& acting national)

Ambition	Aggregate at national scale where that's appropriate, and adapt to sub-national contexts where that's better.
Stakeholders	Ruthlessly calibrate ends to means by sequencing work in different areas, or if necessary by hard-nosed prioritisation. Accept genuine decentralised authority rather than insisting on simple audit trails that end at the top.
Operators	Accommodate regional differences in design, planning and evaluation processes. Resist 'drift' to the capital city and invest in good situational intelligence in areas that are important.

Organisational agility

Ambition	Headquarters and field offices are set up to live out the Virtues in any specific crisis.
Stakeholders	Ensure that financial, political and military resources can be rapidly shifted to meet emerging priorities. Are cautious about excessive specialisation and the constraints that it creates.
Operators	Leverage their situational awareness to connect unmet priorities with outside resources. Where appropriate, can act as a provider of last resort.

Collaborative design

Ambition	Balance deference and support to formal institutions with recognition of their particular vulnerabilities in fragile settings.
Stakeholders	Shape 'inclusive-enough' policy processes that provide entry points for those directly affected, and the partners who will be critical to success.
Operators	Market their area knowledge and local networks as a core selling proposition. Frequently measure public priorities as a reality check on what government and international agencies are saying.

The point is not that these are original insights. With due apologies to Marx: the critics have endlessly analysed the international aid business, and the priority is now to change it.[21] The Virtues are thus more party manifesto than research agenda.

One early lesson in this regard has been that it is counter-productive to speak to abstractions like 'the Congo crisis' or 'the development industry'. This is comfortable for research institutions but it excludes the vast bulk of practitioners, who have no such remit. They find themselves abruptly un-credentialed and cut out of discussions taking place among academics in journals they don't have access to, and institutions they cannot visit. The right unit of analysis is instead the strategic move—the combination of managerial intent, operational innovation and stakeholder bravery to attack an individual policy problem.[22] Better practice then diffuses when we are searching for ways to solve similar problems. Learning becomes part of the ordinary ebb-and-flow of working life. These are basic principles of continuing professional development.

In this light it is encouraging that there are growing numbers of data points under each of the Virtues. One example has already been discussed extensively in Chapters 3 and 5. It turns out that modern survey methods can be applied without excess difficulty in eastern Congo, and this has created a 'short route' to public priorities to complement what formal government institutions are saying.[23] Others have contributed ethnographic-style research on security actors and grass-roots conflict, and tried to market them as basic education for those working in the country.[24] Outside the DRC, meanwhile, smaller organisations are popping up in under-served sectors. One can now find research vendors whose selling point is 'long-term local offices and sustained relationships'.[25] A grant-funded agency can identify its role as insulating the 'autonomy that local leaders need and want', and deliberately target slightly dissident 'intrapreneurs' in established donors.[26] And at the policy level, the Rethink Fragility project rumbles along, in parallel with case-level work by established institutions on 'what counts as progress' in fragile settings.[27]

This is a fitting point to end upon, for the intervention business is frequently caricatured as impervious to self-scrutiny. Studies of peace operations invariably discover cultures of 'secrecy', or 'pretence'.[28] Development insiders lament a false united front, with defensive public relations in 'overdrive trying to either shut up or shut out the objectors'.[29] One well-known economist concluded a micro-survey of technological development in the eighteenth century with the sarcastic aside that he 'can't wait until the Enlightenment arrives in the development community'.[30]

There is just enough truth to these accusations for them to be wounding. We can do better than this. We can take failure seriously, and search around and behind it for our own contributions. To echo a plea written thirty-five years ago:[31]

> Face to face with the ugly and on-going historical reality of Zaire... there is no reason to accept the constituent elements of the prevailing development systems as monolithic and immutable. There are people inside all of the institutions discussed who oppose the human results of the current historical processes. They are reachable, and they need and want the assistance of world citizens.

The language now seems quaint, and the circumstances very different. But Mobutu Sese Seko's dictatorship lasted thirty-five years on the strength of a polite fiction agreed with international backers that 'the major constraint... is the lack of technical experts, direction and management'.[32] The status quo proved remarkably durable. Let us not lose our own sense of urgency to keep overturning it.

A final word

I wrote *Follies in Fragile States* because there is a gap in historical memory. There is a crying need for honest and critical reflection amongst practitioners in the aid business in general, and for aid to fragile states in particular. We must take responsibility for this ourselves rather than leaving it to the think tanks, and academics, who can hear and recount only a tiny part of the story.

If you found the book useful, or interesting, please share, recommend or simply lend it! It is an economic reality that online reviews drive circulation, so please consider this also. For direct feedback I encourage you to get in touch via the Rethink Fragility site, or to find me on Twitter.

In closing, I have to underline that Follies in Fragile States was a collaborative project. The core ideas evolved over countless conversations with practitioners who were dissatisfied with the status quo, and hungry to do better. They were tested with long-suffering Congolese friends and colleagues, who see an endless cycle of well-meaning foreigners coming and going without seeming to build any institutional memory. All these interlocutors have my boundless thanks, and encouragement to 'keep at it'.

Special mention for help with the manuscript and design goes to several formidable colleagues in Hugo de Vries and Spyros Demetriou; and to Dan Fahey, Brie O'Keefe, Lisa Denney, Bryna Griffin, Sam Meikle, and all the others who looked at ever-changing drafts.

Notes & references

Notes to the Prologue

[1] Thottam, J (2011) 'The real lessons of Sri Lanka's war: A global power shift and the end of human rights', *TIME*, 21 November.

[2] Among the better reporting, see Montlake, S (2009) 'Sri Lanka's post-war resettlement stalls', *The Christian Science Monitor*, 19 June; Al Jazeera (2009) 'Sri Lanka defends internment camps', 12 October.

[3] United Nations (2012) 'Report of the Secretary-General's Internal Review Panel on United Nations action in Sri Lanka', November, p19.

[4] Hagopian, A et al. (2013) 'Mortality in Iraq associated with the 2003–2011 war and occupation: Findings from a National Cluster Sample Survey by the University Collaborative Iraq Mortality Study', *PLoS Med.* 10(10): e1001533; Watson Institute (2013) 'Economic costs summary', Costs of War Project, March.

[5] Freemantle, T (2014) 'Decorated marine sergeant scarred again by changes in Iraq', *Houston Chronicle*, 26 January.

[6] Allison, GT and Zellikow, P (1999) 'Essence of decision: Explaining the Cuban missile crisis', Pearson (2nd edn), preface.

[7] Heclo, H and Wildavsky, A (1981) 'The private government of public money', Palgrave Macmillan (2nd edn), p379.

[8] Mosse, D (2005) 'Cultivating development: An ethnography of aid policy and practice', Pluto Press, pxi; Autesserre, S (2014) 'Peaceland: Conflict resolution and the everyday politics of international intervention', Cambridge University Press, Kindle edn at 8897.

[9] Wilson, JQ (1991) 'Bureaucracy: What government agencies do and why they do it', Basic Books, pp37–44. The classic studies of police culture, albeit long since superseded, are: Skolnick, JH (1966) 'Justice without trial: Law enforcement in democratic society', John Wiley & Sons; Westley, WA (1970) 'Violence and the police: A sociological study of law, custom, and morality', The MIT Press.

[10] Lord Malloch-Brown, in the Foreword to Barber, M (2015) 'Blinded by humanity: Inside the UN's humanitarian operations', IB Tauris & Co.

Notes to the Introduction

[1] Gettleman, J (2010) 'Mass rapes in Congo reveal U.N. weakness', *The New York Times*, 3 October.

[2] Rittel, H (1972) 'On the planning crisis: Systems analysis of the "first and second generations"', *Bedriftsøkonomen* 8: 390–396. This is property number 11(!) of wicked problems.

[3] Lagadec, P (1993) 'Preventing chaos in a crisis: Strategies for damage prevention, control and damage limitation', McGraw-Hill.

[4] Charbonneau, L (2012) 'U.N. failed gravely in Sri Lanka—internal review panel', Reuters, 15 November.

[5] Smith, G (2013) 'The dogs are eating them now: Our war in Afghanistan', Counterpoint, p2.

[6] Quick, ID (2013) 'Peacekeeping Agendas dataset', www.rethinkfragility.com.

[7] OECD (2014) 'Fragile states 2014: Domestic revenue mobilization in fragile states', p25.

[8] Independent Commission on Aid Impact (2015) 'Assessing the impact of the scale-up of DFID's support to fragile states', Report 40, February.

[9] International Dialogue on Peacebuilding and Statebuilding (2011) 'A new deal for engagement in fragile states', December.

[10] Quick, ID (2013) 'Peacekeeping Agendas dataset', www.rethinkfragility.com. From 1995 to 2014, seventeen of twenty-five missions covered three or more of the Peacebuilding & Statebuilding Goals. The total figure bundles contiguous missions in a single country into one unit.

[11] GA Res 55/2, 'United Nations Millennium Declaration', 8 September 2000, UN Doc A/RES/55/2.

[12] United Nations (2013) 'A new global partnership: Eradicate poverty and transform economies through sustainable development', The Report of the High-Level Panel of Eminent Persons on the Post-2015 Development Agenda, p52.

[13] Popper, K (1934/1992) 'The logic of scientific discovery', Routledge, p94.

[14] Quick, ID (2013) 'Peacekeeping Resources dataset', www.rethinkfragility.com; World Development Indicators, the World Bank. Defined here as net ODA received as percentage of GNI, 2005–14. For humanitarian funding appeals, see Office for the

Coordination of Humanitarian Affairs, 'Plan d'Action Humanitaire: République Démocratique du Congo', editions of 2008–12.

[15] There were too many scornful reactions to recap here. Among the most virulent was Hatcher, J and Perry, A (2012) 'Defining peacekeeping downward: the U.N. debacle in eastern Congo', *TIME*, 26 November. For a more balanced view: Boutellis, A (2013) 'Will MONUSCO fall with Goma?', *Global Observatory*, 3 December.

[16] Heifetz, R (2009) 'Leadership in a (permanent) crisis', HBR Ideacast, *Harvard Business Review*, 23 July.

[17] BBC News (2014) 'DR Congo ex-fighters "starve in demobilization camp"', 1 October; Human Rights Watch (2014) 'DR Congo: Surrendered fighters starve in camp', 1 October.

[18] International Monetary Fund and International Development Association (2010) 'Enhanced Heavily Indebted Poor Countries Initiative Completion Point Document and Multilateral Debt Relief Initiative', June 15.

[19] Prunier, G (2008/2011) 'Africa's world war: Congo, the Rwandan genocide, and the making of a continental catastrophe', Oxford University Press, p299.

[20] BBC News (2014) 'Second massacre in days leaves 20 dead in east DR Congo', 18 October; Kibangula, T (2014) 'RDC: la situation explosive de Beni expliquée en 4 points', *Jeune Afrique*, 4 November; Reuters (2015) 'At least 21 killed in machete attack in northeast Congo', 4 February.

[21] Hobbes, T (2008) 'Leviathan', Oxford Paperbacks edition, ch. 13.

[22] Vlassenroot, K and Raeymakers, T (2004) 'Conflict and social transformation in Eastern DR Congo', Conflict Research Group, ch. 6.

[23] Coghlan, B, et al. (2009) 'Update on mortality in the Democratic Republic of Congo: Results from a third nationwide survey', *Disaster Med. Public Health Prep.* June 3(2): 88–96.

[24] Vinck, P et al. (2008) 'Living with fear: A population-based survey on attitudes about peace, justice, and social reconstruction in eastern Democratic Republic of Congo', Berkeley-Tulane Initiative on Vulnerable Populations, August, p26.

[25] United Nations (2009) 'Performance report on the budget of MONUC from 1 July 2008 to 30 June 2009', 18 December, UN Doc A/64/583; SC Res 1856 (2008) 22 December, UN Doc S/RES/1856.

[26] Martin, B (2012) 'The protection of civilians in the Democratic Republic of the Congo', *Conflict Trends* 2012(2): 33–40.

[27] United Nations (2012) 'Plan d'Action Humanitaire 2012: République Démocratique du Congo', p5 ('une pauvreté et une précarité générales'), www.unocha.org.

[28] Krasner, SD (2004) 'Shared sovereignty: New institutions for collapsed and failing states', *International Security* 29(2).

[29] SC Res 1856, 22 December 2008, UN Doc S/RES/1856.

[30] SC Res 1925, 28 May 2010, UN Doc S/RES/1925.

[31] Human Rights Watch (2009) 'You will be punished: Attacks on civilians in eastern Congo', 13 December.

[32] Prendergast, J and Atama, N (2009) 'Eastern Congo: an action plan to end the world's deadliest war', The Enough Project, July, p11.

[33] Stearns, J et al. (2013) 'The national army and armed groups in the eastern Congo: Untangling the Gordian knot of insecurity', Rift Valley Institute Usalama Project, p4.

[34] United Nations (2011) 'International Security and Stabilization Support Strategy for the Democratic Republic of the Congo: Quarterly report for April to June 2011', p6.

[35] Padovan, C (2012) 'Life returns to normal in Luvungi, Nord Kivu, thanks to the National Police', press release, MONUSCO Public Information, 8 February.

[36] Heaton, L (2013) 'What happened in Luvungi? On rape and truth in Congo', *Foreign Policy*, March 4; Williams, M and Cragin, W (2013) 'Our experience in Luvungi', *Foreign Policy*, March 5. For the incidents of April–June 2012 see: Radio Okapi (2012) 'Walikale: 27 morts dans les affrontements entre FARDC et Mai-Mai Cheka à Luvungi', 18 April; Le Congolais (2012) 'Nord-Kivu – Les miliciens Maï Maï Cheka occupent une dizaine de villages à Walikale', 18 April; Radio Okapi (2012) 'Nord-Kivu: les FARDC tuent 4 rebelles de Cheka à Ihana', 23 May; United Nations (2012) 'Report of the Secretary-General on MONUSCO', 14 November, UN Doc S/2012/838, para. 13.

[37] Brusset, E et al. (2011) 'Amani labda, peace maybe: Joint evaluation of conflict prevention and peace building in the Democratic Republic of Congo', Synthesis Report, Channel Research.

[38] Fund for Peace, 'Failed States Index', editions of 2007–12; Marshall, MG and Cole, BR, 'Global report on conflict, governance and state fragility', Center for Systemic Peace, editions of 2007, 2008, 2009 and 2011; Norman Patterson School of International Affairs at Carleton University, 'Assessing state fragility: A country indicators for foreign policy report', editions of 2007–2012.

[39] Demetriou, S and Quick, ID (2012) 'The sobering lessons of stabilization in eastern Democratic Republic of the Congo', unpublished manuscript.

[40] Stewart, R and Knaus, G (2012) 'Can intervention work?', Norton Global Ethics Series, p54.

[41] Chandler, D (2006) 'Empire in denial: The politics of statebuilding', Pluto Press; Easterly, W (2014) 'The tyranny of experts: Economists, dictators, and the forgotten rights of the poor', Basic Civitas Books. For the latter argument in respect of the DRC specifically see Autessere, S (2010) 'The trouble with the Congo: Local violence and the failure of international peacebuilding', Cambridge University Press.

[42] Caiden, N and Wildavsky, A (1980) 'Planning and budgeting in poor countries', Transaction Publishers, pxi.

[43] Quick, ID (2011) 'End of assignment report: UN Stabilization Mission in the Democratic Republic of the Congo', internal report.

[44] United Nations (2012) 'Report of the Secretary-General's Internal Review Panel on United Nations action in Sri Lanka', p4.

[45] United Nations (1999) 'Report of the Secretary-General pursuant to General Assembly resolution 53/35: The fall of Srebrenica', 15 November, UN Doc A/54/549; United Nations (1999) 'Report of the Independent Inquiry into the actions of the United Nations during the 1994 genocide in Rwanda', 15 December, UN Doc S/1999/1257.

[46] With some creditable exceptions: Anstee, JM (1996) 'Orphan of the Cold War: The inside story of the collapse of the Angolan peace process 1992–3', Palgrave Macmillan; Ould-Abdullah, A (1999) 'Burundi on the brink, 1993–5: A UN special envoy reflects on preventive diplomacy' United States Institute of Peace.

[47] Toye, J (1987) 'Dilemmas of development', Blackwell, p18.

Notes to Chapter 1

[1] Reyntjens, F (2009) 'The great African war: Congo and regional geo-politics, 1996–2006', Cambridge University Press, p10; Herbst, J and Mills, G (2009) 'There is no Congo', *Foreign Policy*, 18 March; Trefon, T (2011) 'Congo masquerade: The political culture of aid inefficiency and reform failure', Zed Books, p102.

[2] GoDRC (2007) 'Country Assistance Framework 2007–10'; GoDRC (2006) 'Poverty reduction and growth strategy paper', Ministry of Planning, p50; GoDRC (2007) 'Contrat de Gouvernance: Mars-Décembre 2007', Office of the Prime Minister, p4 (author's translation).

[3] United Nations (2007) 'Twenty-fourth report of the Secretary-General on MONUC', 14 November, UN Doc S/2007/671; United Nations / DPKO (2009) 'Report of the technical assessment mission to MONUC: 23 February – 6 March 2009', internal report, March.

[4] Brusset, E et al. (2011) 'Amani labda, peace maybe: Joint evaluation of conflict prevention and peace building in the Democratic Republic of Congo', Synthesis Report, Channel Research, June, p18.

[5] Muzito, P (2009) 'Allocution à l'occasion du lancement des travaux sur le « Plan de Stabilisation et de reconstruction de l'Est de la République Démocratique du Congo »', Office of the Prime Minister.

[6] SC Res 1925, 28 May 2010, UN Doc S/RES/1925, para. 6; United Nations (2010) 'Thirty-first report of the Secretary-General on MONUC', 30 March, UN Doc S/2010/164, paras 80–84.

[7] Polgreen, L (2008) 'A massacre in Congo, despite nearby support', *The New York Times*, 11 December; Human Rights Watch (2008) 'Killings in Kiwanja: the UN's inability to protect civilians', 12 December; PBS (2009) 'Can the UN keep the peace?', *PBS Now*, 15 May.

[8] United Nations (2014) 'Statement of SRSG Martin Kobler to the Security Council: Turning promises into deeds', monusco.unmissions.org.

[9] Personal observations at UN Department of Peacekeeping Operations, 2008–09; MONUC (2009) 'Towards peace and stability: An overview of the UNSSSS for Eastern Democratic Republic of Congo', press booklet, August.

[10] MONUC (2009) 'International Security and Stabilization Support Strategy Integrated Program Framework', Annex 1.

[11] Vlassenroot, K and Raeymakers, T (2004) 'Conflict and social transformation in eastern DR Congo', Academia Press Scientific Publishers, ch. 6. This is a peculiarly

Congolese joke in that the reference is to an obscure, short-lived secessional constitution in 1960, mostly forgotten to history in the shadow of the Katangan civil war.

[12] Schatzberg, MG (1988) 'The dialects of oppression in Zaire', John Wiley & Sons, ch. 4; Trefon, T (2011) 'Congo masquerade: The political culture of aid inefficiency and reform failure', Zed Books, ch. 4. This version of the quote is from Stearns, J (2012) 'Dancing in the glory of monsters: The collapse of the Congo and the great war of Africa', Public Affairs, loc 2000.

[13] Vinck, P et al. (2008) 'Living with fear: A population-based survey on attitudes about peace, justice, and social reconstruction in eastern Democratic Republic of Congo', Berkeley-Tulane Initiative on Vulnerable Populations.

[14] Berghezan, G and Zeebroek, X (2009) 'Small arms in Eastern Congo: A survey on the perception of insecurity', GRIP, *Les livres du GRIP* No. 302–303, loc 2360 in Kindle edition.

[15] Gallup (2008) 'Few urban Congolese have confidence in institutions', May 16; International Legal Assistance Consortium (2009) 'Rebuilding courts and trust: An assessment of the needs of the justice system in the Democratic Republic of the Congo'.

[16] Fund for Peace (2008) 'Failed states index'; Worldwide Governance Indicators (2009) www.govindicators.org; Mo Ibrahim Foundation (2008) 'Ibrahim index of African governance'.

[17] MONUC (2008) 'First steps in extension of state authority: Police deployment', internal working paper (May), Strategic Planning Group.

[18] Quick, ID (2011) 'Why did the "State in a box" approach break down in DRC?', *Peacekeeping Whiteboard*, 31 March; Quick, ID (2011) 'How long does it actually take to deliver the "State in a box"?', *Peacekeeping Whiteboard*, 28 March.

[19] Author conversations with senior UNOPS officials, 2009–10; MONUC (2009) 'Enhancing delivery capacities for stabilization and recovery in Eastern DRC', internal note to file, ODSRSG-RC-HC, September.

[20] GoDRC (2011) 'Plan de travail relatif aux objectives à atteindre', internal planning document (March), Inspection Provinciale du Nord-Kivu.

[21] Tamagnini, A et al. (2010) 'Strategic review of the ISSSS for Eastern DR Congo: Final report', pp27–28. The description is for the town of Nyamilima but also applies to other sites.

[22] Booth, D and Cammack, D (2013) 'Governance for development in Africa: Solving collective action problems', Zed Books.

[23] MONUC (2009) 'Joint Monitoring Team report for week ending 13 May 2009', internal situation report, North Kivu sub-office; MONUC (2009) 'Weekly report for week ending 13 May 2009', internal situation report, North Kivu Brigade; US Department of State (2009) 'Eastern DRC notes – May 15', code cable, via wikileaks / Public Library of US Diplomacy. This was also clear from personal interviews with local officials later in 2009.

[24] Radio Okapi (2009) 'Kinyandoni: une attaque des FDLR fait 2 morts et des blessés', 13 May; MONUC (2009) 'Note to file of 11 July 2009', internal memorandum, ODSRG-RC-HC; Etinga, S (2009) 'Des dizaines de personnes tuées par les FDLR à Walikale et Rutshuru', *Le Potentiel*, 15 May.

[25] MONUC (2009) 'Lessons learned review: Rapid deployment of police to North Kivu under the UNSSSS', internal report (16 September), ODSRSG-RC-HC; MONUC (2009) 'Comment on note to file', internal communication (July), ODSRSG-RC-HC.

[26] Martin, B (2012) 'The protection of civilians in the Democratic Republic of the Congo', *Conflict Trends* 2: 33–40.

[27] MONUC (2009) 'UNSSSS biweekly update: 26 September to 9 October 2009'; MONUC (2009) 'Comment on note to file', internal communication (July), ODSRSG-RC-HC; Bashonga, LP (2009) 'Formation de la Police Territoriale déployée à Rutshuru', *STAREC Infos* 002.

[28] MONUC (2009) 'Lessons learned review: Rapid deployment of police to North Kivu under the UNSSSS', internal report (16 September), ODSRSG-RC-HC.

[29] Author calculations using figures from UNHCR (2011) 'Rapport trimestriel du cluster protection', Protection Cluster.

[30] Oxfam (2012) '"For me, but without me, is against me": Why efforts to stabilise the Democratic Republic of Congo are not working', Oxfam Lobby Briefing.

[31] MONUC (2009) '*Sondage* data', internal report (September), UNPOL North Kivu.

[32] Author conversations with MONUC staff, 2009–10; MONUC (2009) 'Lessons learned review: Rapid deployment of police to North Kivu under the UNSSSS', internal report (16 September), ODSRSG-RC-HC; MONUC (2009) 'Monthly report for August', internal report, Civil Affairs Section.

[33] Tamagnini, A et al. (2010) 'Strategic review of the ISSSS for Eastern DR Congo: Final report', p6.

[34] GoDRC (2010) 'STAREC etat de lieu: L'état de droit', internal briefing document (August), Sécretariat Technique du STAREC (author's translation).

[35] MONUSCO (2012) 'ISSSS Quarterly Report, April–June 2012'; United Nations (2012) 'Report of the Secretary-General on MONUSCO', UN Doc S/2012/355, 23 May. Several magistrates were deployed in mobile teams, the so-called Prosecution Support Cells, but were tasked with military justice only.

[36] MONUSCO (2011) 'ISSSS Monthly Update: 1 to 30 September 2011'.

[37] United Nations (2011) 'Final report of the Group of Experts established pursuant to resolution 1533 (2004)', 2 December, UN Doc S/2011/738, paras 305–306; Radio Okapi (2011) 'Masisi: retour au calme après trois jours de manifestation contre la nomination du chef de la police' 16 August; Digital Congo (2011) 'Goma: Le colonel Zabuloni refuse sa nouvelle affectation', 24 August; Le Congolais (2011) 'Le colonel Ngarunge remplace Zabuloni au commandement de la Police dans le Masisi', 12 October.

[38] United Nations (2011) 'Report of the Secretary-General on MONUSCO', 24 October, UN Doc S/2011/656, para. 14.

[39] MONUSCO (2011) 'Note de synthèse sur la situation à Masisi', internal briefing document (August), Political Affairs Department.

[40] Zabuloni belonged to the Hutu wing of PARECO, many members of which had aligned themselves with the CNDP over the course of 2009–10. Chapter 2 elaborates on this history in detail.

[41] MONUSCO (2011) 'Flash report: Community Liaison Assistant Masisi', internal report (August), Civil Affairs Section.

[42] MONUSCO (2011) 'Masisi CLA's special report', internal report (August), Civil Affairs Section.

[43] GoDRC (2010) 'La nouvelle Police National Congolaise: Presentation of Secrétariat Executif', internal presentation (February), Comité de Suivi de la Réforme de la Police.

[44] 'Peace Agreement between the Government and the Congres National Pour la Defense du Peuple (CNDP)', signed 23 March at Goma, arts 10 and 12.8.

[45] United Nations (2010) 'Final report of the Group of Experts established pursuant to resolution 1533 (2004)', 29 November, UN Doc S/2010/596, para. 160 and annex 16; United Nations (2011) 'Report of the Secretary-General on MONUSCO', UN Doc S/2011/298, 12 May 2011.

[46] MONUSCO (2011) 'Joint Protection Team summary reports', internal reports of 1 June and 30 June, North Kivu sub-office; United Nations (2011) 'Final report of the Group of Experts established pursuant to resolution 1533 (2004)', 2 December, UN

Doc S/2011/738, paras 315–320; International Crisis Group (2012) 'Eastern Congo: Why stabilization failed', *Africa Briefing* 91: 4–5, 4 October.

47 MONUSCO (2011) 'Joint Monitoring Team Masisi: Rapport spéciale', internal report (June), UNPOL North Kivu.

48 Personal communications with provincial command of *Police Territoriale* in 2009–10; MONUC (2009) 'Lessons learned review: Rapid deployment of police to North Kivu under the UNSSSS', internal report (September), ODSRSG-RC-HC; Boutellis, A and Lacaille, G (2011) 'Renewing MONUSCO's mandate: What role beyond the elections?', Issue Brief, International Peace Institute.

49 MONUC (2009) 'Rapport hebdomadaire JMT 3-Rutshuru', internal report (7 April), UNPOL North Kivu. Generally see Stearns, J (2010) 'CNDP tightens control over Masisi', *Congo Siasa*, 21 February; Le Phare (2010) 'La société civile de Masisi réclame la délocalisation des groupes armés', 5 August; United Nations (2010) 'Final Report of the Group of Experts', paras 157–60; Channel Research / iTSCI (2013) 'iTSCi Governance Assessment: Rubaya, North Kivu'.

50 MONUSCO (2011) 'JMT Masisi: Rapport d'activités', internal report (27 April), UNPOL North Kivu; MONUSCO (2011) 'JMT Rutshuru: Rapport d'activités', internal report (28 April), UNPOL North Kivu.

51 Tsongo, AM and Mathieu, P (1998) 'Guerres paysannes au Nord-Kivu (République Démocratique du Congo)', *Cahiers d'études africaines* 38(150–2): 385–416; Mamdani, M (1998) 'Understanding the crisis in Kivu: Report of the CODESRIA Mission to the Democratic Republic of Congo September 1997', Center for African Studies University of Cape Town; Lemarchand, R (2012) 'The dynamics of violence in Central Africa', University of Pennsylvania Press, ch. 1.

52 Van Reybrouck, D (2010/2014) 'Congo: The epic history of a people', Fourth Estate, p282.

53 Young, C and Turner, TE (1985) 'The rise and decline of the Zairian state', University of Wisconsin Press, ch. 8; Callaghy, TM (1984) 'The state–society struggle: Zaire in comparative perspective', Columbia University Press, ch. 4.

54 Callaghy, TM (1984) 'The state–society struggle: Zaire in comparative perspective', Columbia University Press, pp382–388.

55 Sosne, E (1979) 'Colonial peasantization and contemporary underdevelopment: A view from a Kivu village', in Gran, G (ed.) *Zaire: The political economy of underdevelopment*, Praeger, p196.

56 Jumelle, L (1974) 'La réforme administrative au Zaire', *International Review of Administrative Sciences* 40: 171–181; Mpinga-Kasenda and Gould, D (1977) 'Les réformes administratives au Zaire', Presses Universitaires du Zaire; Turner, T (1980)

'Chiefs, bureaucrats and the M.P.R. of Zaire' in Lawson, K (ed.) *Political parties and linkage: A comparative perspective*, Yale University Press.

[57] Beck, J (2012) 'Contested land in the Eastern Democratic Republic of the Congo: Anatomy of the land-related intervention', IFHV Working Paper 2(2).

[58] MacGaffey, W (1982) 'The policy of national integration in Zaire', *Journal of Modern African Studies* 20(1): 87–105.

[59] Callaghy, TM (1984) 'The state–society struggle: Zaire in comparative perspective', Columbia University Press, p261.

[60] L'Etoile (1969) 4–5 October, Kinshasa.

[61] Mamdani, M (1998) 'Understanding the crisis in Kivu: Report of the CODESRIA Mission to the Democratic Republic of Congo September 1997', Center for African Studies, University of Cape Town.

[62] Autessere, S (2010) 'The trouble with the Congo: Local violence and the failure of international peacebuilding', Cambridge University Press, pp158–164.

[63] United Nations (2010) 'Final report of the Group of Experts established pursuant to resolution 1533 (2004)', 29 November, UN Doc S/2010/596, p44.

[64] MONUC (2008) 'UNSSSS Restoration of the state authority: Deployment of the Congolese National Police', internal presentation (March), UNPOL Kinshasa.

[65] GoDRC (2009) 'Comite sectoriel de suivi du Plan de Stabilisation et de Reconstruction de l'Est: Composante police', internal planning document (undated), p2.

[66] UNOPS / GoDRC / Peacebuilding Fund (2010) 'Project document: Soutien à la sélection, à la formation et au déploiement de la Police Nationale Congolaise (PNC)', programme document, accessible via www.mptf.org.

[67] Ibid, p17.

[68] GoDRC (2010) 'Roles et responsabilités des membres du Comité Technique Conjoint (CTC) du STAREC du Nord Kivu', internal working document (undated), North Kivu Governor's office; UNDP / Peacebuilding Fund (2011) 'Appui aux Structures de Coordination du STAREC et l'UNSSSS', programme document, mptf.undp.org. We return to this point in greater detail in Chapter 5.

[69] GoDRC (2011) 'Compte-rendu de la réunion du Comite Technique Conjoint (CTC) du programme STAREC Nord-Kivu', internal minutes (13 April), North Kivu Governor's office (author's translation).

[70] Oxfam (2012) "'For me, but without me, is against me'": Why efforts to stabilise the Democratic Republic of Congo are not working', Oxfam Lobby Briefing, p33.

[71] Paddon, E and Lacaille, G (2011) 'Stabilising the Congo', *Forced Migration Policy Briefing* 8, Refugee Studies Centre, Oxford University, p13.

[72] MONUSCO (2011) 'Note de synthèse sur la situation à Masisi', internal report (15 August), Political Affairs Department.

[73] Kibangula, T (2014) 'Charles Bisengimana, le policier de Kabila', *Jeune Afrique*, 13 January.

[74] UNOPS / Peacebuilding Fund (2014) 'Final programme narrative report: Soutien à la Sélection, à la Formation et au Déploiement de la PNC', accessible via www.mptf.org; MONUSCO (2012) 'International Security and Stabilization Quarterly report: January to March 2012', p31.

[75] Bureau de Coordination des ex-groupes armes du Nord-Kivu (2011) 'Appel a la conscience du Gouvernment: les Accords de Paix de Goma; sont-ils abrogés?', 25 March.

[76] UNOPS / Peacebuilding Fund (2014) 'Final programme narrative report: Soutien à la Sélection, à la Formation et au Déploiement de la PNC', accessible via www.mptf.org.

[77] MONUSCO (2012) 'International Security and Stabilization Quarterly Report: January to March 2012', p31.

[78] MONUSCO (2011) 'International Security and Stabilization Support Strategy for the Democratic Republic of the Congo: Quarterly report for April to June 2011', p18.

[79] AP Photos / Delay, J (2012) 'M23 rebels battle Congolese soldiers', 23 November.

[80] United Nations (2011) 'Report of the Secretary-General on MONUSCO', 12 May, UN Doc S/2011/298, paras 59–63.

[81] I borrow the term from Mann, M (1988) 'States, war and capitalism: Studies in political sociology', Wiley-Blackwell, ch. 1.

[82] International Crisis Group (2012) 'Eastern Congo: Why stabilization failed', Africa Briefing 91, 4 October; International Alert (2012) 'Ending the deadlock: Towards a new vision of peace in eastern DRC'.

[83] Scott, JC (1998) 'Seeing like a state: How certain schemes to improve the human condition have failed', Yale University Press, ch. 1.

[84] MONUSCO (2012) 'International Security and Stabilization Quarterly report: January to March 2012'.

[85] DiMaggio, P and Powell, WW (1983) 'The iron cage revisited: Institutional isomorphism and collective rationality in organizational fields', *American Sociological Review* 48(April): 137–160.

Notes to Chapter 2

[1] *The Economist* (2013) 'Rebel retreat: Can the Congolese army build on a rare victory?', 2 November.

[2] Gettleman, J (2010) 'Mass rapes in Congo reveal U.N. weakness', *The New York Times*, 3 October.

[3] Prunier (2008/2011) 'Africa's world war: Congo, the Rwandan genocide, and the making of a continental catastrophe', Oxford University Press, p305.

[4] International Crisis Group (2006) 'Security sector reform in the Congo', Africa Report 104; Oxfam America (2010) 'No will, no way: US-funded security sector reform in the Democratic Republic of Congo'.

[5] SC Res 1756, 15 May 2007, UN Doc S/RES/1756 (2007), preamble.

[6] GoDRC (2007) 'Contrat de Gouvernance: Mars–Décembre 2007', February, p4.

[7] Human Rights Watch (2007) 'Renewed crisis in North Kivu'; Prendergast, J and Atama, N (2009) 'Eastern Congo: An action plan to end the world's deadliest war', The Enough Project, p11; Paddon, E and Lacaille, G (2011) 'Stabilising the Congo', *Forced Migration Policy Briefing* 8, Refugee Studies Centre, Oxford University, December; International Crisis Group (2012) 'Eastern Congo: Why stabilization failed', Africa Briefing 91; International Alert (2012) 'Ending the deadlock: Towards a new vision of peace in eastern DRC'; Oxfam (2012) '"For me, but without me, is against me": Why efforts to stabilise the Democratic Republic of Congo are not working', Oxfam Lobby Briefing.

[8] ASADHO et al. (2011) 'The Democratic Republic of Congo: Taking a stand on security sector reform', p3. This is a joint report of eight international non-governmental organisations and five Congolese non-governmental organisations.

[9] There is a lot written on this topic. For overviews see: Wolters, S and Boshoff, H (2006) 'The impact of slow military reform on the transition process in the DRC', Institute for Security Studies Situation Report, 10 July; Baaz, ME and Verweijen, J (2011) 'Between integration and disintegration: The erratic trajectory of the Congolese army', paper for the DRC Affinity Group.

[10] Verweijen, J (2010) 'The beer that would not brew: Birth and infancy of the FARDC (2003–2007)', Conference on 'New armies from old. Merging competing military forces after civil wars', 31 August – 1 September 2010, Carlisle, Pennsylvania; Baaz, ME and Verweijen, J (2013) '"The volatility of a half-cooked bouillabaisse": Rebel–military integration and conflict dynamics in the eastern DRC', *African Affairs* 112/449: 563–582.

[11] Stearns, J (2013) 'PARECO: Land, local strongmen and the roots of militia politics in North Kivu', Rift Valley Institute, Usalama Project, p9.

[12] The latter phrase was still being used in 2014. See *Jeune Afrique* (2014) 'Carte interactive des groupes armés du Kivu après la fin du M23', 17 March.

[13] Sources: (1) Mo Ibrahim Foundation (2007–13) 'Ibrahim Index of African Governance'; (2) Fund for Peace (2007–13) 'Failed States Index'; (3) Norman Patterson School of International Affairs at Carleton University (2008–12) 'Assessing state fragility: A country indicators for foreign policy report'. The two Ibrahim indicators are averaged and the scale inverted (subtracted from 100) in order to be visually consistent with the other two indices.

[14] Baaz, ME and Verweijen, J (2013) '"The volatility of a half-cooked bouillabaisse": Rebel–military integration and conflict dynamics in the eastern DRC', *African Affairs* 112/449: 563–582.

[15] Moore, P (2011) 'M23 fighters capture Goma in the DR Congo', Al Jazeera, 23 November

[16] Al Jazeera (2011) 'UN mission to probe DR Congo rape claims', 23 June; CNN (2011) 'Attackers rape more than 170 women in raids on Congo villages, 24 June; Hall, A (2011) 'When rape becomes a game', *Huffington Post*, 5 July.

[17] MONUSCO (2011) 'Joint Protection Team report: Nakiele', internal report (July), South Kivu sub-office; MONUSCO (2011) 'Weekly analytical report', internal report (2 July), South Kivu sub-office; Radio Okapi (2011) 'Fizi: viols massifs à Nyakiele, 70 victimes en une nuit', 22 June; Slate Afrique (2011) 'RDC: plus de 100 victimes de viols et violences dans un village de l'est', 23 June; Stearns, J (2011) 'Military shake-ups could worsen Congo's mass rape problem', *Christian Science Monitor*, 29 June.

[18] Hall, A (2011) 'When rape becomes a game', *Huffington Post*, 5 July; CNN (2011) 'Attackers rape more than 170 women in raids on Congo villages, 24 June; BBC News (2011) 'DR Congo "rape" Colonel "Kifaru" Kulimushi surrenders', 8 July.

[19] Quoted in Stearns, J, Verweijen, J and Erikson Baaz, M (2013) 'The national army and armed groups in the eastern Congo: Untangling the Gordian knot of insecurity', Rift Valley Institute, Usalama Project, p39.

[20] International Crisis Group (2012) 'Eastern Congo: Why stabilization failed', Africa Briefing 91, p4. See also Baaz, ME and Verweijen, J (2013) '"The volatility of a half-cooked bouillabaisse": Rebel–military integration and conflict dynamics in the eastern DRC', *African Affairs* 112/449: 563–582.

[21] MONUSCO (2011) 'Weekly Analytical Report', internal report (14 May), South Kivu sub-office; US Department of State (2011) 'Minembwe update: Dissident groups preparing for integration as Masunzu leaves High Plateau', internal code cable

(21 March), available via wikileaks.org / Public Library of US Diplomacy; Verweijen, J (2011) 'Guest blog: The FRF armed group', *Congo Siasa*, 10 August; Stearns, J (2013) 'Banyamulenge: Insurgency and exclusion in the mountains of South Kivu', Rift Valley Institute Usalama Project.

22 United Nations (2011) 'Final report of the Group of Experts established pursuant to resolution 1533 (2004)', 2 December, UN Doc S/2011/738, paras 508–536.

23 Stearns, J (2011) 'Restructuring of Congolese army produces resentment', *Congo Siasa*, 29 July. The table is modified slightly to fit the paperback format, with the last column dropped. This related to all (combined) Mai-Mai groups, with their total in the bottom row being 3.4% of command assignments.

24 Stearns, J (2013) 'PARECO: Land, local strongmen and the roots of militia politics in North Kivu', Rift Valley Institute, Usalama Project, pp34–37.

25 There is an enormous amount written on this topic. For succinct summaries see Mamdani, M (1998) 'Understanding the crisis in Kivu: Report of the CODESRIA Mission to the Democratic Republic of Congo September 1997', Center for African Studies, University of Cape Town; Prunier, G (2008/2011) 'Africa's world war: Congo, the Rwandan genocide, and the making of a continental catastrophe', Oxford University Press, pp48–50; Huggins, C (2010) 'Land, power and identity: Roots of violent conflict in Eastern DRC', International Alert, pt 2.2.

26 Quoted in Verweijen, J (2014) 'The ambiguity of militarization. The complex interaction between the Congolese armed forces and civilians in the Kivu provinces, DR Congo' (PhD thesis, Utrecht University, Faculty of Humanities, forthcoming).

27 Baaz, ME and Verweijen, J (2013) '"The volatility of a half-cooked bouillabaisse": Rebel–military integration and conflict dynamics in the eastern DRC', *African Affairs* 112/449, p573.

28 United Nations (2011) 'Final report of the Group of Experts established pursuant to resolution 1533 (2004)', 2 December, UN Doc S/2011/738, paras 303–304 and 331, annex 86 (author's translation of the latter).

29 MONUSCO (2011) 'DDRRR weekly report', internal report (12 February), DDRRR section; United Nations (2011) 'Final report of the Group of Experts established pursuant to resolution 1533 (2004)', 2 December, UN Doc S/2011/738, para. 162.

30 United Nations (2011) 'Final report of the Group of Experts established pursuant to resolution 1533 (2004)', 2 December, UN Doc S/2011/738, Annex 31 and paras 171–178.

31 MONUSCO (2011) 'Weekly analytical reports', internal reports of 5 March, 3 April, 23 April, 7 May, South Kivu sub-office.

[32] Vlassenroot, K (2013) 'South Kivu: Identity, territory and power in the eastern Congo', Rift Valley Institute, Usalama Project, chs 3 and 4; Prunier, G (2008/2011) 'Africa's world war: Congo, the Rwandan genocide, and the making of a continental catastrophe', Oxford University Press, ch. 2; Autessere, S (2010) 'The trouble with the Congo: Local violence and the failure of international peacebuilding', Cambridge University Press, pp138–151.

[33] Stearns, J, Verweijen, J and Erikson Baaz, M (2013) 'The national army and armed groups in the eastern Congo: Untangling the Gordian knot of insecurity', Rift Valley Institute, Usalama Project, pp25–26.

[34] Ibid, ch. IV; United Nations (2011) 'Final report of the Group of Experts established pursuant to resolution 1533 (2004)', 2 December, UN Doc S/2011/738, para. 563; United Nations (2012) 'Final report of the Group of Experts established pursuant to resolution 1533 (2004) concerning the Democratic Republic of the Congo', 15 November, UN Doc S/2012/843, paras 116–126.

[35] MONUSCO (2011) 'Mapping of armed groups in South Kivu', internal report (July), South Kivu sub-office; Stearns, J (2011) 'New armed groups appear in South Kivu', *Congo Siasa*, 15 September; Heretiers de la Justice (2013) 'La plaine de la Ruzizi en passe de redevenir une poudrière', 22 August.

[36] MONUSCO (2011) 'Weekly analytical report', internal report (19 March), South Kivu sub-office; United Nations (2011) 'Report of the Secretary-General on MONUSCO', 12 May, UN Doc S/2011/298, para. 16.

[37] MONUSCO (2011) 'DDRRR daily report', internal report (21 March), DDRRR section. See also United Nations (2011) 'Final report of the Group of Experts established pursuant to resolution 1533 (2004)', 2 December, UN Doc S/2011/738, para. 54.

[38] MONUSCO (2011) 'Weekly analytical report', internal report (26 March), South Kivu sub-office.

[39] MONUSCO (2011) 'Support to political process indicators', internal report (July), South Kivu sub-office; MONUSCO (2011) 'DDRRR weekly reports', internal reports (18 June and 1 July), DDRRR section; Le Phare (2011) 'La MONUSCO juge la situation', 22 September.

[40] United Nations (2011) 'Final report of the Group of Experts established pursuant to resolution 1533 (2004)', 2 December, UN Doc S/2011/738, paras 278–283; Stearns, J (2011) 'Restructuring of Congolese army produces resentment', *Congo Siasa*, 29 July; ASADHO et al. (2011) 'The Democratic Republic of Congo: Taking a stand on security sector reform', p9; Baaz, ME and Verweijen, J (2013) '"The volatility of a half-cooked bouillabaisse": Rebel–military integration and conflict dynamics in the eastern DRC', *African Affairs* 112/449, p571.

[41] International Crisis Group (2012) 'Eastern Congo: Why stabilisation failed', Africa Briefing 91, 4 October, p9; Stearns, J (2012) 'From CNDP to M23: The evolution of an armed movement in eastern Congo', Rift Valley Project, Usalama Project, pp41–42.

[42] Stearns, J (2012) 'From CNDP to M23: The evolution of an armed movement in eastern Congo', Rift Valley Project, Usalama Project, pt 4; International Crisis Group (2012) 'Eastern Congo: Why stabilization failed', Africa Briefing 91, pp9–10; United Nations (2012) 'Interim report of the Group of Experts established pursuant to resolution 1533 (2004) concerning the Democratic Republic of the Congo', 21 June, UN Doc S/2012/348, paras 69–71.

[43] Stearns, J (2012) 'From CNDP to M23: The evolution of an armed movement in eastern Congo', Rift Valley Project, Usalama Project, pp49–51; United Nations (2012) 'Final report of the Group of Experts established pursuant to resolution 1533 (2004) concerning the Democratic Republic of the Congo', 15 November, UN Doc S/2012/843, paras 69–81.

[44] ASADHO et al. (2011) 'The Democratic Republic of Congo: Taking a stand on security sector reform'. Some other choice examples include: Oxfam America (2010) 'No will, no way: US-funded security sector reform in the Democratic Republic of Congo'; 'Boshoff, H (2007) 'The demobilization, disarmament and reintegration process in the Democratic Republic of Congo. A never-ending story!', Institute for Security Studies; and 'Melmot, S (2008) 'Candide au Congo: L'échec annoncé de la réforme du secteur de sécurité (RSS)', IFRI Focus stratégique 9, September (author's translation).

[45] Melmot, S (2008) 'Candide au Congo: L'échec annoncé de la réforme du secteur de sécurité (RSS)', IFRI Focus stratégique 9, September (author's translation).

[46] Weber, M (1978) 'Economy and society: An outline of interpretive sociology', University of California Press, p337.

[47] Tilly, C (1985) 'War making and state making as organized crime', in Evans P, Rueschemeyer, D and Skocpol, T (eds) Bringing the state back in, Cambridge University Press, p175.

[48] North, DC, Wallis, JJ and Weingast, BR (1999) 'Violence and social orders: A conceptual framework for interpreting recorded human history', Cambridge University Press, p42.

[49] Stearns J, Verweijen, J and Erikson Baaz, M (2013) 'The national army and armed groups in the eastern Congo: Untangling the Gordian knot of insecurity', Rift Valley Institute, Usalama Project.

[50] SC Res 1794 (2007) UN Doc S/RES/1794, 21 December, para. 13; SC Res 1856 (2008), UN Doc S/RES/1856, 22 December, preamble and para. 3(l).

[51] Radio Okapi (2008) 'DRC security sector reform: Alan Doss recommends coherency in the execution of the programme', 27 February.

[52] United Nations (2008) 'Budget for the United Nations Organization Mission in the Democratic Republic of the Congo for the period from 1 July 2008 to 30 June 2009', 7 April, UN Doc A/62/755; United Nations (2009) 'Performance report on the budget of the United Nations Organization Mission in the Democratic Republic of the Congo for the period from 1 July 2008 to 30 June 2009', 18 December, UN Doc A/64/583.

[53] Boshoff, H (2007) 'The demobilization, disarmament and reintegration process in the Democratic Republic of Congo. A never-ending story!', Institute for Security Studies; Council Joint Action 2007/406/CFSP, 12 June 2007; More, S and Price, M (2010) 'The EU's support to security sector reform in the Democratic Republic of Congo: Perceptions from the field in Spring 2010', Netherlands Institute for International Relations, Conflict Research Unit.

[54] OECD (2005) 'Security sector reform and governance', DAC Guidelines and Reference Series.

[55] Oxfam America (2010) 'No will, no way: US-funded security sector reform in the Democratic Republic of Congo', pp28–30.

[56] Hoebeke, H, Boshoff, H and Vlassenroot, K (2008) 'Assessing security sector reform and its impact on the Kivus', Situation Report, Institute for Security Studies (South Africa); Trefon, T (2011) 'Congo masquerade: The political culture of aid inefficiency and reform failure', Zed Books, pp59–65; Kets, E and de , H (2014) 'Limits to supporting security sector interventions in the DRC', ISS Paper 257.

[57] Oxfam America (2010) 'No will, no way: US-funded security sector reform in the Democratic Republic of Congo', p31.

[58] Melmot, S (2008) 'Candide au Congo: L'échec annoncé de la réforme du secteur de sécurité (RSS)', IFRI Focus stratégique 9, September (author's translation), pp22–3; ASADHO et al. (2011) 'The Democratic Republic of Congo: Taking a stand on security sector reform', p5.

[59] Author interviews with Kinshasa-based diplomats, 2009–10. See indicatively US State Department (2009) 'SSR in the DRC: Embassy convenes Great Lakes Contact Group countries and organizations', internal code cable (8 May), via Wikileaks / Public Library of US Diplomacy; US State Department (2009) 'MONUC head and Great Lakes envoys discuss need for high-level approaches to Kabila', internal code cable (30 December), via Wikileaks / Public Library of US Diplomacy.

[60] United Nations (2012) 'Report of the Secretary-General on MONUSCO', 23 May, UN Doc S/2012/355, paras 57–8.

[61] MONUC (2009) 'SSR–Mil Briefing', internal briefing (19 August), Force Headquarters.

[62] MONUC (2009) 'Aide-mémoire: Propositions pour une réforme limité des FARDC déployées dans les Kivus', internal memorandum (April).

[63] Personal communications with diplomats based in New York around briefing to the Security Council in November 2009; see US State Department (2009) 'Obasanjo on the DRC, Nigeria and African Issues', internal code cable (14 November), via Wikileaks / Public Library of US Diplomacy.

[64] US State Department (2009) 'MONUC head and Great Lakes envoys discuss need for high-level approaches to Kabila', internal code cable (30 December), via Wikileaks / Public Library of US Diplomacy.

[65] Doss, A (2011) 'Great expectations: UN peacekeeping, civilian protection, and the use of force', GCSP Geneva Papers, Research Series No. 4, December.

[66] BBC News (2012) 'UK and the Netherlands withold Rwanda budget aid', 27 July; Al Jazeera (2012) 'Germany latest to suspend Rwanda aid', 28 July; Whitehouse.gov (2012) 'Readout of the President's call with President Kagame', 18 December.

[67] MONUSCO (2011) 'Weekly analytical report', internal report (5 March), South Kivu sub-office.

[68] International Crisis Group (2007) 'Congo: Bringing peace to North Kivu', Africa Report No 133; Wolters, S (2007) 'Trouble in Eastern DRC: The Nkunda factor', Situation Report, Institute for Security Studies (South Africa); US Department of State (2007) 'President Kabila's December 11 meeting with Ambassador and AF Senior Advisor Shortley', internal code cable (12 December), via Wikileaks / Public Library of US Diplomacy.

[69] US Department of State (2008) 'EU ponders military options for DR Congo', internal code cable (16 December), via Wikileaks / Public Library of US diplomacy; Traynor, I (2008) 'UK blocking European Congo force', *Guardian* (UK), 12 December; ICG (2009) 'Congo: Five priorities for a peacebuilding strategy', Africa Report 150, Pts 1–3.

[70] Braeckman, C (2009) 'Le double pari de Kabila et Kagame', *Le Soir* (Belgium), 27 January; United Nations (2009) 'Report of the Secretary-General on MONUC', 27 March, S/2009/160, paras 2–16; United Nations (2009) 'Interim Report of the Group of Experts established pursuant to resolution 1533 (2004)', 18 May, UN Doc S/2009/253, pts III–IV; International Crisis Group (2010) 'Congo: Pas de stabilité au Kivu malgre le rapprochement avec le Rwanda', Rapport Afrique 165; Stearns, J (2012) 'From CNDP to M23: The evolution of an armed movement in eastern Congo', Rift Valley Project, Usalama Project, pts 2–3.

[71] SC Res 1925, 28 May 2010, UN Doc S/RES/1925, para. 11; SC Res 1991, 28 June 2011, S/RES/1991 para. 1.

[72] Martin, B (2012) 'The protection of civilians in the Democratic Republic of the Congo', *Conflict Trends* 2012(2): 33–40.

[73] United Nations (2009) 'Report of the Secretary-General on MONUC', 4 December, UN Doc S/2009/623, paras 9–16.

[74] Guehenno, JM (2009) 'Robust peacekeeping: Building political consensus and strengthening command and control', in Center for International Cooperation, *Robust Peacekeeping: The politics of force*, p8.

[75] Johnstone, I (2006) 'Dilemmas of robust peace operations', in Center for International Cooperation, *Robust Peacekeeping: The politics of force*, p76.

[76] Quoted in Neustadt, RE (1960/1990) 'Presidential power and the modern presidents: The politics of leadership from Roosevelt to Reagan', The Free Press, p10.

[77] Mr Brahimi led UN teams in Haiti, Afghanistan, Iraq and Syria, along with the landmark review of UN peace operations that bears his name. Quote from Brahimi, L and Ahmed, S (2008) 'In pursuit of sustainable peace: The seven deadly sins of mediation', in Center for International Cooperation, *Robust Peacekeeping: The politics of force*, p56.

[78] Booth, D and Unsworth, S (2014) 'Politically smart, locally led development', Discussion Paper, Overseas Development Institute.

Notes to Chapter 3

[1] Roeykens, PA (1876) 'Léopold II et la Conférence géographique de Bruxelles' cited in Hothschild (1998/2006) *King Leopold's ghost: A story of greed, terror and heroism in colonial Africa*, pp45–60.

[2] Glave, EJ (1892) 'In savage Africa; or, Six years of adventure in Congo-land'; Bateman, C (1889) 'The first ascent of the Kasai: Being some records of service under the lone star'.

[3] Conrad, J (1999/2006) 'Heart of Darkness', Project Gutenberg edn, p172.

[4] Donovan, S (2006) 'Touring in extremis: Travel and adventure in the Congo', in Youngs, T (ed) *Travel writing in the nineteenth century: Filling in the blank spaces.*

[5] Vandervelde, E (1909) 'Les derniers jours de l'Etat du Congo: Journal de voyage', Juillet–Octobre 1908.

[6] Wrong, M (2001) 'In the footsteps of Mr Kurtz: Living on the brink of disaster in the Congo'; Sundaram, A (2014) 'Stringer: A reporter's journey in the Congo'; Naipaul, VS (1979) 'A bend in the river'; O'Hanlon, R (1998) 'No mercy: A journey into the heart of the Congo'; Salbi, Z and Shannon, L (2010) 'A thousand sisters: My journey into the worst place on Earth to be a woman'.

[7] Pricewaterhouse Coopers (2013) 'Africa gearing up: Future prospects in Africa for the transportation and logistics industry', at www.pwc.com/africagearingup.

[8] World Bank (2008) 'Project appraisal document: High-priority roads reopening and maintenance project (ProRoutes)', 25 February, p4.

[9] Reported in Kandolo, M (2014) 'Sénat: Fridolin Kasweshi interrogé sur l'état des routes', *Forum des AS*, 18 November.

[10] European Union Delegation in the Democratic Republic of the Congo (2014) 'Présentation: Les infrastructures de transports: la priorité des chantiers', at eeas.europa.org, 19 June (author's translation).

[11] For Security Council usage see SC Res 1856, 22 December 2008, UN Doc S/RES/1856, para. 2.

[12] GoDRC (2009) 'STAREC: Enjeux, défis et perspectives', internal memorandum (undated), Cellule de mobilisation des ressources.

[13] The total gazetted area for the STAREC ended up at 700,000km^2. See GoDRC (2010) 'Ordonnance No. 10/072', *Journal Officiel de la République Démocratique du Congo*, 1 November 2010.

[14] GoDRC (2009) 'Programme de stabilisation et de reconstruction des zones sortant des conflits armés', June, p5.

[15] This section is drawn from SC Res 1794, 21 December 2007, UN Doc S/RES/1794, para. 2; SC Res 1856, 22 December 2008, UN Doc S/RES/1856, para. 2; SC Res 1925, 28 May 2010, UN Doc S/RES/1925, para. 6; SC Res 2098, 28 March 2013, UN Doc S/RES/2098, para. 11 and preamble.

[16] I assume here that the mandate for Province Orientale included the districts of Ituri and Haut-Uéle, and excluded Bas-Uéle and Tshopo. Population figures are definitely approximate given the paucity of reliable data.

[17] Tamagnini, A et al. (2010) 'Strategic review of the International Security and Stabilization Support Strategy for Eastern DR Congo: Final report', July, p13.

[18] GoDRC (2005) 'Monographie de la province du Nord Kivu', Ministère du Plan; author calculations. There is always a good deal of guesswork in demography in eastern Congo due to lack of updated census data.

[19] Herbst, J (2000) 'States and power in Africa: Comparative lessons in authority and control', p11.

[20] Galula, D (1964/2006) 'Counterinsurgency warfare: Theory and practice', Kindle edn, loc 463.

[21] I take this term from Bafilemba, F et al. (2013) 'Mary Robinson's next steps to help end Congo's deadly war', Enough Project.

[22] Stearns, J (2014) 'A year after its defeat, could the M23 make a comeback?', *Congo Siasa*, 9 November.

[23] Acemoglu, D and Robinson, J (2013) 'The roads of the Congo', *Why Nations Fail blog*, 15 August.

[24] Crawford, Y and Turner, T (1985) 'The rise and decline of the Zairian State', Kindle edition, loc 5382–94.

[25] Guevara, EC (1965 / 2012) 'Letter to Fidel Castro, 5/10/1965', in *Congo Diary*, Centre de Estudios Che Guevara.

[26] Prunier, G (2008/2011) 'Africa's world war: Congo, the Rwandan genocide, and the making of a continental catastrophe', Oxford University Press, ch. 4; Stearns, J (2012) 'Dancing in the glory of monsters: the collapse of the Congo and the great war of Africa', Public Affairs, ch. 9.

[27] Vlassenroot, Koen and Raeymaekers, Timothy (2008) 'New political order in the DR Congo? The transformation of regulation', *Afrika Focus* 21: 39–52.

[28] The best overview is Stearns, J (2012) 'Dancing in the glory of monsters: the collapse of the Congo and the great war of Africa', Public Affairs, ch. 17. See also Africa Rights (2000) 'The cycle of conflict: Which way out in the Kivus?', December.

[29] There are few publicly available accounts of the military dimensions. See International Crisis Group (2009) 'Congo: A comprehensive strategy to disarm the FDLR', Africa Report 151, 9 July, part II; United Nations (2009) 'Final report of the Group of Experts on the Democratic Republic of the Congo', 23 November, UN Doc S/2009/603; US Department of State (2010) 'Operation Amani Leo: Old wine in a new bottle?', internal code cable (January), via WikiLeaks / Public Library of US Diplomacy.

[30] Human Rights Watch (2009) '"You will be punished": Attacks on civilians in eastern Congo', December, p15. See also Congo Advocacy Coalition (2009) 'Letter to Sir John Holmes', 6 February.

[31] International Crisis Group (2012) 'Eastern Congo: Why stabilization failed', Africa Briefing 91, 4 October, p5.

[32] For one recent estimate see Vogel, C (2014) 'Mapped armed groups in eastern Congo, 4th edition', 1 November, at christophvogel.net.

[33] MONUC (2009) 'Security and Stabilization Support Strategy for Eastern DRC'.

[34] MONUSCO (2010) 'I-SSSS: Integrated Programme Framework 2009–12', January; MONUSCO (2009), 'International security and stabilization support strategy: Outputs & results', internal working document (December), ODSRSG-RC-HC.

[35] MONUSCO / Alao, B (2011) 'Sud-Kivu province: Opening Shabunda to the world a daunting task', Featured News, 4 July 2011.

[36] MONUSCO (2011) 'Report: Joint mission Bukavu-Shabunda, 12–17 June 2011', internal report, South Kivu sub-office.

[37] MONUSCO (2009) 'Rapport de mission de l'équipe mixte de protection: 17–19 juin 2009', internal report, South Kivu sub-office.

[38] Stearns, J et al. (2013) 'Raia Mutomboki: The flawed peace process in the DRC and the birth of an armed franchise', Rift Valley Institute, Usalama Project, p39; Vogel, C (2014) "Contested statehood, security dilemmas and militia politics: The rise and transformation of Raia Mutomboki in eastern DRC', Annuaire des Grand Lacs 2013/2014, pp299–324; Hoffman, K and Vlassenroot, K (2014) 'Armed groups and the exercise of public authority: The cases of the Mayi-Mayi and Raya Mutomboki in Kalehe, South Kivu', Peacebuilding 2(2): 202–220.

[39] Vogel, C (2014) 'Trouble all over—Where is Raia Mutomboki headed to?', 16 August, christophvogel.net; United Nations (2012) 'Report of the Secretary-General

on MONUSCO', 14 November, UN Doc S/2012/838, paras 11–25; International Crisis Group (2012) 'Eastern Congo: Why stabilization failed', Africa Briefing 91, Appendix E.

40 United Nations (2012) 'Report of the Secretary-General on MONUSCO', 26 January, UN Doc S/2012/65, para. 24; United Nations (2012) 'Report of the Secretary-General on MONUSCO', 23 May, UN Doc S/2012/355, paras 16, 45, 67; MONUSCO (2012) 'International Security and Stabilisation Support Strategy for the DRC: Quarterly Report for January to March 2012'.

41 UNDP (2013) 'Shabunda (Sud Kivu): le défi de la restauration de l'autorité de l'Etat', *Nos Histoires*, September (author's translation).

42 GoDRC (2010) 'Comité sectoriel de suivi du plan de stabilisation et de reconstruction de l'est: composante police / Plan opérationnel', internal draft (April); GoDRC (2009) 'STAREC: Enjeux, défis et perspectives', internal memorandum (undated), Cellule de mobilisation des ressources.

43 United Nations (2007) 'Twenty-fourth report of the Secretary-General on MONUC', 14 November, UN Doc S/2007/671, paras 58–59; United Nations (2009) 'Report of the technical assessment mission to MONUC: 23 February – 6 March 2009', internal report (March), DPKO, paras 102–109.

44 SC Res 1906, 23 December 2009, UN Doc S/RES/1906 (2009), para. 19.

45 Personal communications 2010–11, notably with Protection Cluster in North Kivu and agencies working under Return, Recovery and Reintegration component of the International Security and Stabilisation Support Strategy.

46 Oxfam GB (2014) 'More harm than good? UN's Islands of Stability in DRC', 8 May.

47 Sawyer, I (2013) 'Unbroken violence in Congo', *Foreign Policy*, 25 November.

48 Prendergast, J and Atama, N (2009) 'Eastern Congo: An action plan to end the world's deadliest war', The Enough Project, p9.

49 OECD (2013) 'Upstream implementation of the OECD due diligence guidelines for responsible supply chains of minerals from conflict-affected and high-risk areas: Final report on one-year pilot implementation of the supplement on Tin, Tantalum and Tungsten', p24. For one attempt to map the sector see Spittaels, S and Hilgert, F (2013) 'Analysis of the interactive map of artisanal mining areas in Eastern DR Congo', IPIS.

50 Matthysen, K and Montejano, AZ (2013) '"Conflict minerals" initiatives in DR Congo: Perceptions of local mining communities', IPIS / Humanity United / EurAC, p38.

[51] Tegera, A et al. (2014) 'An open letter' [regarding conflict minerals], September; Matthysen, K and Montejano, AZ (2013) '"Conflict minerals" initiatives in DR Congo: Perceptions of local mining communities', IPIS / Humanity United / EurAC.

[52] Global Witness (2012) 'Coming clean: How supply chain controls can stop Congo's minerals trade fuelling conflict', p15.

[53] Human Rights Watch (2003) 'Ituri covered in blood: Ethnically targeted violence in northern DRC'.

[54] United Nations (2004) 'Operation Artemis: The lessons of the Interim Emergency Multinational Force', Military Division Peacekeeping Best Practices Unit.

[55] Van Reybrouck, D (2010/2013) 'Congo: The epic history of a people', Fourth Estate, p472.

[56] On this period see: United Nations (2003) 'Second special report on MONUC', 27 May 2003, UN Doc S/2003/566; International Crisis Group (2003) 'Congo crisis: Military intervention in Ituri', 13 June; Tamm, H (2013) 'FNI and FRPI: Local resistance and regional alliances in north-eastern Congo', Rift Valley Institute Usalama Project, ch. 3.

[57] International Crisis Group (2003) 'Congo crisis: Military intervention in Ituri', p9.

[58] Senior MONUC official quoted in Autessere, S (2010) 'The trouble with the Congo: Local violence and the failure of international peacebuilding', Cambridge University Press, p208.

[59] Ituri is allotted just a single paragraph in United Nations (2007) 'Twenty-fourth report of the Secretary-General on MONUC', 14 November, UN Doc S/2007/671 (para. 21). Quotation from United Nations (2008) 'Twenty-fifth report of the Secretary-General on MONUC', 2 April, UN Doc S/2008/218.

[60] Human Rights Watch (2007) 'Renewed crisis in North Kivu'; Prendergast, J and Atama, N (2009) 'Eastern Congo: An action plan to end the world's deadliest war', The Enough Project, p11; Paddon, E and Lacaille, G (2011) 'Stabilising the Congo', *Forced Migration Policy Briefing* 8, Refugee Studies Centre, Oxford University, December; International Crisis Group (2012) 'Eastern Congo: Why stabilization failed', Africa Briefing 91; International Alert (2012) 'Ending the deadlock: Towards a new vision of peace in eastern DRC'; Oxfam (2012) '"For me, but without me, is against me": Why efforts to stabilise the Democratic Republic of Congo are not working', Oxfam Lobby Briefing.

[61] United Nations (2008) 'Plan d'action humanitaire 2008: République Démocratique du Congo', Office for the Coordination of Humanitarian Affairs; United Nations

(2009) 'Plan d'action humanitaire 2009: République Démocratique du Congo', Office for the Coordination of Humanitarian Affairs.

[62] Vinck, P et al. (2008) 'Living with fear: A population-based survey on attitudes about peace, justice, and social reconstruction in eastern Democratic Republic of Congo', Berkeley-Tulane Initiative on Vulnerable Populations.

[63] Autessere, S (2010) 'The trouble with the Congo: Local violence and the failure of international peacebuilding', Cambridge University Press, p128.

[64] Adapted from Ghemawat, P (2007) 'Redefining global strategy: Crossing borders in a world where differences still matter', Harvard Business Review Press, ch. 2.

[65] Mamdani, M (1998) 'Understanding the crisis in Kivu: Report of the CODESRIA Mission to the Democratic Republic of Congo September 1997', Center for African Studies, University of Cape Town.

[66] Vinck, P and Pham, PN (2014) 'Searching for lasting peace: Population-based survey on perceptions and attitudes about peace, security and justice in eastern Democratic Republic of the Congo', Harvard Humanitarian Initiative / United Nations Development Programme.

[67] Fahey, D (2013) 'Ituri: Gold, land and ethnicity in north-eastern Congo', Rift Valley Institute Usalama Project, p13.

[68] Mamdani, M (1998) 'Understanding the crisis in Kivu: Report of the CODESRIA Mission to the Democratic Republic of Congo September 1997', Center for African Studies, University of Cape Town.

[69] Pottier, J (2003) 'Emergency in Ituri, DRC: Political complexity, land and other challenges in restoring food security', FAO International Workshop on Food Security; Vlassenroot, K and Huggins, C (2005) 'Land, migration and conflict in Eastern DRC', Institute for Security Studies, pp161–74; van Puijenbroek, J and Ansoms, A (2011) 'A Legacy from the past hindering the future: Land conflicts in Ituri (DRC)', in Ansoms, A and Marysse, S (eds) *Natural Resources and Local Livelihoods in the Great Lakes Region of Africa*, p62.

[70] Tamm, H (2013) 'FNI and FRPI: Local resistance and regional alliances in north-eastern Congo', Rift Valley Institute Usalama Project.

[71] Human Rights Watch (2003) 'Ituri covered in blood: Ethnically targeted violence in northern DRC'; Reyntjens, F (2009) 'The great African war: Congo and regional geopolitics 1986–2006', Cambridge University Press, pp216–221.

[72] Prunier, G (2008 / 11) 'Africa's World War: Congo, the Rwandan genocide, and the making of a continental catastrophe', Oxford University Press, ch. 8.

[73] Muchukiwa, B (2006) 'Territoires ethniques et territoires étatiques: Pouvoirs locaux et conflits interethniques au Sud Kivu (R.D. Congo)', L'Harmattan; Vlassenroot, K (2013) 'South Kivu: Identity, territory, and power in the eastern Congo', Rift Valley Institute Usalama Project.

[74] Vlassenroot, K and Huggins, C (2005) 'Land, migration and conflict in Eastern DRC', Institute for Security Studies, p116.

[75] International Crisis Group (2013) 'Understanding conflict in Eastern Congo (I): The Ruzizi Plain', Africa Report 206, 23 July, pp10–11.

[76] Verweijen, J (2013) 'Anatomy of a feeble analysis: a critical reading of Crisis Group's latest report on the DR Congo', 30 July, at matsutas.wordpress.com.

[77] Ibid.

[78] Huggins, C (2010) 'Land, power and identity: Roots of violent conflict in Eastern DRC', International Alert; Autessere, S (2010) 'The trouble with the Congo: Local violence and the failure of international peacebuilding', Cambridge University Press, ch. 4.

[79] Verweijen, J (2013) 'Anatomy of a feeble analysis: a critical reading of Crisis Group's latest report on the DR Congo', 30 July, at matsutas.wordpress.com; Tegera A et al. (2014) 'An open letter' [regarding conflict minerals], September.

[80] Autessere, S (2010) 'The trouble with the Congo: Local violence and the failure of international peacebuilding', Cambridge University Press, pp42, 91–92, 102–125.

[81] SC Res 1856, 22 December 2008, UN Doc S/RES/1856; SC Res 1906, 23 December 2009, UN Doc S/RES/1906; SC Res 1925, 28 May 2010, UN Doc S/RES/1925; SC Res 1991, 28 June 2011 UN Doc S/RES/1991.

[82] GoDRC (2007) 'Country Assistance Framework 2007–10'.

[83] The sole exceptions are mining and roads, where it was impossible to be vague on this point.

[84] GoDRC (2007) 'Plan d'action pour la réforme de la justice RDC', Ministry of Justice; and GoDRC (2008) 'Feuille de Route', Ministry of Justice, December.

[85] European Commission (2006) 'The European Commission contributes to the restoration of justice in the East of the Democratic Republic of Congo', press release IP/06/845, 26 June.

[86] Klimis, E (2006) 'La justice en RDC (brainstorming)', Groupe de recherche en appui aux politiques de paix, Working Paper 2006/2.

[87] Respectively: Brusset, E et al. (2011) 'Amani labda, peace maybe: Joint evaluation of conflict prevention and peace building in the Democratic Republic of Congo', Synthesis Report, Channel Research; European Court of Auditors (2013) 'EU support for governance in the Democratic Republic of the Congo', Special Report 9. See also European Union (2009) 'Rapport d'évaluation à mi-parcours', March.

[88] European Union (2009) 'Convention de Financement (République Démocratique du Congo): Programme d'appui à la Réforme de la Justice', FED 2009/021351, Annex.

[89] GoDRC (2009) 'Plan de stabilisation et de reconstruction de l'est de la République Démocratique du Congo: Atelier 3, Justice', internal planning document (May), Office of the Prime Minister; GoDRC (2009) 'Programme de stabilisation et de reconstruction des zones sortants de conflits armées (STAREC)'.

[90] GoDRC (2009) 'Plan de stabilisation et de reconstruction de l'est de la République Démocratique du Congo: Atelier 1, Extension de l'autorité de l'état', internal planning document (May), Office of the Prime Minister; GoDRC (2009) 'STAREC: Enjeux, défis et perspectives', internal memorandum (undated), Cellule de mobilisation des ressources.

[91] MONUC (2010) 'International Security and Stabilisation Support Strategy: Integrated Program Framework 2009–12', p9. This comprises less than 1% of a 24,000-word document.

[92] Personal communications with stabilisation coordination officers for North Kivu and South Kivu; author's own experience in Maniema province.

[93] See e.g. MONUC (2011) 'Quarterly report for the International Security and Stabilisation Support Strategy', April–June; GoDRC (2010) 'Fiche de projet: Appui à la sensibilisation des populations pour la restauration de l'autorité de l'Etat pour le retour de l'administration légale dans l'axe Bunia-Boga, Ofaye, Chabi et Mitego', project concept, Bureau du District de l'Ituri, December.

[94] Paddon, E and Lacaille, G (2011) 'Stabilising the Congo', *Forced Migration Policy Briefing* 8, Refugee Studies Centre, Oxford University.

[95] Oxfam (2012) '"For me, but without me, is against me": Why efforts to stabilise the Democratic Republic of Congo are not working', Oxfam Lobby Briefing.

[96] Fahey, D (2012) 'What's happening in Ituri?', *Texas in Africa*, 20 February.

[97] Mbambi, VK et al. (2009) 'Les conflits fonciers en Ituri: de l'imposition à la consolidation de la paix', RCN Justice et Démocratie, September, pt 3. On total caseload see Mongo, E et al. (2009) 'Conflits fonciers en Ituri: Poids du passé et défis pour l'avenir de la paix', Reseau Haki na Amani / IKV Pax Christi, December, ch. 4.

[98] Mugangu, S (2007) 'Appui à la consolidation de la justice et de la paix sociale en Ituri: Evaluation de l'impact des activités du projet', RCN Justice et Démocratie, July (author's translation.)

[99] Ibid, p39.

[100] Personal communications with staff from UNHABITAT, REJUSCO and the UN Group of Experts, 2011-14.

[101] UNHABITAT et al. (2011) 'Projet pilote de sécurité foncière intégrée en Ituri', February (author's translation). On the Land Commission see International Crisis Group (2008) 'Congo: Four priorities for sustainable peace in Ituri', Africa Report 140, 13 May; Vircoulon, T and Liégois, F (2010) 'Violences en brousse: Le 'peacebuilding' international face aux conflits fonciers', IFRI Programme Afrique subsaharienne, pp20–21.

[102] de Vit, PV (2012) 'Program evaluation: Land conflict prevention and mitigation program, Eastern Democratic Republic of the Congo, UN Habitat', February; author copies on file of program documents from Reseau Haki Na Amani, Bunia.

[103] Reseau Haki na Amani / International Alert (2010) 'Guide pratique de résolution et de prévention des conflits fonciers', September, p22.

[104] Vircoulon, T and Liégeois, F (2012) 'How to create a public policy in a failed state: The challenge of securing land rights in eastern Congo', IFRI Sub-Saharan Africa Programme. See also International Alert (2012) 'Ending the deadlock: Towards a new vision of peace in Eastern DRC', September, pp42–43.

[105] Mbambi, VK et al. (2009) 'Les conflits fonciers en Ituri: de l'imposition à la consolidation de la paix', RCN Justice et Démocratie, September, p57; van Puijenbroek, J and Ansoms, A (2011) 'A Legacy from the past hindering the future: Land conflicts in Ituri (DRC)', in Ansoms, A and Marysse, S (eds) *Natural Resources and Local Livelihoods in the Great Lakes Region of Africa*; Fahey, D (2011) 'The trouble with Ituri', *African Security Review* 20(2): 108–113; International Alert (2012) 'Ending the deadlock: Towards a new vision of peace in Eastern DRC', September, pp42–43; personal communications with UNHABITAT staff working on land conflict mediation.

[106] Ibid.

[107] MONUC/ODSRSG-RC-HC (2009–11) 'ISSSS restauration de l'autorité de l'état: sommaire', from August 2009 through January 2011; MONUC (2012) 'International Security and Stabilisation Support Strategy for the DRC: Quarterly Report for January to March 2012'.

[108] MONUC (2009) 'Points arising from visits to Haut Uele and Ituri in Province Orientale', internal note to file, Eastern Coordination, February; personal

communications with MONUC Civil Affairs and UNDP Bunia, 2009–11. This was still ongoing in 2014: see Radio Okapi (2014) 'Les notables de Walendu-Bindi protestent contre la suspension du programme Ilot du stabilité', 27 September.

[109] MONUC (2010) 'Weekly situation report: 19 December', internal report, Bunia sub-office; also editions of 8 January 2011, 22 January 2011, 11 March 2011; MONUC (2011) 'Report for JPT mission to Aveba, 26–29 May 2011', internal report, Bunia sub-office.

[110] Stanley, HM (2013) 'In Darkest Africa: Or, the quest, rescue and retreat of Emin Governor of Equatoria', cited in Fahey, D (2013) 'Ituri: Gold, land and ethnicity in north-eastern Congo', Rift Valley Institute Usalama Project.

[111] United Nations (2012) 'Final report of the Group of Experts established pursuant to resolution 1533 (2004) concerning the Democratic Republic of the Congo', 15 November, UN Doc S/2012/843, paras 82–89; Tamm, H (2013) 'FNI and FRPI: Local resistance and regional alliances in north-eastern Congo', Rift Valley Institute Usalama Project; Radio Okapi (2013) 'Ituri: l'armée et le FRPI s'engagent à assurer la sécurité des déplacés à Walendu Bindi', 4 September.

[112] Paddon, E and Lacaille, G (2011) 'Stabilising the Congo', *Forced Migration Policy Briefing* 8, Refugee Studies Centre, Oxford University; International Alert (2012) 'Ending the deadlock: Towards a new vision of peace in Eastern DRC', September; Oxfam (2012) '"For me, but without me, is against me": Why efforts to stabilise the Democratic Republic of Congo are not working', Oxfam Lobby Briefing.

[113] Quote from Finer, SE (1997) 'The history of government from earliest times', vol. 1; quoted in Herbst, J (2000) 'States and power in Africa: Comparative lessons in authority and control' Herbst, J (2000) 'States and power in Africa: Comparative lessons in authority and control'. Latter terms from Jackson, R (1990) 'Quasi-states: Sovereignty, International Relations and the Third World; Kopytoff, I (1989) 'The African frontier: The reproduction of traditional african societies'.

[114] United Nations (2014) 'Report of the Secretary-General: Peacebuilding in the aftermath of conflict', 23 September, UN Doc A/69/399-0S/2014/694.

[115] Quick, ID (2011) 'A transactional model of sovereignty', *Peacekeeping Whiteboard*, September; Quick, ID (2012) 'A bad man model of public institutions', *Peacekeeping Whiteboard*, May.

Notes to Chapter 4

[1] G7+ (2010) 'Statement of the G7+ Heads of State', 20 September. See also International Dialogue on Peacebuilding and Statebuilding (2010) 'Dili declaration: A new vision for peacebuilding and statebuilding', 10 April.

[2] OECD (2010) 'Fragile States Principles Monitoring Survey: Global Report', via oecd.org/dacfragilestates. The African Union's estimate was even higher: African Union (2010) 'Multi-disciplinary mission for evaluation of post-conflict reconstruction and development needs in DRC and Burundi', via peaceau.org.

[3] European Court of Auditors (2013) 'EU support for governance in the Democratic Republic of the Congo', Special Report 9, via eca.europa.eu.

[4] Brusset, E et al. (2011) 'Amani labda, peace maybe: Joint evaluation of conflict prevention and peace building in the Democratic Republic of Congo', Synthesis Report, Channel Research.

[5] International Dialogue on Peacebuilding and Statebuilding (2011) 'A new deal for engagement in fragile states'. See as background: International Dialogue on Peacebuilding and Statebuilding (2009) 'Concept paper for the international dialogue on peacebuilding and statebuilding' and (2010) 'Dili Declaration: A new vision for peacebuilding and statebuilding'.

[6] SC Res 1756, 15 May 2007, UN Doc S/RES/1756; SC Res 1856, 22 December 2008, UN Doc S/RES/1856; SC Res 1925, 28 May 2010, UN Doc S/RES/1925; SC Res 2098, 28 March 2013, UN Doc S/RES/2098. See Quick, ID (2013) 'The Security Council's (perpetual) struggle to get a handle on DRC', *Rethink Fragility*, 12 April.

[7] United Nations (2000) 'Note of guidance on relations between Representatives of the Secretary-General, Resident Coordinators and Humanitarian Coordinators', 30 October; United Nations (2006) 'Note from the Secretary-General: Guidance on integrated missions', 9 February; United Nations (2006) 'Integrated Missions Planning Process (IMPP): Guidelines endorsed by the Secretary-General in 2006', 13 June; United Nations (2008) 'Decision No. 2008/24—Integration', 25 June.

[8] SC Res 1906, UN Doc S/RES/1906 (2009), para. 2.

[9] Stearns, J (2010) 'As peace returns to the Congo, the UN leaves', *Congo Siasa*, 5 March 2010; Boshoff, H (2010) 'MONUC to leave the DRC, mission unaccomplished?', Institute for Security Studies (Pretoria), 26 April 2010; Hara, F (2010) 'Time to pull out UN troops in Congo? Not so fast', *Christian Science Monitor*, 14 May 2010; BBC News (2010) 'Can DRC cope without UN force?', 28 May 2010.

[10] United Nations (2010) 'Thirty-first report of the Secretary-General on MONUC', 30 March, UN Doc S/2010/164, para. 101.

[11] Security Council Report (2010) 'Monthly forecast', April; Security Council Report (2010) 'Special research report no. 2: Seeking a new compact: Resolution 1906 and the future of MONUC'; United Nations (2010) 'Briefing to the UN Security Council by Alan Doss', internal remarks, 13 April.

[12] MONUC (2010) 'Weekly analytical reports', internal reports of 13 March, 27 March, 17 April, 8 May, North Kivu sub-office; MONUC (2010) 'Daily report', internal report (13 April), Ituri sub-office; MONUC (2010) 'Weekly assessment report', internal report (8 May), Ituri sub-office; MONUC (2010) 'Weekly analytical reports', internal reports of 1 May, 8 May, 29 May, South Kivu sub-office.

[13] DRC Protection Cluster (2010) 'Briefing note to the Security Council: Protection of civilians needs continued international engagement', May; MONUC (2010) 'MONUC drawdown and the ISSSS', internal memorandum (April), ODSRSG-RC-HC. Personal communications with UN agencies and non-governmental organisations based in Goma and Bukavu in 2010.

[14] US Department of State (2010) 'Testimony of Assistant Secretary for Bureau of African Affairs: The Great Lakes Region: Current conditions and US policy', House Foreign Affairs Subcommittee on Africa and Global Health of House Foreign Affairs Committee, 25 May 2010.

[15] SC Res 1925, 28 May 2010, UN Doc S/RES/1925, para. 1.

[16] SC Res 1906, 23 December 2009, UN Doc S/RES/1906, para. 2.

[17] United Nations (2010) (2010) 'Thirty-first report of the Secretary-General on MONUC', 30 March, UN Doc S/2010/164, para. 33.

[18] United Nations (2010) 'Budget for MONUC for the period from 1 July 2010 to 30 June 2011', 16 February, UN Doc A/64/670, Annex III, Organization Chart A.

[19] This section is a close reading of United Nations (2010) 'Thirty-first report of the Secretary-General on MONUC', 30 March, UN Doc S/2010/164. I take the term 'factoring' from Jones, BD (1994) 'Reconceiving decision-making in democratic politics: Attention, choice and public policy', University of Chicago Press, pp161–164.

[20] United Nations (2012) 'Evaluation of the Technical Assessment Mission (TAM) process', internal report, Division of Policy, Evaluation and Training; MONUSCO (2011) 'End of assignment report: Ian D Quick', internal report (30 August), ODSRG-RC-HC. The term is sometimes used elsewhere: see Mintzberg, H (1994) 'The rise and fall of strategic planning: Reconceiving roles for planning, plans, planners', The Free Press, ch. 2.

[21] Landau, M (1973) 'On the concept of a self-correcting organization', *Public Administration Review* 33(6): 536.

[22] SC Res 671, UN Doc S/2007/671, para. 53; SC Res 160, UN Doc S/2009/160, paras 38–39; SC Res 472, UN Doc S/2009/472, para. 78.

[23] United Nations: (2007) 'Twenty-third report of the Secretary-General on MONUC', 20 March, UN Doc S/2007/156; (2007) 'Twenty-fourth report of the Secretary-General on MONUC', 14 November, UN Doc S/2007/671; (2008) 'Twenty-fifth report of the Secretary-General on MONUC', 2 April, UN Doc S/2008/218; (2008) 'Fourth special report of the Secretary-General on MONUC', 21 November, UN Doc S/2008/728; (2009) 'Twenty-seventh report of the Secretary-General on MONUC', 27 March, UN Doc S/2009/160; (2009) 'Twenty-ninth report of the Secretary-General on MONUC', 18 September, UN Doc S/2009/472; (2009) 'Thirtieth report of the Secretary-General on MONUC', 8 December UN Doc S/2009/626; (2010) 'Thirty-first report of the Secretary-General on MONUC', 30 March, UN Doc S/2010/164; (2010) 'Report of the Secretary-General on MONUSCO', 8 October, UN Doc S/2010/512; (2011) 'Report of the Secretary-General on MONUSCO', 17 January, UN Doc S/2011/020; (2011) 'Report of the Secretary-General on MONUSCO', 12 May, UN Doc S/2011/298; (2011) 'Report of the Secretary-General on MONUSCO', 24 October, UN Doc S/2011/656; (2012) 'Report of the Secretary-General on MONUSCO', 26 January, UN Doc S/2012/65; (2012) 'Report of the Secretary-General on MONUSCO', 23 May, UN Doc S/2012/355; (2012) 'Report of the Secretary-General on MONUSCO', 14 November, UN Doc S/2012/838.

[24] The reports in question were United Nations (2011) 'Report of the Secretary-General on MONUSCO', 17 January, UN Doc S/2011/20, para. 67; and United Nations (2011) 'Report of the Secretary-General on MONUSCO', 12 May, UN Doc S/2011/298, paras 36–37.

[25] Remark of Sir Samuel Goldman, a former Treasury Secretary in the United Kingdom, cited in Heclo, H and Wildavsky, A (1974/1981) 'The private government of public money', Palgrave Macmillan, p24.

[26] United Nations (1999) 'Report of the Secretary-General to the Security Council on the Protection of Civilians in Armed Conflict', 8 September, UN Doc S/1999/957, para. 68.

[27] For the Sierra Leone mandate see SC Res 1270, 22 October 1999, UN Doc S/RES/1270, para. 14. For the DRC mandate see SC Res 1291, 24 February 2000, S/RES/1291, para. 8.

[28] For succinct overview of this period see Holt, V and Taylor, G (2009) 'Protecting civilians in the context of UN peacekeeping operations', Department of Peacekeeping / Office for the Coordination of Humanitarian Affairs, pp241–287; Boutellis, JA (2013) 'From crisis to reform: Peacekeeping strategies for the protection

of civilians in the Democratic Republic of the Congo', *Stability: International Journal of Security and Development* 2(3): 1–11.

[29] United Nations (2008) '6024th meeting of the Security Council', 26 November, UN Doc S/PV/6024.

[30] SC Res 1794, 21 December 2007, UN Doc S/RES/1794, para. 5. The same formula was repeated in successive mandates over the next few years.

[31] United Nations (2010) 'UN system-wide strategy for the protection of civilians in the Democratic Republic of the Congo', January, p2.

[32] Martin, B (2012) 'The protection of civilians in the Democratic Republic of the Congo', *Conflict Trends* 2012(2): 33–40.

[33] Ibid; Boutellis, JA (2013) 'From crisis to reform: Peacekeeping strategies for the protection of civilians in the Democratic Republic of the Congo', *Stability: International Journal of Security and Development* 2(3): 1–11; Mahoney, L (2013) 'Non-military strategies for civilian protection in the DRC', Fieldview Solutions.

[34] A non-exhaustive list includes: the Kofi Annan International Peacekeeping Training Centre; the US-based Peace Operations Training Institute; the UN Institute for Training and Research; the Rwanda Peace Academy; the Nigerian Army Peacekeeping Centre; the Brazilian Peace Operations Joint Training Centre; and the Department of Peacekeeping's own Integrated Training Service.

[35] Quick, ID (2013) 'Tactical success, strategic failure: UN peacekeeping and the protection of civilians', *Rethink Fragility*, 13 December.

[36] DRC Protection Cluster (2013) 'Protection cluster and protection of civilians: Protection of civilians in the DRC', fact sheet; DRC Protection Cluster (2011) 'Manuel de bonnes pratiques pour la protection humanitaire et la Cluster Protection en RDC', p36. Both via globalprotectioncluster.org.

[37] United Nations (2012) 'Protection of civilian (POC) resource and capability matrix for implementation of UN peacekeeping operations with POC mandates', Department of Peacekeeping Operations, February.

[38] Holt, V and Taylor, G (2009) 'Protecting civilians in the context of UN peacekeeping operations', Department of Peacekeeping / Office for the Coordination of Humanitarian Affairs; Mahoney, L (2013) 'Non-military strategies for civilian protection in the DRC', Fieldview Solutions.

[39] Whitman, T (2010) 'Joint Protection Teams: A model for enhancing civilian security', Institute for Inclusive Security; United Nations (2012) 'Protection of civilians: Coordination mechanisms in UN Peacekeeping Missions, DPKFO/DFS Comparative Study and toolkit', Department of Peacekeeping Operations /

Department of Field Support; Martin, B (2012) 'The protection of civilians in the Democratic Republic of the Congo', *Conflict Trends* 2012(2): 33–40.

[40] International Crisis Group (2012) 'Open letter to the United Nations Security Council on the situation in the Democratic Republic of Congo', 11 June.

[41] Polgreen, L (2008) 'A massacre in Congo, despite nearby support', *The New York Times*, 11 December; PBS America (2009) 'Can the UN keep the peace?', transcript, 15 May; Howden, D (2010) 'We have failed, admits UN, as fresh wave of Congo rapes emerges', *The Independent* (UK), 9 September. For NGO briefs see, among many others, Human Rights Watch (2009) '"You will be punished": Attacks on civilians in eastern Congo', December 13, ch. VII; Refugees International (2010) 'Last line of defence: How peacekeepers can better protect civilians', 24 February; Oxfam GB et al. (2010) 'Ghosts of Christmas past: Protecting civilians from the LRA', Joint NGO briefing paper, 14 December.

[42] Human Rights Watch (2008) 'Killings in Kiwanja: The UN's inability to protect civilians', December 11, pt VII.

[43] Kemp, E (2012) 'DRC protection cluster co-facilitation—lessons learned', accessible via humanitarianresponse.info.

[44] United Nations (2010) 'UN system-wide strategy for the protection of civilians in the Democratic Republic of the Congo'; United Nations (2012) 'Protection of civilians: Coordination mechanisms in UN Peacekeeping Missions, DPKFO/DFS Comparative Study and toolkit', Department of Peacekeeping Operations / Department of Field Support. For general accounts see Culbert, V (2011) 'Protection cluster co-facilitation in the DRC: Lessons learned for Oxfam's Protection Cluster Support Project' and Kemp, E (2012) 'DRC protection cluster co-facilitation— lessons learned', accessible via humanitarianresponse.info. For sample outputs see Cluster Protection (2012) 'Rapport trimestriel du cluster protection au sud Kivu— avril/juin 2012', via globalprotectioncluster.org.

[45] See, among others, United Nations (2009) 'Lessons learned note on the protection of civilians in un peacekeeping operations: dilemmas, emerging Practices and Lessons', internal report, DPKO/DFS; Holt, V and Taylor, G (2009) 'Protecting civilians in the context of UN peacekeeping operations', Department of Peacekeeping / Office for the Coordination of Humanitarian Affairs.

[46] United Nations (2013) 'Review of the reporting by United Nations peacekeeping missions on the protection of civilians: Report of the Office of Internal Oversight Services', 15 March, UN Doc A/67/795, paras 52–59; United Nations (2014) 'Evaluation of the implementation and results of protection of civilians mandates in United Nations peacekeeping operations: Report of the Office of Internal Oversight Services', 7 March 2014, UN Doc A/68/787.

[47] Quick, ID (2011) 'What are peacekeepers looking for? (According to their routine reporting)', *Peacekeeping Whiteboard*, 18 October.

[48] United Nations (1999) 'Report of the Secretary-General to the Security Council on the Protection of Civilians in Armed Conflict', 8 September, UN Doc S/1999/957.

[49] See Chapter 2, section 1. I have been much too categorical on this myself: see Quick, ID (2011) 'Poor man's COIN: On counter-insurgency in fragile states', *Peacekeeping Whiteboard*. The phrase, *bellum omnium contra omnes*, comes from the most famous passage in Hobbes' *Leviathan* (1651).

[50] Prendergast, J and Atama, N (2009) 'Eastern Congo: An action plan to end the world's deadliest war', The Enough Project.

[51] Security Council Report (2008) 'Cross-cutting report No 2: Protection of Civilians', pt 6(h); Holt, V and Taylor, G (2009) 'Protecting civilians in the context of UN peacekeeping operations', Department of Peacekeeping / Office for the Coordination of Humanitarian Affairs, pp241–287.

[52] 'The Democratic Republic of Congo: Taking a stand on security sector reform' (2011) p3. This is a joint report of eight international and five Congolese non-governmental organisations.

[53] MONUSCO (2011) 'Atelier de travail sur la stabilisation', internal agenda document (June), ODSRSG-RC-HC. Recapped in MONUSCO (2011) 'ISSSS Monthly Update: 1 to 30 June'; MONUSCO (2011) 'Quarterly report on the International Security and Stabilisation Support Strategy: April to June 2011'.

[54] Summarised in MONUSCO (2011) 'Fiches de projets statistics', internal record (August), ODSRSG-RC-HC.

[55] MONUSCO (2011) 'ISSSS Indicateurs: Révision de 31 Juillet 2011', internal working document, ODSRSG-RC-HC.

[56] Bailey, S (2011) 'Humanitarian action, early recovery and stabilization in the Democratic Republic of Congo', Humanitarian Policy Group, HPG Working Paper, p7.

[57] Coghlan, B et al. (2009) 'Update on mortality in the Democratic Republic of Congo: Results from a third nationwide survey', *Disaster Med. Public Health Prep.* 3(2): 88–96.

[58] Author conversations, 2009–12. See Autessere, S (2010) 'The trouble with the Congo: Local violence and the failure of international peacebuilding', Cambridge University Press, pp193–202, 220–221.

[59] See United Nations (2009) 'Report of the Secretary-General on peacebuilding in the immediate aftermath of conflict', 11 June, UN Doc A/63/881-S/2009/304, para. 33; Ball, N and van Beijnum, M (2009) 'Review of the Peacebuilding Fund', Joint evaluation for Canada, the Netherlands, Norway, Sweden and the United Kingdom; Campbell, S et al. (2014) 'Independent external evaluation: UN Peacebuilding Fund project portfolio in Burundi', 2007–13', pp49–50.

[60] Eide, EB et al. (2005) 'Report on integrated missions: Practical perspectives and recommendations', independent study for the expanded UN ECHA Core Group, pp19–20.

[61] MONUSCO (2011) 'Quarterly report on the ISSSS: April to June 2011'.

[62] UNDP / Multi-Partner Trust Fund Office (2011) 'Deuxième rapport annuel consolidé d'activités du Fonds pour la Stabilisation et le Relèvement de la République Démocratique du Congo', available via www.mptf.org, p9.

[63] United Nations (2009) 'Report of the Secretary-General on peacebuilding in the immediate aftermath of armed conflict', 11 June, UN Doc A/63/881-S/2009/304.

[64] Smith, D et al. (2004) 'Towards a strategic framework for peacebuilding: Getting their act together', Overview report of the Joint Utstein Study of Peacebuilding, Norweigan Ministry of Foreign Affairs, pp10–11; United Nations (2012) 'Civilian capacity in the aftermath of conflict: Independent report of the Senior Advisory Group', para. 14, available via www.civcap.info.

[65] Booth, D and Unsworth, S (2014) 'Politically smart, locally led development', Overseas Development Institute, Discussion Paper, p4.

[66] MONUSCO (2010) 'I-SSSS: Integrated Programme Framework 2009–12', pp8–9.

[67] Tamagnini, A et al. (2010) 'Strategic Review of the International Security and Stabilization Support Strategy for Eastern DR Congo: Final report'.

[68] Paddon, E and Lacaille, G (2011) 'Stabilising the Congo', *Forced Migration Policy Briefing* 8, Refugee Studies Centre, Oxford University; International Crisis Group (2012) 'Eastern Congo: Why stabilization failed', Africa Briefing 91, pt C; Oxfam (2012) '"For me, but without me, is against me": Why efforts to stabilise the Democratic Republic of Congo are not working', Oxfam Lobby Briefing.

[69] MONUC (2010) 'Presentation to Security Council on Integrated Strategic Framework', internal presentation (February), ODRSG-RC-HC.

[70] United Nations (2008) Policy Committee decisions of 25 June 2008 and 2 June 2009; SC Res 1906, 23 December 2009, UN Doc S/RES/1906, para. 40. MONUC's 2010–11 budget lifted its lifetime total to USD 10.2bn before adjusting for inflation: Quick, ID (2014) 'Peacekeeping agendas dataset', held by author.

[71] MONUC (2009) 'Integrated strategic framework version 0.0', internal draft, September.

[72] Personal communications with New York based staff, 2010–11; United Nations (2010) 'Thirty-first report of the Secretary-General on MONUC', 30 March, UN Doc S/2010/164, paras 18–21.

[73] This is referred to obliquely in (2010) 'Thirty-first report of the Secretary-General on MONUC', 30 March, UN Doc S/2010/164, para. 99.

[74] MONUSCO (2011) 'UN Transitional Framework for DRC', internal planning document, ODSRSG-RC-HC. See also UN Development Group (2012) '2011 Resident Coordinator Annual Report', available via www.undg.org.

[75] Pirandello, L; Musa, M (tr) (1995) 'Six characters in search of an author', DigiReads, Acts I–II.

[76] Baumgartner, FR, Jones, BD and Mortensen, PB (2014) 'Punctuated equilibrium theory: Explaining stability and change in public policy-making', in Sabatier, PA and Weible, CM (eds) *Theories of the policy process*, Westview Press.

[77] Simon, HA (1997) 'Administrative behavior: A study of decision-making processes in administrative organisations', 4th edn, the Free Press.

[78] United Nations (2012) 'Protection of civilians coordination mechanisms in UN peacekeeping missions: DPKO/DFS comparative study and toolkit', Department of Peacekeeping Operations / Department of Field Support; Martin, B (2012) 'The protection of civilians in the Democratic Republic of the Congo', *Conflict Trends* 2012(2): 33–40; Mahoney L (2013) 'Non-military strategies for civilian protection in the DRC', Fieldview Solutions.

Notes to Chapter 5

[1] MONUC (2010) 'Integrated strategic framework version 2.0', internal draft, ODSRSG-RC-HC.

[2] MONUC (2008) 'Background briefing: UN support for security and stabilization of eastern DRC', internal briefing note, ODSRSG-RC-HC; MONUSCO (2010) 'I-SSSS: Integrated Programme Framework 2009–12', January.

[3] Among public documents see: MONUC (2009), 'Towards peace and stability', fact sheet, 2009; MONUSCO (2010) 'I-SSSS: Integrated Programme Framework 2009–12', January; MONUSCO (2010) 'ISSSS Quarterly Report, September–December 2010'; MONUSCO (2011) 'ISSSS Quarterly Report, January to March 2011'; MONUC / ODSRSG-RC-HC (2010) 'International Security and Stabilisation Support Strategy: General Briefing', internal presentation, March.

[4] MONUC (2010) 'International Security and Stabilisation Support Strategy: General Briefing', internal presentation (March), ODSRSG-RC-HC; MONUSCO HC (2011) 'Presentation to Heads of Office Conference: Stabilisation Support Unit', internal briefing (July), ODSRSG-RC-HC.

[5] MONUSCO (2011) 'ISSSS Quarterly report', internal code cable (February), ODSRSG-RC-HC; MONUSCO (2011) 'High-level meeting on stabilization', internal code cable (February), ODSRSG-RC-HC; MONUSCO (2011) 'High-level meeting on stabilization', internal code cable (May), ODSRSG-RC-HC.

[6] UNDP / Multi-Donor Trust Fund Office (2009) 'Stabilization and Recovery Funding Facility for the Democratic Republic of Congo: Terms of reference', 5 November.

[7] OECD-DAC (2008) 'The Paris Declaration on Aid Effectiveness and the Accra Agenda for Action', via www.oecd.org.

[8] G7+ (2010) 'Statement of the G7+ Heads of State', 20 September. See also International Dialogue on Peacebuilding and Statebuilding (2010) 'Dili declaration: A new vision for peacebuilding and statebuilding', 10 April.

[9] Rorison, S (2008) 'Congo: Democratic Republic', Bradt travel guides.

[10] GoDRC (2011) 'Invitation à le réunion des partenaires STAREC/ISSSS', internal correspondence (3 February), Cabinet du Vice-Premier-Ministre.

[11] Author's personal notes from event; MONUSCO (2010) 'Réunion des Partenaires ISSSS / STAREC': 15–16 fevrier 2011', internal agenda document, ODSRSG-RC-HC. Recapitulated in MONUSCO (2011) 'ISSSS Monthly report: 1 to 28 Feb 2011'; MONUSCO (2011) 'ISSSS Quarterly Report, January to March 2011'.

12 MONUSCO (2011) 'Réunion des partenaires ISSSS/STAREC', internal presentation (February), ODSRSG-RC-HC. Excluding three title slides.

13 MONUSCO (2011) 'High-level meeting on stabilization', internal code cable (February), ODSRSG-RC-HC.

14 Copy of remarks on file with author. No public minutes were issued for this meeting.

15 MONUC (2010) 'Note de discussion sur la Stratégie de Restauration de l'Autorité de l'état dans le contexte du STAREC/ISSSS', internal briefing document (March), ODSRSG-RC-HC; MONUSCO / GoDRC (2010) 'STAREC état de lieu : l'état de droit', internal briefing document (August), STAREC Technical Secretariat.

16 MONUSCO (2010) 'ISSSS Update for 16 August to 15 September 2010'; MONUSCO (2011) 'ISSSS Quarterly Report, April to June 2011'.

17 Paddon, E and Lacaille, G (2011) 'Stabilising the Congo', *Forced Migration Policy Briefing* 8, Refugee Studies Centre, Oxford University, December.

18 Ordonnance no. 10/072, 30 October 2010, Journal Officiel de la République Démocratique du Congo, no. 21. See also Ordonnance no. 09/051, 29 June 2009, Journal Officiel de la République Démocratique du Congo, numéro spécial de 8 juillet 2009.

19 Constitution de la République Démocratique du Congo, May 2005, Title III, via wikisource.fr.

20 GoDRC (2009) 'Compte rendu de la première réunion du comité de suivi du STAREC', 22 October; GoDRC (2010) 'Compte rendu de la deuxième réunion du comité de suivi du STAREC', 1 April; GoDRC (2010) 'Compte rendu de la troisième réunion du comité de suivi du STAREC', 13 December; GoDRC (2011) 'Compte rendu de la quatrième réunion du comité de suivi du STAREC', 15 May.

21 Personal observations, 2009–12. The first such report was MONUSCO (2010) 'International Security and Stabilisation Support Strategy: Report to the Stabilisation Funding Board'.

22 UNDP/GoDRC (2008) 'Soutien a la stratégie de sécurité et la stabilisation a l'est de la RDC', internal programme document, April; UNOPS/USAID (2008) 'Support to stabilization strategy along the Rutshuru–Ishasha axis', internal project document, September.

23 Personal communications with ministers in North Kivu and Maniema provinces. For similar findings see: GoDRC (2010) 'Compte rendu de la deuxième réunion du comité de suivi du STAREC', 1 April; Paddon, E and , G (2011) 'Stabilising the Congo', *Forced Migration Policy Briefing* 8, Refugee Studies Centre, Oxford University;

Oxfam (2012) "'For me, but without me, is against me": Why efforts to stabilise the Democratic Republic of Congo are not working', Oxfam Lobby Briefing, pp31–32.

[24] GoDRC (2011) 'Plan d'action', internal memorandum (March), STAREC Technical Secretariat.

[25] Bashonga, PL (2010) 'L'interview de la semaine', *STAREC Infos* 17 (author's translation).

[26] The official figure was USD 20m but this could never be verified. Personal communications with UNDP and MONUSCO staff from 2013–14; MONUSCO (2012) 'ISSSS Quarterly Report, January to March 2012'.

[27] Generally on this point see GoDRC / European Union (2008) 'Mesure de la performance de la gestion des finances publiques en République Démocratique du Congo, selon la méthodologie PEFA', pp21–22; available via europa.eu. The 2012 edition suggests little change.

[28] Autessere, S (2010) 'The trouble with the Congo: Local violence and the failure of international peacebuilding', Cambridge University Press, p98; Demetriou, S and Quick, ID (2012) 'The sobering lessons of stabilization in eastern Democratic Republic of Congo', unpublished manuscript; personal communications with diplomatic staff in Kinshasa and Goma, 2008–11.

[29] United Nations (2010) 'Budget for MONUSCO for the period from 1 July 2010 to 30 June 2011', UN Doc A/64/670; personal communications with MONUSCO staff. Calculated as sum of grades D1–D2 and ASG–USG.

[30] Autesserre, S (2014) 'Peaceland: Conflict resolution and the everyday politics of international intervention', Cambridge University Press, Kindle edn at 3568, 2847.

[31] Tamagnini, A et al. (2010) 'Strategic review of the International Security and Stabilization Support Strategy for eastern DR Congo: Final report'.

[32] Personal communications with MONUSCO's South Kivu coordination team; MONUSCO (2010) 'CTC Liste de présence', internal record (August), South Kivu sub-office; MONUSCO (2010) 'CTC 17 Aout 2010: Compte rendu', internal record, South Kivu sub-office; Radio Okapi (2010) 'Marcellin Cishambo: « Le Starec n'a pas encore atteint sa vitesse de croisière »', 25 August.

[33] On the formal requirements see UNDP / Multi-Donor Trust Fund Office (2009) 'Stabilization and Recovery Funding Facility for the Democratic Republic of Congo: Terms of reference', available via mptf.undp.org. For comments by senior officials see DigitalCongo (2011) 'Le programme de stabilisation en RDC suscite espoir malgré les défis à relever, affirme Adolphe Lumanu', 25 May; La Référence, 'Muzito fixe les priorités d'avenir pour l'Est', 28 May.

[34] Radio Okapi (2010) 'Marcellin Cishambo: « Le Starec n'a pas encore atteint sa vitesse de croisière »', 25 August.

[35] MONUSCO (2010) 'Stabilisation and Recovery Funding Facility: Briefing note on procedures', August; GoDRC/MONUSCO (2010) 'Format fiche de projet'; MONUSCO/ODSRSG-RC-HC (2010) 'Proposition de projets ISSSS / Financement de projets ISSSS', fact sheet.

[36] MONUSCO/ODSRSG-RC-HC (2010) 'ISSSS biweekly update: 1 to 15 October 2010' and 'ISSSS biweekly update: 16 to 31 October'; MONUSCO/ODSRSG-RC-HC (2011) 'ISSSS monthly report: 1 to 28 Feb 2011' and 'ISSSS monthly report: 1 to 31 April 2011'.

[37] UNDP / Peacebuilding Fund (2011) 'Appui aux Structures de Coordination du STAREC et l'UNSSSS', programme document, available via mptf.undp.org; UNDP/UNOPS/GoDRC (2010) 'Renforcement des capacités des agents de l'administration publique en zones récemment stabilisées et réhabilitation/construction et équipement de bâtiments administratifs stratégiques', programme document, available via mptf.undp.org.

[38] MONUSCO (2011) 'ISSSS Quarterly Report: January to March 2011', p22.

[39] MONUSCO (2011) 'Fiches de projets statistics', internal records (to December), ODSRSG-RC-HC.

[40] Personal communication in 2010. See also MONUSCO (2010) 'Etat de lieu STAREC/ISSSS in Maniema', internal mission report (October), ODSRSG-RC-HC; Bashonga, LP (2009) 'L'interview de la semaine', *STAREC Infos* 2.

[41] GoDRC (2011) 'Procès verbal de la réunion du CTC/STAREC, province de Maniema, tenue à Kindu le 10 et le 12 février 2011', internal minutes, Maniema Office of the Governor.

[42] Schattschneider, EE (1960) 'The semi-sovereign people'; Cobb, RW and Elder, CD (1983) 'Participation in American politics: The dynamics of agenda-building'; Baumgartner, FR and Jones, BD (1991) 'Agenda dynamics and policy subsystems', *Journal of Politics* 53: 1044–1074.

[43] Figures via UNDP / Multi-Partner Trust Fund Office, mptf.undp.org, verified January 2015.

[44] UNDP / Multi-Partner Trust Fund Office (2011) 'Deuxième rapport annuel consolidé d'activités du Fonds pour la Stabilisation et le Relèvement de la République Démocratique du Congo', p9.

[45] GoDRC/MONUSCO (2011) 'Compte-rendu de la réunion du Comité Technique Conjoint (CTC) du programme STAREC Nord-Kivu', internal minutes (May), North Kivu Office of the Governor.

[46] MONUC (2009) 'Towards peace and stability', fact sheet; MONUSCO (2010) 'ISSSS quarterly report, July to September 2010'; MONUSCO (2012) 'ISSSS quarterly report, January to March 2012'.

[47] GoDRC (2011) 'Agenda Comité de Suivi STAREC/ISSSS: 24 Mai 2011', internal agenda document, STAREC Technical Secretariat; MONUSCO (2011) 'Mot de cloture de M. Sarassorro', internal record of remarks, ODSRSG-RC-HC. The original phrasing was deliberately ambiguous: *des priorités provinciales, sur lequel nos interventions futures vont pouvoir être basées* ('provincial priorities, on which we will be able to base future interventions'). For the three previous meetings see GoDRC (2009) 'Compte rendu de la Première réunion du comité de suivi du STAREC', 22 October; GoDRC (2010) 'Compte rendu de la deuxième réunion du comité de suivi du STAREC', 1 April; GoDRC (2010) 'Compte rendu de la troisième réunion du comité de suivi du STAREC', 13 December.

[48] Personal communications with provincial Governors and Ministers from 2010–11; Bashonga, PL (2010) 'Marche du Starec dans les provinces: Le Nord-Kivu s'approprie le leadership', *STAREC Infos* 17, 28 May; DigitalCongo (2010) 'Plaidoyer pour le renforcement de la coordination entre les gouvernements central et provinciaux', 25 May; MONUSCO/ODSRSG-RC-HC (2010) 'Etat de lieu STAREC/ISSSS in Maniema', internal mission report, October.

[49] United Nations (2010) 'Thirty-first report of the Secretary-General on MONUC', 30 March 2010, UN Doc S/2010/164, paras 98–108; SC Res 1925 para. 12(m) and (n), 28 May 2010, UN Doc S/RES/1925.

[50] Kets, E and de Vries, H (2014) 'Limits to supporting security sector interventions in the DRC', ISS Paper 257. For similar perspectives see Boshoff, DH et al. (2010) 'Supporting SSR in the DRC: Between a rock and a hard place', Clingendael Conflict Research Unit; Oxfam America (2010) 'No will, no way: US-funded security sector reform in the Democratic Republic of Congo'; ASADHO et al. (2011) 'The Democratic Republic of Congo: Taking a stand on security sector reform'; International Crisis Group (2012) 'Eastern Congo: Why stabilization failed', Africa Briefing 9.

[51] Personal communications, UN and UK officials in Kinshasa; MONUSCO (2010) 'Support for FARDC garrisoning', internal project concept (October), ODSRSG-RC-HC. On completed facilities see MONUSCO/IOM (2009) 'Appui a la Réinstallation du Personnel Militaire et de leur dépendants', internal project concept; MONUSCO (2012) 'ISSSS Quarterly Report, January–March 2012'.

[52] Bashonga, LP (2009) 'Lancement du STAREC: Priorité aux axes routières', *STAREC Infos* 1 (author's translation); MONUSCO (2012) 'ISSSS quarterly report, January–March 2012'.

[53] International Crisis Group (2010) 'Congo: A stalled democratic agenda', Africa Briefing 73, pt 3; Trefon, T (2011) 'Congo masquerade: The political culture of aid inefficiency and reform failure', Zed Books, pp71–78; Weiss, HF and Nzongola-Ntalaja, G (2013) 'Decentralization and the DRC – an overview', paper prepared for the DRC Affinity Group, available via www.ssrc.org.

[54] Kabila, J (2009) 'Discours du Président de la République sur l'Etat de la Nation', Kinshasa, 7 December 2009; quoted in International Crisis Group (2010) 'Congo: A stalled democratic agenda', Africa Briefing 73.

[55] Englebert, P (2011) 'Décentralisation, incertitude, et despotisme de proximité en République Démocratique du Congo', Papier préparé pour le Projet RDC – Provinces-Décentralisation du Musée Royal de Tervuren (section Histoire du Temps Présent), Belgique (author's translation.)

[56] Kayandi, T (2010) 'L'interview de la semaine', *STAREC Infos* 34, 11 November.

[57] DigitalCongo (2009) 'Rétrocession de 40% des recettes aux provinces: gouverneurs et députés provinciaux prêts à traduire le gouvernement devant la justice', 17 June; Le Potentiel (2009) 'La Conférence des gouverneurs a tranche rétrocession des 40%: rien n'a changé', 27 June; Devey, M (2011) 'Moise Katumbi: Je gère le Katanga comme une entreprise', *Jeune Afrique*, 24 May.

[58] Tamm, H (2013) 'FNI and FRPI: Local resistance and regional alliances in north-eastern Congo', Rift Valley Institute Usalama Project.

[59] MONUSCO (2010) 'Rapport de mission à Bunia de l'équipe STAREC', internal report (October), ODSRSG-RC-HC.

[60] European Court of Auditors (2013) 'EU support for governance in the Democratic Republic of the Congo', Special Report 9, para. 73.

[61] Brusset, E et al. (2011) 'Amani labda, peace maybe: Joint evaluation of conflict prevention and peace building in the Democratic Republic of Congo', Synthesis Report, Channel Research.

[62] International Dialogue on Peacebuilding and Statebuilding (2010) 'Dili declaration: A new vision for peacebuilding and statebuilding', April; Tamagnini, A et al. (2010) 'Strategic review of the International Security and Stabilization Support Strategy for eastern DR Congo: Final report', p23.

[63] Patrick, S and Brown, K (2007) 'Greater than the sum of its parts? Assessing 'whole of government' approaches' to fragile states', International Peace Academy.

64 GoDRC / United Nations (2009) 'Compte rendu de la Première Réunion du Comité d'Administration du Fonds de Stabilisation', 6 November; GoDRC / United Nations (2010) 'Compte rendu du Réunion du Comité d'Administration du Fonds de Stabilisation', 14 July.

65 Oxfam (2012) '"For me, but without me, is against me": Why efforts to stabilise the Democratic Republic of Congo are not working', Oxfam Lobby Briefing, p15; Demetriou, S and Quick, ID (2012) 'The sobering lessons of stabilization in eastern Democratic Republic of Congo', unpublished manuscript; de Vries, H (2015) 'Going around in circles: Peacekeeping and stabilization in the DR Congo 2008–2015', forthcoming.

66 Bailey, S (2011) 'Humanitarian action, early recovery and stabilization in the Democratic Republic of Congo', Humanitarian Policy Group, HPG Working Paper.

67 Ibid; Goodhand, J and Atkinson, P (2001) 'Conflict and aid: Enhancing the peacebuilding impact of international engagement: A synthesis of findings from Afghanistan, Liberia and Sri Lanka', International Alert; Bennett, J et al. (2010) 'Multi-donor evaluation of support to conflict prevention and peacebuilding activity in Southern Sudan 2005–2010', ITAD and Channel Research; Overseas Development Institute (2013) 'What is the evidence on the impact of employment creation on stability and poverty reduction in fragile states? A systematic review'.

68 UNDP (2011) 'Compagne de sensibilisation de la population sur la restauration de l'Autorité de L'Etat: Axe Rutshuru–Ishasha du 14 au 17 Juin 2011', internal presentation. No press release or official photographs followed the visit.

69 GoDRC/UNDP/MONUSCO (2010) 'Renforcement des capacités des agents de l'administration publique en zones récemment stabilisées et réhabilitation/construction et équipement de bâtiments administratifs stratégiques', project document, available via mptf.undp.org.

70 MONUSCO (2008) 'Stratégie UNSSSS: Plan d'action pour la restauration et l'extension de l'autorité de l'état', internal planning document, Civil Affairs Section.

71 MONUSCO (2009) 'UNSSSS Biweekly 26 September to 9 October'; MONUSCO (2010) 'ISSSS quarterly report, September–December 2010'; UNDP/UNOPS (2014) 'Rapport de fin du projet: PBF/COD/E-3/00075962', available via mptf.undp.org.

72 MONUSCO (2011) 'ISSSS quarterly report, April–June 2011'.

73 Le Potentiel (2011) 'Mashako Mambo échappe à la mort à Rutshuru: les FDLR frappe au coeur du gouvernement', 9 May; Radio Okapi (2011) 'Insécurité au Nord Kivu: la société civile interpelle la communauté internationale', 10 May; Radio Okapi (2011) 'Rutshuru: Les FDLR tuent 6 personnes à Katwiguru', 26 May.

[74] Societé Civile / Forces vives du Nord Kivu (2011) 'Appel à la responsabilité internationale et nationale', press release of 9 May (author's translation). See also ACPD-CAPD (2011) 'Rapport sur les violations massives des droits de l'homme en province du Nord Kivu, Mai 2011', a report of a Goma-based network.

[75] MONUSCO (2011) 'Weekly report: 14 May' and 'Weekly report: 21 May', internal situation reports, North Kivu sub-office; Radio Okapi (2010) 'Rutshuru: la population dans la rue après une embuscade meurtrière', 10 May; La Réference (2011) 'Cyprien Iyamulemye peint le drame sécuritaire dans le Rutshuru', 13 May; Digital Congo (2011) 'Lutte contre l'insécurité au Nord-Kivu : Rutshuru abrite momentanément le gouvernement provincial, annonce l'autorité provinciale', 10 May

[76] Pothin, A (2010) 'Les agents de l'administration publique de l'Ituri et de Rutshuru formés', STAREC Infos 36; MONUSCO (2011) 'JMT Rutshuru: Rapport d'activités du 14 au 16 juin 2011', internal situation report, UNPOL North Kivu (author's translation in both cases).

[77] Personal communications in North Kivu, Ituri and Maniema, 2009–10; Radio Okapi (2009) 'Nord Kivu: Starec, la lenteur des activités inquiète la société civile', 10 November; Ngwamba, M (2011) 'STAREC: la Société civile appelée à un dialogue serein et rationnel avec l'Etat Congolais', La Réference, 6 September; Coordination de la Société Civile de Beni-Lubero (2011) 'Notre plaidoyer à monsieur le coordinateur inter-provincial du programme Starec en R.D. Congo', open letter.

[78] Oxfam (2012) '"For me, but without me, is against me": Why efforts to stabilise the Democratic Republic of Congo are not working', Oxfam Lobby Briefing.

[79] International Crisis Group (2010) 'Congo: No stability in Kivu Despite a rapprochement with Rwanda', Africa Report N°165, November; Paddon, E and Lacaille, G (2011) 'Stabilising the Congo', Forced Migration Policy Briefing 8, Refugee Studies Centre, Oxford University, December MONUSCO (2012) 'International Security and Stabilization Support Strategy for Democratic Republic of Congo: Generating a joint political approach to stabilization', internal strategic review, June; International Alert (2012) 'Ending the deadlock: Towards a new vision of peace in Eastern DRC', September, pp36–38.

[80] Tamagnini, A et al. (2010) 'Strategic review of the International Security and Stabilization Support Strategy for eastern DR Congo: Final report', p5.

[81] Personal communications with civil officials in Kinyandoni 2009–10; MONUC (2009) 'Comment on note to file', internal communication (11 July), ODSRSG-RC-HC. This remained a live issue up to date of final revisions in mid-2015.

[82] Vinck, P and Pham, PN (2014) 'Searching for lasting peace: Population-based survey on perceptions and attitudes about peace, security and justice in eastern Democratic Republic of the Congo', Harvard Humanitarian Initiative, United Nations Development Programme.

[83] Gambino, T (2011) 'Testimony before Senate Committee on Foreign Relations Subcommittee on African Affairs', available via foreign.senate.gov.

[84] For the six 'strategic axes' prioritised in 2008 the figures are: Irumu 15%, Masisi 8%, Rutshuru 23%, Kalehe 13%, Shabunda 21% and Fizi 15%. Peacebuildingdata.org (2014) 'Interactive map: DRC 2014, Territories', via peacebuildingdata.org.

[85] Ibid. The figures are Rutshuru 48%, Masisi 40%, Goma 43% and Fizi 67%.

[86] At a formal level see GoDRC (2010) 'Rôles et responsabilités des membres du comité technique conjoint (CTC) du STAREC du Nord Kivu', internal draft (June), North Kivu Office of the Governor; GoDRC (2010) 'STAREC: Le Comité Technique Conjoint (CTC) Termes de Référence', internal draft (July), South Kivu Office of the Governor. As to practice: MONUSCO (2011) 'CTC liste des Contacts', internal contact directory, ODSRSG-RC-HC; alongside minutes of individual meetings on file with author.

[87] Roy, A (2014) 'The NGO-ization of resistance', *Massalijn*, 4 September.

[88] MONUSCO (2010) 'Processus de soumission et d'allocation des fonds pour les ONGs et les institutions de l'Etat dans le cadre du STAREC/SSSS', information note, February; MONUSCO (2010) 'NGO participation in the (UN)ISSSS/STAREC', internal note to file (December), ODSRSG-RC-HC; MONUSCO (2011) 'ISSSS monthly update: 1 to 31 April 2011'; MONUSCO (2011) 'Q & A Stabilization Meeting with INGOs', internal note to file (July), ODSRSG-RC-HC.

[89] MONUSCO (2010) 'Survey of public opinions regarding stabilisation', internal concept note (October), ODSRSG-RC-HC.

[90] PNUD/GoDRC (2010) 'Appui aux Structures de Coordination du STAREC et l'UNSSSS', programme document, available via www.mptf.org; MONUSCO (2012) 'International Security and Stabilization Support Strategy for Democratic Republic of Congo: Generating a Joint Political Approach to Stabilization', internal strategic review, June.

[91] Autesserre, S (2014) 'Peaceland: Conflict resolution and the everyday politics of international intervention', Cambridge University Press, Kindle edn, ch. 4 and loc 4161.

[92] United Nations (2012) 'Protection of civilians coordination mechanisms in UN peacekeeping missions: DPKO/DFS comparative study and toolkit', Department of Peacekeeping Operations / Department of Field Support; MONUSCO (2014) 'CLA Best Practice Review', internal working document, Civil Affairs Section.

[93] Ibid. CLA posts were graded at GL-5 under the Common System of Salaries, Allowances and Benefits. Many of these staff members were graduates with extensive management experience.

[94] Schjörlien, JS and Berts, H (2010) 'Review of civilian observer component of the MONUC Joint Monitoring Teams in eastern Democratic Republic of the Congo', Stockholm Policy Group.

[95] Author conversations with Senior Civilian Observer and JMT Team Leaders from 2009–11; MONUSCO (2009) 'Priorities and action plan: Joint Monitoring Teams', internal memorandum, ODSRSG-RC-HC; MONUSCO (2009) 'Reinvigorating functioning of JMTs', internal memorandum, ODSRSG-RC-HC; MONUSCO (2010) 'ISSSS Joint Monitoring Teams: Options for management and coordination', internal memorandum, ODSRSG-RC-HC. For public sources see MONUSCO (2010) 'UNSSSS update for 6 Feb to 20 Feb 2010'; Tamagnini, A et al. (2010) 'Strategic review of the International Security and Stabilization Support Strategy for eastern DR Congo: Final report'; MONUSCO (2011) 'ISSSS Monthly Report: 1 to 31 May 2011'; University of Oslo (2011) 'NORDEM Annual report 2011', p12.

[96] Whitman, T (2010) 'Joint Protection Teams: A model for enhancing civilian security', Institute for Inclusive Security; United Nations (2012) 'Protection of civilians: Coordination mechanisms in UN Peacekeeping Missions, DPKFO/DFS Comparative Study and toolkit', Department of Peacekeeping / Department of Field Support; Martin, B (2012) 'The protection of civilians in the Democratic Republic of the Congo', *Conflict Trends* 2012(2): 33–40.

[97] MONUSCO (2011) 'Report of JPT/JIT mission to Kikozi and Muranvya', internal report (April), South Kivu sub-office.

[98] MONUSCO (2011) 'Report of JPT mission to Kalembe', internal report (February), North Kivu sub-office.

[99] Vinck, P and Pham, PN (2014) 'Searching for lasting peace: Population-based survey on perceptions and attitudes about peace, security and justice in eastern Democratic Republic of the Congo', Harvard Humanitarian Initiative, United Nations Development Programme.

[100] Pothin AE (2009) 'STAREC: Les choses avancent!', *STAREC Infos* 1; Pothin, AE (2010) 'Une année de plus, Un espoir de plus!', *STAREC Infos* 9.

[101] Personal communications with Cellule de communication STAREC, 2009–11.

[102] Personal observations 2008–11; UNDP / Peacebuilding Fund (2011) 'Appui aux Structures de Coordination du STAREC et l'UNSSSS', programme document, available via mptf.undp.org; MONUSCO / GoDRC (2011) 'Projet de sensibilisation au programme STAREC', project concept note.

103 Author search of radiookapi.net from January 2008 to December 2012, accurate at January 2015.

104 Scott, JC (1998) 'Seeing like a state: How certain schemes to improve the human condition have failed', Yale University Press, pp5, 94.

105 MONUC (2008) 'Background briefing: UN support for security and stabilization of Eastern DRC'; MONUC (2009) 'Towards peace and stability: An overview of the United Nations Support Strategy for Security and Stabilization of Eastern DRC', fact sheet; UN Peacebuilding Fund (2009) 'Priority Plan for the Democratic Republic of Congo (DRC)', via www.mptf.org; MONUC (2010) 'ISSSS Integrated Programme Framework'.

106 Demetriou, S and Quick, ID (2012) 'The sobering lessons of stabilization in eastern Democratic Republic of Congo', unpublished manuscript.

107 International Dialogue on Peacebuilding and Statebuilding (2011) 'A new deal for engagement in fragile states', accessible via www.newdeal4peace.org.

108 7143rd meeting of the Security Council, 19 March, UN Doc S/PV.7143; United Nations (2010) 'Review of the United Nations peacebuilding architecture', UN Doc A/64/868- S/2010/393, 21 July, p20; United Nations (2012) 'Report of the Secretary-General: Peacebuilding in the aftermath of armed conflict', 8 October, UN Doc A/67/499-S/2012/746.

109 United Nations (1945) 'Charter of the United Nations and statute of the International Court of Justice', ch. 1, art. 2, accessible via www.un.org.

Notes to the Epilogue

[1] Wildavsky, A (1987/2007) 'Speaking truth to power: The art and craft of policy analysis', Transaction Publishers, p26.

[2] United Nations / Office of the Special Envoy of the Secretary-General for the Great Lakes Region of Africa (2013) 'A Framework of hope: The peace, security and cooperation framework for the Democratic Republic of Congo and the region', February.

[3] Reid, SA (2014) 'Did Russ Feingold just end a war?', *Politico*, 11 March; UN News Centre (2014) 'Ban appoints Algerian diplomat Said Djinnit as envoy for Great Lakes region', 17 July. No disrespect is intended to Mr Djinnit, a highly capable official, but these things matter among diplomats.

[4] United Nations (2013) 'Statement of SRSG Martin Kobler to the Security Council', 21 October, via radiookapi.net; United Nations (2014) 'Statement of SRSG Martin Kobler to the Security Council', 14 March, via monusco.unmissions.org; Kobler, M (2014) Tweet timestamped 2205 14 March 2014, via twitter.com.

[5] UN News Center (2014) 'UN concerned about growing displacement of people in DR Congo's Katanga province', 29 January; BBC News (2014) 'Second massacre in days leaves 20 dead in east DR Congo', 18 October; Kibangula, T (2014) 'RDC: la situation explosive de Beni expliquée en 4 points', *Jeune Afrique*, 4 November; Nienaber, G (2014) 'Woolgathering catastrophe in Congo', *Huffington Post*, 24 November; AFP (2014) 'When home is Congo's "triangle of death"', 1 December; Reuters (2015) 'At least 21 killed in machete attack in northeast Congo', 4 February.

[6] RTGA World TV (2015) 'Joseph Kabila Renonce a l'aide de la Monusco contre les FDLR', 15 February, available via youtube.be; Borreau, M and Bangré, H (2015) 'RDC: recherche de compromis entre Joseph Jabila et la Monusco', *Le Monde*, 18 February.

[7] Mende, L (2014) 'Pourquoi Scott Campbell devait quitter la RDC', *Le Phare*, 23 October.

[8] Dewey, J (1927/1991) 'The public and its problems', p81.

[9] Ramalingam, B (2013) 'Aid on the edge of chaos: Rethinking international cooperation in a complex world', Oxford University Press, ch. 19; Doing Development Differently Manifesto Community (2014) 'The manifesto', via doingdevelopmentdifferently.com.

[10] Booth, D and Unsworth, S (2014) 'Politically smart, locally led development', Overseas Development Institute, Discussion Paper, pVI.

[11] Heifetz, R (1994) 'Leadership without easy answers', Harvard University Press, ch. 4.

[12] This language originates with Block, P (1981/2000) 'Flawless consulting: A guide to getting your expertise used', Jossey-Bass/Pfeiffer, ch. 10.

[13] Grindle, MS (2004) 'Good-enough governance: Poverty reduction and reform in development countries', *Governance* 17(4), pp525–548; Booth, D and Unsworth, S (2014) 'Politically smart, locally led development', Overseas Development Institute.

[14] Currion, P (2015) 'The invisible lesson of invisible children', IRIN, 3 February.

[15] Independent Commission for Aid Impact (2015) 'Assessing the impact of the scale-up of DFID's support to fragile states', p9.

[16] Ibid, pp9, 27; Anderson, M (2015) 'Aid billions yet to make a difference in fragile states, UK watchdog says', *The Guardian*, 12 February.

[17] Magee, H (2015) 'The aid industry—what journalists really think', International Broadcasting Trust, p8. See Easterly, W (2014) 'The tyranny of experts: Economists, dictators, and the forgotten rights of the poor', Basic Civitas Books; Moyo, D (2011) 'Dead aid: Why aid is not working and how there is another way for Africa', Penguin.

[18] Ramalingam, B (2013) 'Aid on the edge of chaos: Rethinking international cooperation in a complex world', Oxford University Press, p362.

[19] Heifetz, RA and Linsky, M (2002) 'Leadership on the line: Staying alive through the dangers of leading', Harvard Business School Press, ch. 5.

[20] Quick, ID (2014) 'The Five Virtues: For better decisions in fragile states', *Rethink Fragility*, 9 November.

[21] Marx K / Engels F (1888) 'Theses on Feuerbach', # XI.

[22] Adapted from Kim, WC and Mauborgne, R (2004) 'Blue ocean strategy', *Harvard Business Review*, October.

[23] Vinck, P and Pham, PN (2014) 'Searching for lasting peace: Population-based survey on perceptions and attitudes about peace, security and justice in eastern Democratic Republic of the Congo', Harvard Humanitarian Initiative, United Nations Development Programme.

[24] Rift Valley Institute (2015) 'Course Prospectus'; 'Usalama project: Understanding Congolese armed groups', both via www.riftvalley.net. The latter has been cited extensively throughout *Follies in Fragile States*, particularly in Chapter 2.

[25] Integrity Research & Consultancy (2015) 'Our values', via integrityresearch.com.

[26] Faustino, J (2014) 'Doing development differently', presentation at Center for International Development, via youtube.com; Faustino, J and Booth, D (2014) 'Development entrepreneurship: How donors and leaders can foster institutional change', Asia Foundation / Overseas Development Institute, pt 6.

[27] Rethink Fragility (2014) 'About us', October, via rethinkfragility.com; Valters, C, Rabinowitz, G and Denney, L (2014) 'Security in post-conflict contexts: What counts as progress and who drives it?', Development Progress / Overseas Development Institute.

[28] Pouligny, B (2006) 'Peace operations as seen from below: UN missions and local people', Kumarian Press, ch. 6; Autesserre, S (2014) 'Peaceland: Conflict resolution and the everyday politics of international intervention', Cambridge University Press, Kindle edn at 8897.

[29] Humphries, D (2014) 'Consensus is the death of development innovation and here's why', 14 November.

[30] Easterly, W (2014) 'The tyranny of experts: Economists, dictators, and the forgotten rights of the poor', Basic Civitas Books, p287.

[31] Gran, G (1979) 'An introduction to Zaire's permanent development crisis', in Gran G (ed.) *Zaire: The political economy of underdevelopment*, p20.

CPSIA information can be obtained at www.ICGtesting.com
Printed in the USA
LVOW07s1835191115

463349LV00033B/1675/P